Dedic

We'd like to dedicate this bc
leading us on our pilgrimage
years.

It turns out that by chance this is the first such book published in the post-Sir Bobby Robson era.

At the time of writing, it's too early to know whether or not the directors' decision will be vindicated. Perhaps what we can say is that, if by the end of what would anyway have been Sir Bobby's last season we finally have a trophy of some kind, then maybe they will be able to look us in the eyes and say they feel that their action was justified. Though perhaps Sir Bobby would also have delivered the same result; no-one will ever know.

If we have nothing to show for the upheaval, then was it really the right thing to do in the wider scheme of things? Our stock in the eyes of many of the committed and also in the opinion of the vast majority of neutrals certainly has gone down in these last few strange days of August 2004.

Still, and as always:
Good luck and many thanks to Sir Bobby,
Good luck and great success to our new manager,
and Howay the Toon!

Toon Tales

A Euro-Geordie Pilgrimage

(The football fan's essential if desultory guide to comparative linguistics and European history - in Black and White)

'Ranks with the satanic verses' – sunderland Sentinel

'Now we know what Magpie droppings look like' – Boro Bugle

'Topical yet timeless' - anon

Photographs

Front cover photo: UEFA Cup Final at Ullevi Stadium, Gothenburg with (from left to right) Sarah, Phil, Chris, Emilie, Don, Pete, Jiri, Barry, Lilly, Brian, Harvey, Sarah

Centre photos: people and places along the pilgrims' trail (courtesy of Don Faulds, Chris & Sarah Wilkie, Richard Biggs, & the authors)

toon tales

A Euro-Geordie Pilgrimage

as told by

Peter Cain

and

Barry Robertson

First published in Great Britain in 2004 by
Toon Publishing Limited
129/131 New Bridge Street
Newcastle Upon Tyne NE1 2SW

e-mail : toonpublishing@yahoo.co.uk
website : http://www.freewebs.com/toonpublishing/

1 3 5 7 9 10 8 6 4 2

A CIP catalogue record for this book is available from the British Library

ISBN 0-9548357-0-0

Printed and bound in Great Britain
by Biddles Ltd, King's Lynn, Norfolk

Contents

Acknowledgments

Our many thanks go to all of the following: Malcolm Colling for advice, inspiration, and proof-reading; Brian Robertson for cover and website development; Don Faulds, Chris and Sarah Wilkie, and Richard Biggs for additional photos; Didier de Almeida for computer wizardry; Ian Rosenvinge and Bruce Renwick for additional anecdotes; Niall and Biffa at nufc.com and Mark Jensen at The Mag for their wise words; Tony Faux at Biddles for printing expertise; Ian Robertson for the company set-up; and of course to wives, families, and friends; not forgetting the big happy family that is the Toon Army.

An introduction – plus the authors' apology for this book

John Bunyan apologised for his *Pilgrim's Progress*, and we thought that we should do the same. So here goes: we apologise for John Bunyan's *Pilgrim's Progress*.

It's funny how some things in life go in cycles, rather like the *Tour de France*. A cyclical phenomenon closer to Geordie hearts, however, is Newcastle United - in fact many people's lives literally revolve around the Toon. When they look back over the years God gave them, the milestones by which they measure their time on Earth are not always family birthdays. They are more likely to mark the ebb and flow of Newcastle's (mis)fortunes - home, away and abroad. One such milestone was the Quarter Final of the 1969/70 Fairs Cup when we, the holders, were knocked out by RSC Anderlecht on the away goals rule. We had gone down two-nil in Brussels but Keith Dyson's goal, our third on that crisp March night of the return leg, had taken us into an aggregate lead and now there seemed to be just seconds to go. Then they pulled one back and we were oot. Just another statistic for millions, but devastating for us. A defining moment in life.

Back in those days, the whole European adventure was so new and so exotic. As thirteen and fourteen year-olds, we had no chance of getting to the away legs. Howay man, who had the money? But you followed it all avidly in the Journal and the Chronicle, and of course on the radio (when it was on). And in those colour specials that the Daily Express produced (to be plastered across the bedroom wall). Off they'd headed in 68/69 to Rotterdam, Lisbon, Zaragoza, Setubal (or in fact to Lisbon again), Glasgow (even that sounded pretty exotic then) and finally behind the Iron Curtain to Budapest. What wouldn't we have given to have been there! For some of us on Tyneside, that European adventure by proxy kindled what was to become a lifelong passion for languages and a fascination for all things European. So thank you, NUFC!

Anderlecht is a curate's egg of a suburb in Brussels, and one of the better parts is the Parc Astrid where the football ground stands. And as we all know, the Prince, Philippe Albert (everyone knows his name), came to us from Anderlecht, and the transfer deal included a pre-season friendly in Brussels in the summer of 1996. That game marked Alan Shearer's third appearance in his first week for Newcastle (after his début at Lincoln and the Charity Shield four-nil débacle). He spent a long time signing autographs before the match down by the wire fence at the northern end of the Reine Astrid stadium where the faithful had congregated. And Philippe naturally got a great reception from all sides of the ground. We won two-nil with goals from Tino and Ginola.

Watching in the summer evening sunshine were Geordies from all over the place. Some lads and lasses were on a camping holiday in Holland, not a million miles away from Brussels. Others lived in that city itself, like Barry, son Brian, and mate Neale. Now they were less than anonymous on account of their gi-huge Magpie hats, trophies of that very Charity Shield game only a few days earlier. And there was nothing wrong with Pete's lungs, two rows behind, despite the three-hour drive from Luxembourg: 'With an N and an E and a Wubble-U C....' and 'Toon Toon, Black and White Army.' Soon the Magpie hats (and the whole stand) were joining in. The crack at half-time revealed that they had a lot in common: exiled Geordies working on the continent for many years, following the Toon around, born within a year of each other, mothers born on the same day, April 17th. You can learn a lot in fifteen minutes! It was that accidental meeting, appropriately or fatefully enough at Anderlecht, that eventually produced this book:

Toon Tales is a travelogue of the 2003/04 UEFA Cup pilgrimage. We didn't win the trophy but, hey, we had great fun criss-crossing the map of Europe – from snow-covered

Nordic wastes to sun-kissed Mediterranean beaches (where actually it stotted doon). Wherever our journey took us, we soaked up the local colour, culture and raindrops, spoke a bit of the local lingo and supped plenty of the local beer. The Toon Army is such a rich tapestry of friendly and often hilarious characters that somebody just had to write a book about their continental adventures. So here it is!

But while you're reading this, please bear in mind that we don't claim to be football experts. (This is the apology bit!) We're just fans - Toon Army wallahs. So we're not trying to analyse the why's and wherefores of every game; nor are we attempting detailed match reports, because the media in their various forms do that better than we can; what we're trying to do is give a taste of what it was like being there (before, during and after), sometimes a couple of hundred yards away from the action (like at the Camp Nou) where you could hardly make out who was who, sometimes within touching distance, and always with all the distractions of being in the middle of a boisterous crowd. Sometimes we say things just for effect - there's such a thing as irony so we don't always mean exactly what we say; if you're non-anglo, we know some of you have a particular problem in spotting irony, so don't get too upset: it's your fault not ours (did you spot it?); stereotypes are useful and fun, so we use them, but don't read too much into them - there's always some element of truth in them, but by no means everyone conforms to the same trait. We didn't start taking notes or writing this until after Mallorca and we don't have perfect memories, so some details may not be quite right; if you spot any mistakes, let us know, and we'll be grateful. There are two people writing this (Magpie-hat Barry and Nothing-wrong-with-his-lungs Pete), and sometimes we ramble on in different directions over the same ground. Collaborating on the writing has been a great experience and big fun: you learn a lot; including that sometimes identities need to blur to keep the narrative flowing, so the 'I' in this book is often a composite person, neither one of us nor the other, but both of us (and sometimes maybe it's you!); we all create our own personal realities and meanings from our different experiences of the same events – no two histories are the same – just read a match report of a game you went to yourself to see what we mean. You might think some of the language isn't real enough - well, we thought long and hard about that and decided in the end to err on the side of inviting your mothers and ours to read it too!

Setting out

Things have changed since the pioneering days of the 1968/69 Inter-Cities Fairs Cup run. Today's travelling fans think nothing of organising their next trip to even the most obscure and far-flung of destinations. Look at me for instance; here I am sitting in a plane writing this on my way back from another of Newcastle's forays into Europe. The Internet makes it easy to weigh up alternatives to suit the time you have available to take days off and your travel budget. Why, only a few months ago, I was quite seriously working out the best route to some small town on the Turkish-Syrian border for a possible match in the first round of the 2003/04 UEFA Cup.

You might quite rightly question this, because you and I know that Newcastle never played in that particularly exotic location. Well, they easily could have done, and for an hour or so it seemed a distinct possibility to anyone like me who'd been logged on to the UEFA official website looking at the groupings for the live draw. The draw usually takes place in Geneva around lunchtime, and they have a very slick website where you can follow it live on streamed video or audio, with the grid of all the ties updated in real time. There are so many conditions attached to the early round draws - such as not playing a team from your own country, segregating seeded and un-seeded teams, teams that share the same ground can't play at home the same night, and so on - that UEFA has to pre-allocate teams into groups even before the draw is made. This means that you know in advance that your range of possible opponents is narrowed down to one of perhaps four or eight teams out of the eighty or so that might still be in the competition. On this occasion, Malatyaspor appeared in the short-list alongside other more recognisable or at least pronounceable names such as Basel and Breda.

Booking your travel to places like those is simple – you just open up a new window on your computer and search the net for the cheapest flights, ferries or trains and a convenient hotel and then straight away you book on-line or phone directly to the hotel at the number you find on their website. You haven't got a match ticket yet, but within half an hour of the draw being confirmed, you're fixed up with everything else you need.

But Malatyaspor would have been different: a two-legged flight to Istanbul then Ankara, or a charter flight to some Turkish Mediterranean resort, to be followed by a train or a bus or a hike overland to Malatya. Much more expensive and time-consuming, but still bookable within an hour or so. Waiting for the draw, I'd got the route worked out and had even found a hotel in Malatya through their own Internet site. The *Altin Kayisi* sounded fine: rooms at eighty dollars, satellite TV, 'non-stop' hot water (though I hope you can stop it now and then), and they took credit cards. All sounded very normal – nowhere in UEFA land is too much of a culture shock nowadays. The name translates to Hotel Golden Apricot, which I suppose is akin to the Golden Tulip chain of hotels you get in Holland and elsewhere – it turns out that apricots are to Malatya what tulips are to Amsterdam. As fate - or in this case I suppose Allah - would have it, we missed out on Malatyaspor and instead it was going to be an hour in the car to Breda, just over the border from Belgium into Holland. So we swapped the prospects of the Golden Apricot for the Golden Tulip. What kind of car gets you from Newcastle to Holland in an hour? Not mine, for sure, but many years ago I made advance preparations for easier trips around Europe by joining the massed ranks of Geordies in exile, in my case in Belgium.

Someone else got the trek to Malatya. And you know who it was? Basel, whom we met in the following round, after they had just scraped past Malatyaspor three-two with a silver goal in extra time. It would be interesting to hear their travellers' tales, because it could be us going there next year. Maybe they could report back on what they thought of the

Altin Kayisi Hotel – we didn't meet anyone who'd been there while we were in Basel.

Back in the 1968/69 season, you needed to be really determined if you were planning to follow the team into Europe under your own steam. And it really was like that, because back then they still had steam trains to get to some of the places on the route to the Final. So these were major expeditions. Living in the North-East of England has always meant that our fans travelled more miles in a season than just about anyone else's to support the team in the domestic league. Living in the North-West corner of Europe, and with the steely might of the North Sea to cross first, meant trips often measured in thousands of kilometres and lasting days not hours. And having to think in foreign kilometres instead of old money was a new experience in itself.

With all of the difficulties in arranging things yourself, the way to go for nearly all fans was on trips organised by the club. Back then, travel was relatively speaking much more expensive than now, so it needed more thinking about, not only on how to get there, but also on whether you could afford it, and whether you could persuade your lass to let you out to play. But once you had overcome these barriers and you'd chosen the club trip, all you had to do was turn up at the coach and go with the flow - just about the whole deal was organised and you didn't even have to know which one of Zaragoza or Ujpest Dosza was in Spain and which was in Hungary. In fact, when you got to your destination the local brews were so exotic that you would never know which country you were in anyway. Some things never change, I suppose. We had encountered one such scene on our travels in 2002.

Palaver and palabras in Barcelona

'It's f***in' typical o' these bast***d'n Italians!' The words were spoken not in hatred but out of sheer exasperation 'An' aal the soddin' money aa've spent on beer! Wasted!' And quite frankly the lad had a point (as well as a pint in his hand). All the trouble he'd gone to - the time off work, the row with their lass, the beer money - and the game had been postponed because of a few drops of rain. Well, a downpour actually, more like a sodding monsoon. Trouble was, we weren't in Italy at all. This was Barcelona, and we'd been given proof positive of the old adage that the rain in Spain falls mainly when Newcastle are playing there. Mind you, maybe he had inside information denied to the rest of us. Perhaps the groundsman was Italian and hadn't done his job properly. Who knows? Who cares? Either way, the game was off and there was nothing for it but to trek back from the *Camp Nou* to *las Ramblas* and get some serious drinking done. And you know what? *Ramblas* comes from an Arabic word meaning 'torrents', and to the Toon Army the words certainly are synonymous. Ah yes, *las Ramblas:* the Bigg Market of Barcelona; though sadly the lasses strutting their stuff there in summer wear far more than their Toon cousins do in November. We and a few hundred more of the advance guard of the Toon Army had bivouaced in a big Irish bar, possibly called Flanagan's, at the downstream end of the torrent the night before. Sweet timing had provided us with a big-screen feast of a losing relegation battle for the mackems against Man City, who have never been supported so loudly, yet so ironically.

As for the Camp Nou, what a crap hole that much vaunted venue is. Okay, so it holds 110,000. But it has a bog of a pitch and barely any cover, for crying out loud. From our experience it's always raining in Spain, so they need to fix themselves up with a roof for the next time we come. Real Mallorca could do with one too. For us, it wasn't such a problem because in an effort to blend in with the locals we'd equipped ourselves with sombreros – beautiful examples selected for their waterproofing qualities from the finest on offer on Las Ramblas' souvenir strip. We bought big ones to keep our *maracas* dry. We'd thought we'd been hearing the locals saying *maracas* all day, but we eventually found out that they were saying *urracas* which is Spanish for magpies.

They also liked calling us Geordies, because Jordi is just about the most popular Catalan boys' name. Johan Cruyff chose the name for his son who was born there.

The Camp Nou facilities (at least those offered to us away fans) were reminiscent of the old Gallowgate end (that's where Tony Blair used to sit as a kid, watching Jackie Milburn, remember?). The bogs were awful, and the catering arrangements pitiful. No doubt about it, we are well and truly pampered at the Gallowgate Colosseum these days. To be sure, the best thing that can be said about the Camp Nou is that it is linguistically intriguing; they're not even sure whether to call it Nou Camp or Camp Nou (what about 'Monsoon Now?').

The first time I went to the Camp Nou was while my colleague Big Brian and I were at a robotics conference with about two thousand other people from all over the world, including plenty of Americans and Japanese, in the Barcelona Fira Exhibition Centre, out by the Plaça Espana. It's at the foot of the hill of the Parc Montjuic, and as you climb the hundreds of stairs up the hill and look back down you get a view of the waterfalls and the fountain that they set dancing in coloured lights two or three evenings a week. If you want to escape the heat of the city, take a couple of hours and try this walk through the fresh and shady pines.

At the top is a beautiful old concert hall, the Palau Nacional, which had just been renovated when we were there in spring 1993. As you go further up through the pine forest you find yourself standing before the Olympic Stadium and the Olympic Swimming Pool and the outdoor Diving Pool. You'll have seen the famous views of divers who seem to be diving into space and down into the city – that's the Barcelona pool. It was just a few months after the Olympics and everything was gleaming new; the pool's changing rooms have certainly suffered since.

I've ended up going to games a couple of times with people who've never seen a football match before, not even on the television. One time I was at a meeting in London with my friends Eric from Denmark and Doug from Boston, and I took them both to see Gazza play at Arsenal one dark night in the mid-eighties. We lost. I don't think they've been to a game since. This time, Big Brian and I had found out that there was a Spanish league game and somehow we ended up going with Dave from South Carolina, I seem to remember, whom we'd met at the conference. The tickets are dirt cheap and easy to buy at the ground, though you tend to end up sitting on the rim of the bowl, stratospherically remote from the pitch. To give you an idea of the view, go up to the last row of Level 7 with some binoculars and look through the wrong end. Anyway, Barcelona was a good team at the time with players like Laudrup and Stoichkov and they were three goals up after ten minutes. Dave, our American friend was really getting into it and came up with 'Gee, guys, this is just like basketball. What kind of scores do you get in sahccer?' Dave thought that this scoring rate must be normal and that he was in for a score well into double figures. It could have been, but Barcelona relaxed and amazingly got pegged back to a three-all draw by the end of the match. It was all over too fast for Dave, who'd been looking forward to the popcorn and Bud breaks and the pom-pom girls. Anyway, it was a good introduction to real football, and a non-believer was converted; it's all part of the pilgrimage.

On the same trip, we bumped into Mark Knopfler sitting at the table beside us when we went for a late meal. I think he'd been giving a concert in the Palau and recording in Barcelona. Talent nurtured in Gosforth. Years later, in 2003, he was to wave (back) to us at the start of the Great North Run. The restaurant was Los Caracoles, which means 'The Snails'. Don't let the name put you off. It's a very busy, touristy but good restaurant on a corner site in Escudellers, a little side street on the left as you ramble down towards the harbour end of Las Ramblas. You walk through the furnace-hot kitchens to get to your table. Ask them to bring you a plate of Pato Negra and Manchego and a bottle of Faustino I to start your meal off, while you work out what to have from the menu; roast suckling pig is a good bet. Tasting the Faustino is fine, but saying the word's even better when you're ordering it in Barcelona – they remember Tino's hat-trick. What they should make is Faustino III in honour of his exploit, not just Faustino I, V, and VII. The crowd atmosphere that night was possibly the best ever at the all-seater St James's. Asking for a Faustino in Barcelona is an affront of the same order as making a Parisian ask for a ticket to Waterloo on the Eurostar. I'm sure that someone high up deliberately decided the Channel Tunnel was going to end up at Waterloo, not St Pancras or Euston or Kings Cross, just to annoy the Frogs.

But it was Mark Knopfler, not Tino, who wrote and performed the Local Hero theme, which the lads run out to at every home game, as well as the theme music for the second and fourth series of Auf Wiedersehen Pet. Why aye man! And he wrote Tunnel of Love 'like the Spanish City to me, when we were kids' – pity they've pulled most of it down now. He also plays guitar on Carlsbergly one of, if not the greatest song about Newcastle ever written, Jimmy Nail's 'Big River': 'this was a big river, ... the coaly Tyne.'

By the time we're drawn to play Barcelona again, I've got a feeling you're going to be in need of a haircut, and I know where you should head for. Look for the Plaça Universitat, a five minutes walk from the top of Las Ramblas, then take a few paces up Ronda Sant Antoni, one of the streets leading out of the square where you'll find an old-fashioned barbers; a narrow, deep room with about fifteen barber's chairs lined up facing the mirror stretching down one wall. For every chair, there's a barber, so you hardly ever need to wait. I don't much like waiting to get my hair cut, and I would never go to a barber where you have to book an appointment, so this is my kind of place. Like the barbers on High Bridge, where all you have to say on a Monday morning is 'aye', and depending on your intonation they know you mean 'what a cracking result!' or 'they were shite, weren't they?'. The chances of not talking about NUFC in there are zero. And both are lightning fast in action; five minutes and you're out, half an inch shorter, a few ounces of clippings and a couple of pounds lighter. When I first discovered this place (the one in Barcelona, that is), it cost two hundred and fifty pesetas, about a pound, but with the passing of time and the coming of the euro, the price has reached its current dizzy heights. Spanish barbers are special; in the holidays, I used to go to one not far from Malaga run by a really old grandpa and his fairly old son where you got a *copa* of *jerez* (sherry) to sip while you got your hair cut. Class.

After your five minutes in the barbers, head back down Tallers, a narrow street which leads you back to Las Ramblas past a string of record, guitar, and hippy shops of varying degrees of weirdness, and make your way down to la Boqueria covered market, where you can choose and eat your lunch while you walk around marvelling at the choice of fruit, vegetables, fish and meat and then rest up on a high stool for a *cava* and a *café con leche* at one of the *tapas* stalls. Remember how in Spender or Get Carter or Byker Grove, they turn a corner and are suddenly transported from one part of the town to another miles away? Well the Newcastle equivalent of this Spanish stroll would be getting your hair cut in High Bridge, stepping out of the doorway into the much regretted Handyside Arcade (how did they dare pull it down and replace it with characterless chain store mall mediocrity?) and ending up in the characterful Grainger Market. Sugar cone 99 at Mark Toney's? Yes please! All these places have something in common in the metonymic way that they embody the spirit of their respective cities.

The Daily Mirror took a more than imaginative geographical liberty in their back-page report on Celtic's triumph over Barcelona, which happened on the same night as our away leg at Real Mallorca (in fact we bumped into a good few Celtic supporters at Brussels and Madrid airports on the outward and return journeys). The Mirror informed its readers that Celtic's next opponents were going to be Villarreal, a Spanish town three hundred metres (!) south of

Barcelona. So presumably a lot of the Celtic fans had been drinking in Villarreal's bars, before strolling along to the Camp Nou!

Barcelona may be in Spain, but it's also the capital of the region of Catalonia. The Catalans have a strong separatist tradition and have their own language, Catalan. It is a sort of cross between Spanish and French with some Italian thrown in for good measure. I reckon that if the Kingdom of Northumbria had held out for a couple of centuries more, instead of caving in around 870 AD, Geordie would now have been at least as distinct from standard English as Catalan is from Castillian Spanish and would have a meaningful written tradition. The Catalans all speak Spanish as well, but monolingual Castillian speakers can have major difficulties understanding Catalan at the spoken level. Come to think of it, the same still goes for Geordies versus the southerners. If you have a reasonable knowledge of French and Spanish, you'll have no bother reading signs and should be able to cope with the main news and footie stories in the local paper, as we found out after buying one in Catalan by mistake. *Camp Nou* simply means the New Ground or Stadium, Camp coming from the Latin *Campus* (a field), and 'nou' lying somewhere between the French *nouveau* and the Spanish/Italian *nuevo/novo*.

'So what?' the lad who'd been rueing his bad luck might well have replied. 'They're all just a bunch of greasy *dagos* anyway.' And after a fashion he'd have been right. Though in his normal parlance he would have called the Italians 'Spics' or 'Wops'. But, generically, they were all 'dagos' to him. Why is that? How come such similar languages are spread right across the Mediterranean basin? Indeed, what would happen if someone were to pull the plug? It's all down to the mighty hand of Rome.

Once upon a time, much of present-day Spain, Portugal, France, Britain and Ireland, plus chunks of Germany and Northern Italy were populated by Celtic tribes. They all went happily about their business (relieving any boredom with an internecine massacre or two) until the Roman Empire decided it was about time for another enlargement. The Roman legions started putting themselves about in a big way, and before long, after Julius Caesar finally subdued the whole of Gaul not long before the birth of that other JC, they were under the Roman yoke and in the fullness of time became well and truly Romanised.

Of course the Romans came up our way as well. The local Geordie tribe of the time were known as the *Votadini*, which was a Latinised version of a native Celtic word meaning 'Those beer swilling heedbangers who daub themselves with black and white warpaint and whose womenfolk go around wearing next to bugger all even in the coldest of winters'. For reasons best known to themselves, the Romans never mixed in quite the same way in Britannia as they did in Gallia and Hispania (maybe the weather had something to do with it) and when they left Wallsend (Segedunum), the locals were still speaking their own lingo. The Vikings soon put paid to that, however, and bequeathed us our current dulcet tones. More of that later, when we get to Oslo.

So anyway, there we were (Barry and Pete, by the way, pleased to meet yiz) in this *Ramblas* bar packed to the gunwales with disappointed, but in no way angry, Toon Army wallahs. On the way there, as we streamed out of the ground, we had crossed the path of some English tourists. One of them asked, in his quaint cockney (well, south of the Tees) accent, what the matter was. We told him the game had been postponed because of the weather. This in fact is something we all should have realised a trifle earlier, as it had been pissing down the whole day, including during our one-hour-long jog down the *Ramblas* through *El Born* and the *Mare Nostrum* and along the beach to the Hotel Arts' big whale and back at nine o'clock that morning. 'Well,' said our new southern friend, 'if that had been Arsenal or Man. U, there would have been a riot.' 'Yes, but this is Newcastle United,' was the Geordie reply, 'we don't do riots, we just have fun.' And fun aplenty was being had in the bar all right.

There they were on their mobiles, sorting out flights, telling the wives to ring in the next morning with some excuse, determined to stop over another day ON THE OFF-CHANCE the game would be played (which really didn't look at all likely). The atmosphere in the bar was all sweetness and light, our dripping sombreros notwithstanding.

There then arose what can only be described as a potentially explosive situation. One of the greatest possible crimes against (Geordie) humanity had been perpetrated by a hapless Barcelona barman (he may well have been called Manuel). Even if he'd had a hap, he wouldn't have had a hope. The bottled beer (*San Miguel*, of course) was beyond its 'best by' date. Not that anyone would have noticed by the taste, mind. Well, you don't even notice the taste after the first few, do you? Nevertheless, notice it some enterprising soul did, and upon the uttering of the words 'Ya norron bonny lad', there was a deadly silence. Poor Manuel, you had to feel sorry for him. A lone Spanish bar steward in a sea of less than sober black and white. But all the lad from Gateshead wanted was free beer, of course, and to his credit that is what he secured for himself and the rest of us. After he left the bar, we quietly slipped the bar owner the price of the beers. Leave a good impression, we say.

The next morning, nursing just the mildest of hangovers, we tappy-lappied from our *Hotel Colon* to *Estruch*, the nearest *tapas* bar for breakfast. The *Colon* sounds like a shitty hotel, doesn't it, but it's quite the opposite. *Colon* is Spanish for Columbus, who set sail from Barcelona (amongst other places) to *colon*ise the New World. Armed with our Spanish-English dictionaries, we pounced upon the local papers for an account of … the postponement, much to the amusement of the locals. After several false starts and possible mistranslations (especially of the headlines, which are always a bugger, ask any translator), we were confident that we had understood the message. Yes, we were getting there, eventually: '*El partido...*' yes, got it, the game … '*fue* *abandonado'*... yes, was abandoned... hang on, it wasn't abandoned, it didn't even get started, okay they must mean 'postponed', great: 'The game was postponed...' *'a causa de las condiciones meteorológicas'* ... yes, we were getting very close now, '... because of the meteorological conditions'... 'Bollocks, ' – or *cojones*, as we were already beginning to think in Spanish - it just means 'weather'. There we have it: 'The game was postponed because of the weather'. A roar of triumphant laughter from us. We had cracked it. Yes, no doubt about it: the game had indeed been postponed because of the weather. There it was in black and white. Slapping-each-other-on-the-back time, I'd say. Our efforts to wade (ho ho) through this headline had not gone unnoticed in the bar, whose clientèle included a few Brits, though we were the only Geordies. 'But surely you knew already that ze game 'ad been called off?', the barman ventured. He had a point...

Pete, or *Pedro* by now (we always go a little native, you see, me and *Barrio Gotico,* the better to absorb the local colour) couldn't stay on because of work but hoped to see the game live on ITV that night. In fact the plan was to get back home in time for the Mike Neville Show or Look North for some of the pre-match build-up. Home, by the way, being Trier, Germany. But thanks to the wonders of satellite telly you can stay firmly in touch with what is happening back in the Holy Land these days. There were a few hundred others at the airport who hadn't managed to stay on either. Reached Deutschland in time to see the match on the box. Thought we were unlucky to go down three-one.

Me too, Pete, maybe a draw would have been a fairer result, and certainly Kieron Dyer's dozing tea-pot impersonation should never have happened, which would have brought it down to two-one, and a little bit of luck for Shola or Lua Lua could have made it twos apiece, as they were livewires on the night. Maybe a half or more of the Toon Army stayed on for the match, and a lot more Barça fans turned up than had the night before, when they'd obviously been sitting at home or in the bars laughing like drains (ha ha) at the *guiris,* which is what the *dagos* call us foreigners, who'd gone along to the ground imagining that the game might ever be played. A lot more turned up than had for the Dalglish-era rain game too, when we'd almost outnumbered them to see Aaron Hughes' début in the one-nil defeat. This time it was the turn of another of our young players, Michael Chopra to make his début; let's hope he goes on to be as successful as Aaron Hughes. Of course in that first match it had bucketed down as well, and it was as a direct result of the downpour that the famous big Newcastle flag never saw the light of day again. When I left the ground that first time, I was walking back up the avenue in the pouring rain and spotted a huge black lump lying abandoned in the gutter. It was the flag. I went over and had a look. It was the dead weight of ten men – no wonder they'd dumped it there. I half toyed with the idea of calling a taxi and trying to take it back for them, but the excess baggage would have been too much! I wonder whatever became of it. The last few times it had passed over my head before matches, it had begun to smell pretty badly, so maybe it was just as well. It was probably a health risk.

Most of the Newcastle fans this time were at one end of the ground, but a hundred or so, including me, somehow ended up at the other end, nearly half a kilometre away; it's a big place, especially when you're looking down from the rim of the giant soup bowl. There was plenty of noise coming out of the far end, and you could make out snatches of topical songs made up for the occasion of skiving an extra day off work; things like 'Stand up if you've got the sack' and 'We're supposed to be at home'. The best one down at our end was 'Figo is a Geordie'. Even some of the fans who would have liked to stay on for the match couldn't because their organised trips' flights couldn't be changed at such short notice, and they'd reluctantly had to go back at the originally booked time. So this was at least one occasion when travelling independently had its advantages, because it gave the lucky ones the flexibility to decide for themselves 'should I stay or should I go?'

That's the ticket

Back in the old days, a few intrepid fans who for various reasons couldn't use the club transport did it under their own steam (travel, that is), like we do now. It wasn't so difficult to get to Feyenoord – there was the ferry from Hull straight there; and obviously Rangers was a piece of cake – twelve thousand made the trip up to Glasgow; but Budapest or Zaragoza were not the easiest places to get yourself to back then. You needed visas and such like, for a start.

Organised trips are great if you live in the region. They're like a charter holiday, a city break, but with the key differences that there are lots of familiar, friendly faces around and everyone is united in a common purpose: to support the team, and have a very good time doing it. The club's own trips have the added attraction, which becomes more and more useful as you progress through the rounds and more people want to come on the trips, that they even get you a guaranteed match ticket thrown in with the package, neatly by-passing the hurdle of tickets going to those who have the best recent away-match attendance record. But there are many of us who are exiles living abroad in other parts of the UK, Europe and further afield, and we're never going to get very far up that particular league table of away-match attendance, and we're not able to take advantage of the club trips either, so we're doubly penalised. We have to be lucky and inventive to find tickets for the most popular games or the smallest grounds.

Newcastle's Euro Cup matches and pre-season tours in recent years have opened up new holiday possibilities for the whole family. Why waste time poring over holiday brochures when all you need to do is wait and see where the lads are heading during the pre-season and, as long as it's not somewhere too outlandish like Kuala Lumpur, just tag along. The same applies when any of the mid-season Euro away games coincide with autumn and spring half-term breaks or Easter holidays. The lads'll take you to places you'd never have dreamed about going otherwise. How else would you ever have thought of a nice summer holiday in Lokeren and Anderlecht in Belgium, or Troyes in France, or Rotterdam, Enschede, Helmond, Den Bosch, Deurne, Capelle, or Veenendael in Holland (there aren't many teams left in Holland that we haven't played now, except perhaps for those enigmatic Go-Ahead Eagles!!) or Munich and Bochum in Germany, or a mid-term break in Oslo or Gothenburg? You just announce that you've decided it would be nice to have a family touring holiday of the Netherlands or the west coast of Sweden or a skiing holiday in Norway. And by the way, Pet, since we're going to be in the vicinity anyway, wouldn't it be nice to fit in one, or four if it's a Holland pre-season tour, of the Toon's matches?

Let me just break at this point to let you know that while I am sitting typing this up, I've just seen that Chelsea have got knocked out of the Champignons League by Monaco, so we're now the last surviving UK team in the 2003/04 European competitions, at least until tomorrow when we face Marseille. Which is in itself quite an achievement, no matter what happens. Actually I'd better go to bed soon or I'll miss the early call for the TGV. By the way, here's a case in point: we haven't got tickets yet, so tomorrow's going to be a busy day. You and I will find out what happened later.

Booking your travel is the easy part, getting your tickets can be an adventure in itself. We're lucky enough to have been born into the welcoming arms of one of the best-supported clubs in existence, albeit one of the least supporter-friendly ones. But this can be a double-edged sword when it comes to that most vital of concerns: the support is the best, so the demand is the highest, and so you're never really sure that you're going to get a ticket. Many a time and oft, especially for small grounds with small away ticket allocations, demand out-strips supply and if you don't plan ahead, you have to scramble around at the last minute to find an alternative solution.

From previous bitter experience of not getting tickets from the club allocation, our conclusion is that it's best to try several routes right from the outset. Not only do you apply in the normal way to the NUFC Box Office, but you also see if by lucky chance you have a friend living in the locality of the opponents who can order tickets from their club, or you can try through the local NUFC Supporters Club, if they have one. It's surprising how many countries have supporters clubs for UK teams, and we're not just talking about the Singapore chapter of Man Utd or Real Madrid. In one case on this particular pilgrimage, the local supporters club proved invaluable to us and we managed to source enough tickets from them early enough to be able to make a family holiday of it, as the match coincided with the half-term school holidays. So thanks very much to Christian at the Norwegian NUFC Supporters Club for the eight Vålerenga tickets!

With this belt and braces approach, you minimise the risk of losing out on a ticket, but it can result in you ending up with one or two spares. It's clear that we're not the only ones playing for safety, as you often bump into other people also trying to off-load surplus tickets on match day. These are not ticket touts; these are good honest supporters who for one reason or another have a ticket left over. In our general experience, all they ever ask for is the face value of the ticket, and in many cases even less. So sometimes it is worth travelling in hope. Mind, Marseille supporters are different – we were offered two tickets through e-Bay first of all for one hundred and eighty euros, but he then pretended he had been offered two hundred and twenty euros, and asked for a better offer. It was obviously some tout, so we initially decided to bail out. But then came the thought that there could be scope to turn the tables on him...

One time we ended up giving away our spare tickets to two local lads who were autograph hunting at the team hotel in Basel – it was getting near kick-off, and the tickets were only going to go to waste otherwise. And it fitted in well with our credo as good pilgrims to do our best to leave a warm glow behind in the hearts and minds of any town that the Toon passes through. It was a small gesture, but the two kids were genuinely grateful, and after getting permission by mobile phone from their parents, they joined the crowd on the tram to the ground.

When it comes to ordering match and travel tickets, you're forced into making arrangements in the wrong order. For one thing, there is sometimes only one week between getting through one round and the first leg of the next round. The club box office does an amazing job of getting tickets out to people, but with all their speed, the tickets might still only arrive at best a couple of days before the match, and often later, which can mean you're waiting for the morning post with your plane ticket in your hand! Luckily, the club have a very efficient back-up system in case your tickets don't get to you before you have to leave, as we found out when we had to leave to get to the Champignons League game at Feyenoord before the tickets came. (That wasn't a typo just there by the way; it's just that I hate to call it by its official name, as it has mushroomed beyond the champions. Why don't UEFA get real and call it something like the Euro League?) You phone the Box Office and let them know your problem and they take a note of your application details, and they specify a meeting point at the away ground an hour or so before the match. When you get there you find you're not alone, and that there are maybe ten other supporters with the same problem, all waiting for the NUFC representative. You show him your application form and some ID and then you're grouped together with your fellow travellers and ushered into the ground by the host club's stewards. All very smooth and efficient. Can you imagine what it would have been like to miss that last minute three-two win?

Gannin' Dutch again

What a great occasion that was. It was also a case of history repeating itself, or even coming full circle, as

Feyenoord were of course our very first opponents in a European competition way back in 1968.

That was the year of student uprising all around Europe and it fittingly marked a new departure for Newcastle United. At last the Mags could start tilting at windmills, eating frogs' legs at a snail's pace and generally going all continental. But let's not forget: the only reason we got in in the first place was because two clubs from the same city could not enter, so many thanks to our Scouse friends.

We had been far too young to travel then of course (where would we have got the money anyway?), so we had to be content with the home games. But this time, here we were in the famous (and famously unpronounceable) *Kuyp*. It's a pity Johan Cruyff hadn't still been around somewhere to add to the tongue-twisting fun.

We had planned our rendezvous in Rotterdam with our usual military-like precision. Chris and Sarah were flying over from London, and Pete was driving up from Trier (via Luxembourg and Belgium) to pick them up at Rotterdam's tiny but cosy airport. The three of them were staying at a hotel called *'t wapen van marion* in a little village on the coast called Oostvuurne. The area around Rotterdam is surprising for a number of reasons. You have the ultra-modern city of Rotterdam itself: the reason why there are so few old buildings in the city centre is that the Germans bombed the shit out of them. This was particularly tragic as the Dutch had already surrendered a couple of hours before the first bomb fell. For some reason, the order to abort the mission didn't get through to the pilots in time. We all know the song: 'when it's spring again I'll bring again tulips from Amsterdam.' Well Ajax supporters (Ajax being the big Amsterdam club, remember) sing their own quaint variation on that. Instead of '*Als de lente komt dan breng ik jouw tulpen uit Amsterdam.*' They sing:

'*Als de lente komt dan gooien wij bommen op Rotterdam*' = 'When it's spring again we'll hoy again bombs onto Rotterdam.'

But let's not mention the war.

The new-fangled glass-plate fronted buildings of downtown Rotterdam seem to be jutting out at all angles and some of them seem to defy their centre of gravity. They've even got some flats which are cubes balancing on one of their corners like tumbling dice. It must be acrobats who live in them – maybe Lua Lua could be interested. You'd think they might fall down on you at any minute.

Then there is Europoort about twenty clicks away from the city centre. This is the biggest port in the world. Let's draw breath and run through that again, shall we? The biggest port in the whole wide world! It is megablastically gi-huge!!! Oil terminals here, container-laden trains there. Construction work under way seemingly everywhere. More and more oil tanks as you scan the horizon. It's home to the spot market for oil. Let's hope nobody ever starts hoying bombs on this little lot. The overall impression in this neck of the woods is one of grime and grottiness. Yet just around the corner from it all is the toy-town village of Oostvuurne. Like all villages on the Dutch coast, it is spotlessly well kept, and the brightly marked streets are so narrow that you expect to see Noddy and Big Ears driving their car past you any minute. The hotel called 't wapen van marion is great value for money. Check out their website (www.wapenvanmarion.nl), it's a good one. They charge two-star prices for four-star comfort, which includes an indoor pool and tennis courts. The hotel is just a few hundred yards away from a sandy beach. And while you're jogging along that beach to build up an appetite for breakfast you can see the Europoort refineries in the distance. It's a very convenient base for blasting along the motorway into the heart of Feyenoord territory.

And that is just what Sarah, Chris and Pete did around tea-time on match-day to meet up with Barry and his son Brian. Thank goodness for mobiles, which enabled us to home in very effectively and rendezvous on a supermarket/cinema car park just across the road from the *Kuyp*, thus making for a speedy get-away back to our respective destinations of Oostvuurne and Brussels after the match.

But there were still a few hours to go before kickoff, and we decided to follow the Club's advice and head for the *Ouwe haven* (old port) district for the pre-match bevs. When we got there (by taxi) we found the place heaving with Toon wallahs and felt immediately at home. We had hoped to wear something suitable for the occasion but it was just as well we weren't shod with clogs, because as we were sipping the cool Heineken (Brian his coke), we heard the unwelcome sound of the dregs of Dutch society seeking to start a riot, and we had to be pretty fleet of foot! A hundred or so came charging into the black and white throng. Glasses were flying and breaking, and we saw at least one lad who'd got hurt. Fortunately, there were plenty of cloggy Edgar Wallaces (polisses) on hand just around the corner (in Dutch that's *om de hoek*) and the scum that had set out to spoil our fun were quickly stamped on.

But that sort of thing always leaves a bad taste in your mouth. We just don't need these morons. In fact the human gene pool doesn't need them either. Wouldn't it be great if they would just spontaneously combust or collectively drown themselves in the North Sea? They'd be flaming Fleming lemmings.

When we got to the ground, we went to the main entrance, where the rest of the late or lost ticket Toon were waiting, and sure enough the NUFC rep showed up and we were escorted to the end where the faithful were gathered. The *Kuyp* was pretty impressive, all right. True to its name, it is a great big bowl. What we saw right in the middle of that bowl was not cornflakes waiting for the milk to be poured but, bizarrely and surreally, a couple of red pianos. We thought we were about to be treated to some pre-match musical entertainment, but in fact we were to be subjected to a form of torture designed to leave us at least temporarily brain-damaged.

The tunes and the songs were of the sort you normally associate with Germans who are pissed out of their square heads at carnival time, linking arms and swaying to and fro in their beer halls. In German they call that *schunkeln*, which is a bit like the 'shuggy' in 'shuggy boat', if you see what I mean.

The seats we were in were, of course, never going to be used as such. But when we stood, we realised that the sides of the *Kuyp* were also suitable for the cornflakes bowl analogy. Boy, were they steep! But fortunately no accidents occurred, and the acoustics were excellent for the in-form Toon Army. Unkindly, we also sang (to the tune of 'she'll be coming round the mountain when she comes'): 'If it wasn't for the British you'd be Krauts!' Unkind, perhaps, but essentially true. The reason the Dutch are called Dutch in the first place is because they were taken to be *deutsch*, i.e. German. And in America, the people known as the Pennsylvanian Dutch are actually German. Funny, isn't it? To avoid possible confusion, the Germans' nickname for a Dutchman is *käsekopf*, which translates as cheese-head. This solves all problems, of course.

It was a big night for the Toon. You know the story. We had to win to have any chance of staying in the Champignons League, but even then we were relying on Juventus beating Kiev for us. After we had gone two-one up through a Viana screamer and with us looking good, the Dutch came back and equalised. With literally just seconds on the clock, Dyer shot, the goalkeeper parried, but it broke loose to Bellamy who thumped it off the prostrate goalkeeper (not the goalkeeper's prostate) into the net. With Juventus winning too, we were through to the next stage and Bloater and Gloater could laugh at us all the way to the bank, as usual.

First steps on the path

With tickets arriving just before you leave, you have no alternative but to book your travel before you're sure of having a match ticket. Booking a flight early is more important than ever now, with the volatility of the ticket prices from the new cheap airlines. When they see that demand is going up, they put the prices up, and dramatically. In fact I wouldn't be at all surprised if they don't also tune into the UEFA draws and when they see that they fly to airports near where the UK teams are going to be playing, they put the prices up as fast as they can. If you look the next day, the prices can easily have gone up by a factor of ten.

To beat this, there's a way: in the later rounds, the draw is made all the way from the last sixteen through to the final, so you know that you are going to play one of a pair of teams in the following round if you get through the current one, and they even plan ahead which is the home and which is the away leg. So some people buy cheap tickets to the two places, knowing that if you wait to see if you get through and which of the two possible next-round opponents you will play, you stand to pay a lot more. Whatever you lose on the wrong guess can be dwarfed by the price hikes on the right guess. And if the worst comes to the worst and your team doesn't get through, you'll have lost the cost of maybe two six- or ten-pound tickets, but you stood to save ten times or more, and hey, there's not going to be a match so you've saved the price of match entry, which puts you ahead, doesn't it... ? Maybe not.

If you don't want to gamble, the other way to get around it is to be ready with your Internet booking forms primed on-screen for all the possible opposing teams and ready to submit as soon you know the draw and which is the away leg. Then when your opponents are chosen, you switch to the right window and hit the 'submit' button. A lot of people do this kind of thing, you know. There's a sort of competition going on between supporters to see who can devise the cleverest short cuts or trickiest and cheapest ways of getting to the matches. And it forms quite a popular subject of conversation on match day. 'How did you get here?' 'That's nothing, I came via such and such and mine only cost fifty pence each way.'

There's more than one way to travel and there are hundreds of choices of where to stay. For the travel, you tend towards whatever's easy and convenient and doesn't take too long. Obviously, you look for a good price, which sometimes might even mean having to stay a Saturday night after a Thursday night match, although that old condition that airlines used to apply in the days when they had a near cartel on prices has largely been sucked out of the aircraft window in recent years. Of course it depends on where you'd have to stay for an extra day, as some places are worth seeing, and others really aren't, and in any case you have extra accommodation costs to pay for. You also find that planes at unpopular times of the day can be far cheaper, so if you don't mind getting up or arriving at an unearthly hour, then this can have its rewards. As we were to find out in Mallorca...

Being based on the continent also gives us more scope to travel by car or better still by train, which I prefer anyway to planes. I'm no Denis Bergkamp, but I can sympathise with his feelings when it comes to planes. One time I was in a Sabena propeller plane called a Brasilia Embraer that took off and climbed steadily, but then the engine note lowered and it levelled off instead of continuing to climb. This plane had a computerised voice system giving out messages and it started to regale us with the insistent message 'warning: door open.' Not good. Anyway, the plane started to circle and we eventually got back down on the ground.

I was later told that if it had been a jumbo jet, where more than three quarters of the take-off weight is fuel, it couldn't have gone straight back down and landed because the airframe isn't designed for the forces, so they either have to circle for ages to use up the fuel or go out and jettison the fuel over the sea. It's a long way to the sea from Brussels, so I was glad that it was a little propeller plane that time. The crew called the maintenance people, who proceeded to 'solve' the problem with what looked a bit like a toffee hammer.

After a few good whacks, they announced that all was well and we could proceed to a second take-off. They did however offer everyone the chance to get off and catch another plane that hadn't been whacked with a hammer. Everyone looked at each other, but nobody got up to go. I had the impression that if one person had stirred, there would have been a stampede for the door, but no-one did, me included. But I felt like it.

Nevertheless, I'm on another plane writing this now, because sometimes there's no alternative. In this case, it's the fastest way out of Manchester, which is certainly the right direction to be headed.

UEFA rules state that generally about five per cent of ground capacity has to be allocated to the away supporters. So something else you can do on the Internet to occupy yourself in the build-up to the draw for the next round is to look at the websites of the possible opponents. If you draw a team with a good-sized ground, you can generally breathe a sigh of relief as this boosts your chances of being successful in getting a match ticket. But you have to be careful of being too cheered because quite often UEFA puts extra restrictions on the crowd size for security and safety reasons by creating wide swathes of no-man's land either side of the away supporters, taking a few thousand off the ground capacity. So five per cent can represent anything from barely a thousand tickets against little teams to three or even five thousand when it's a really big Italian or Spanish stadium. And the big teams often give a bigger percentage, because we're considered as low box-office potential for their own supporters, so they think they might as well give us some extra places to boost their revenue. Who can forget the wall of twelve thousand fans at Inter Milan in the second round of the Champignons League in 2002/03? Give them a few more seasons, and continental clubs will know what to expect when they are drawn against the Toon!

The Breda tale

Isn't the UEFA Cup a fantastic invention? In a way it's a bit like the FA Cup, with huge differences between the levels of the leagues and the teams who take part. On the one hand you've got teams like Valencia, Inter Milan, Barcelona and Liverpool, and on the other hand you've got teams you've never heard of like Vålerenga. The romance of the Cup! The big difference of course is that the FA Cup is unseeded, so if you're lucky you can get right through to the Final without ever playing a decent team and by playing all your games at home, while the UEFA Cup is very much more controlled through seedings, and you have to play games home and away. The first-round draw brought us up against NAC Breda. What a fine name, NAC: our aim became precisely that – to knack Breda. From our point of view, this was an ideal draw, because it was just around the corner, and a nice little town we'd passed through before.

Of course when you're on the outside looking in, when you fail to qualify, it's vaguely annoying to see unheard-of teams playing against Barcelona and the like. If sunderland ever get in, they'll be viewed exactly in this way by supporters who find themselves having to make arrangements to get there. You can hear them now, '*Donde? Qué? Où? Was ist das?* Who on earth and where in hell is sunderland?? Is that where they hang monkeys? We were hoping to draw a team on the Turkish-Syrian border, now we have to go to somewhere far less developed. Do they have an airport (above us only a monkey's heed)? Is there a hotel nearby? Should we take our own food and drinks with us? What language do they speak? What injections do you need to go there? Should we take our own water?'

Only joking, mackems, good luck to you. Anyway don't worry, you continentals, it's not going to happen.

So, Breda. No need for complicated travel arrangements, and just the one afternoon off work needed. And the same

29

went for Harvey, also based in Brussels, and for Pete coming from work in Luxembourg. Tickets could have been a problem as the ground capacity was very low at seventeen thousand and reduced still further by UEFA safety restrictions. We asked around and came up with quite a group of us who wanted to go, so we downloaded the European away leg ticket application forms off the official site and sent in our applications. Despite the restricted numbers, we were lucky and got all the tickets that we asked for, so there we were: Pete, Barry and son Brian, Graham, Harvey, Neale and Don. At the last minute Graham and Neale had to cry off, but we were still a happy band that set off on a sunny Thursday lunchtime in October.

First stop sprout-side was at school to pick up Brian – by magical good luck he had the afternoon off (maybe the headmaster was wanting to go too?), then over to Harvey's *maison de maître*, then to Brussels Zaventem Airport ('above us always rain - good for the sprouts'), to rendezvous with Don who was flying in from Gatwick ('above us only southern nothingness'). Here's one great thing about Brussels Airport: would you believe it's got a good-sized replica of the Angel of the North? Well it has: in Terminal A on a pedestal to the left of the landing between the escalators taking you below ground and under the runways. It's about one-tenth scale, I guess. I don't think many people much liked it when they first saw it (the real one), but somehow it grows on you, don't you find? Now I actually quite like seeing it in the distance as you head up the motorway on the last leg of the journey for a visit back home. A bit like seeing Penshaw Monument a bit earlier or the Tyne Bridge a bit later, they're signs that you're almost back. Anyway, can I encourage you to rub the foot of the replica Angel for good luck any time you pass through Brussels Airport? I do, and I'm by no means the only one to do it, as the Angel's feet are getting quite polished by now. Pity, I should have taken the plane instead of the TGV to Marseille, so I could have paid homage to the magic toes and the result might have been different....

We spent the journey talking about old times, the North-East, and other Newcastle games in Europe. Don is a truly seasoned Euro traveller and he's seen action in other obscure places and competitions such as Bari for the Anglo-Italian Cup – yes, we actually know someone who attended an Anglo-Eyetie Cup away game!!! And he lives in Brighton but has a season ticket, and makes it up to a lot of the games. That's dedication for you. As for Harvey, well he was born in Whitley Bay but then he had the misfortune to have to leave for exile in Oxfordshire while he was still in Junior School, and while he's been just about everywhere in the world since, including sharing private airplane trips with film stars to Cannes and Geneva in his previous job as the Hollywood film industry's European representative, he's never been back to the Promised Land. He's a fiercely proud supporter of the lads, nonetheless, and he's done his best to convert Clint Eastwood, Ewan MacGregor, Michael Douglas, Catherine Zeta Jones, and the like. So don't be surprised if you see them in the Gallowgate now and then.

Reunions like this always get you reminiscing over old times and schooldays. At Brian's school now, they don't seem to have nicknames for the teachers, maybe because there's such a big turnover that there's no time for traditions to become established. Whereas we had some great ones: probably the best one was Scotch Mist Macleod, who attempted to teach us the noble art of boxing. At the end of the term, he organised a tournament. Even in those days, the fight game was open to the evils of match-fixing, and my bout was stopped for lack of aggression – we'd agreed beforehand that I wouldn't punch my opponent if he wouldn't punch me, so we took up our three minutes with a few Ali shuffles and some desultory bobbin' and a-weavin'. But also a couple of kids who hated each other got paired together, and that was a bloodbath. Another teacher, whose initials - unfortunately for him but gloriously for us - were W.C., inescapably became Bogs, while another was a railway fanatic who got called Stoker. One new kid had only ever heard his nickname and when he went to the first lesson, he piped up with 'Please Mr Stoker …' - a bad start. At least he taught us the Five W's: 'Warm Wet Westerly Winds in Winter', and 'Yeess boyz, constant revision, constant revision'. Don's class was crazier than mine: he told us about the time that they were waiting for Stoker to arrive for the lesson and they upset a load of books off the shelves over the floor and then half the class braced themselves against the wall, as if they were propping it up and when he walked in they all shouted 'Please Sir, help! The wall's collapsing!' He turned on his heels and left!

As you travel seamlessly from Belgium into Holland, you might wonder what really is the difference between the Flemish-speaking Belgians and the Dutch. Well, it's all rather artificial, because for hundreds of years it used to be united, albeit under the rule of an ever-changing array of distant kings, emperors and kaisers including Burgundians, Spaniards, Hapsburgs, and Prussians. After the Battle of Waterloo, things got confused for fifteen years until 1830 when they got fed up, asked if they could split in two and had a bit of a revolution. As a result, Belgium was set up by the Prussians and British as a buffer state on top of France. They found a convenient minor royal in Prussia called Leopold Saxe-Coburg to be its new king, convenient because he was future Queen Victoria's uncle and wasn't doing anything in particular at the time. That's very unusual for a Royal, of course, as they usually have such a busy schedule, bless them.

Julius Caesar wrote in his campaign diaries about a particularly pesky tribe of workie-tickets called the Belgae, so that gave someone a good clue for the new name. Roughly speaking, the Dutch speakers who ended up still being in Holland were the Protestants, while the Dutch Catholics ended up in Belgium. They still speak very much the same language although the Belgian Flemish version has been Frenchified in some of the grammar and in borrowing quite a few words and expressions. Flemish also flows along more mellifluously while Dutch is more jagged, especially when they wrap their tonsils around a *ch* or a *g*, which come out sounding more like they're trying to clear a particularly tenacious glob of phlegm out of their throat. It's the Dutch who should be called the 'Phlegmish', come to think of it. It's little wonder then that Flemish songs are much more pleasant to hear than Dutch.

Apart from getting them to sing a song, another foolproof way of telling them apart is to put them in two cars and watch them drive away. The one who hooks up a caravan then lurches out to overtake without warning or indicating and who uses the accelerator pedal like an on-off switch is Dutch, while the one to whom any absolutely predictable motoring incident comes as a complete surprise and who then crashes is a Belgian. That's why you can't get much more than about fifteen per cent overall no-claims bonus in Belgium.

The trouble with all these artificial solutions to border problems is that by trying to solve one problem they create another, and for Belgium the problem which has simmered for almost two hundred years is that the French speakers in the South and the Flemish in the North basically don't get along very well with each other (that's diplomatic speak for 'hate each other's guts'), and neither bunch is particularly sympathetic towards the people who live in Brussels. Then you've got an enclave of German-speakers over in the Ardennes to make it even more complicated. The end result is that each has its own little regional government within an overall federal setup, leading to a triplicated or even quadruplicated civil service and endless petty jealousies and arguments. You should see the electoral lists when they're voting – there are getting on for twenty different parties because you have Flemish and French versions of each one, and some German ones too for good measure.

It's funny how a lot of names don't seem to be what they should be. While we've established pretty clearly already that the Dutch should be the Phlegmish, what we call Holland should really be called the Netherlands. It's only the two coastal provinces North and South Holland that actually have this name. It's as if Dutch people would start calling England Northumberland. And as we noted earlier, wouldn't Dutch be a better name for Germans (or was it the other way round?), since they call their country Deutschland? It's hard to make sense of some of these names, isn't it?

By mid-afternoon, we'd chosen a good space in the shelter of a Tynemouth-registered tour coach in the massive car park beside the ground, donned the colours, coloured the Don and headed off on the twenty-minute walk into town. As we were approaching the main square, a local couple stopped us and, looking at little Brian, advised us to hide our shirts and not to go any closer to the town centre as there was a lot of trouble going on. Apparently a group of Dutch fans from one of Breda's local rivals had decided to come to town to spoil the atmosphere, and they'd succeeded. So we took the couple's advice and skirted the centre and found a nice pavement café with a few tables and chairs outside. On our later trip to Mallorca, Harvey told me that he'd noticed that Brian was more hoping to sit inside, but I was as usual oblivious to any chill in the air, having been brought up on wearing shorts until I was well past Brian's age and going on five-mile runs in the snow and slush across the Town Moor, so we settled down in the open air. Maybe that explains why Brian pointedly ordered a big mug of hot chocolate, while we got in the *Amstels*. *Amstel* ... from *Amster*dam.

Whenever I go to Holland, I can't resist an *Uitsmijter*. 'What kind of drink is that?' I hear you ask, 'something like a *Jägermeister*?' Well actually, no, but it goes down a treat with an *Amstel*. If you find somewhere that does a good one, and there are a few places in both Breda and Eindhoven that'll do you proud, then you get a big plate loaded with slices of toast overlaid with ham and cheese and then topped off with a few fried eggs, and a load of salad surrounding them. And by the way, the name itself is one of its finer points, because it means 'chuck out' - it's the name for Dutch leftovers. So it was *uitsmijters* all round. While we were tucking in to our chuck-outs, Don spotted one of his friends who'd been at the Royal Antwerp game, of which more anon.

Whatever trouble there had been had dissolved away as we joined the flow of good-humoured Toon Army and NAC'ers making our way together back up to the ground. This was going to be a bit of a nail-grower, because we'd already won the first leg five-nil, so it was supposed to be more of a gentle run-out for the lads. That win had started us off on our season's best run of seven matches where we won every game except the narrow loss three-two away at Arsenal, and even that had been at least a moral victory as we'd come back twice to equalise for twos each only to give away a very unfortunate penalty for a deliberate handball by JJ when we were looking the more likely to get the winner.

I'd been up at St. James's Park for the home leg against Breda, as the match had been a few days after the Great North Run, and that was to be the only home leg I made it to, because I decided to use my spare holidays to go to all the away legs - the atmosphere is much better. The NAC fans had a great time in Newcastle, sitting out in the beautiful autumn sunshine (they were lucky), playing football in Old Eldon Square with the Goths, having a pre-match Chinky in Stowell Street, singing their hearts out before, during, and after the game, and they didn't mind too much about losing, though maybe we needn't have rubbed it in so hard.

For the return leg Shay Given, Gary Speed and Alan Shearer were all being rested, so Steve Harper, Hugo Viana and Shola were in. Like all the good teams now, we've got some excellent players who would surely hold down regular places in other teams, and many might say they should be regulars for us too. This question of squad rotation is a tricky one, and some teams seem to be more successful than others at keeping on winning while at the same time keeping more than eleven players happy with a regular starting place. Steve Harper, Hugo Viana and Shola are good examples. Maybe Viana has had more difficulty in adapting but he's shown at times that he is a player of real quality; we wouldn't have got into the second round of the 2002/03 Champignons League without his fabulous goal in Feyenoord. Shola is arguably the closest of the three to becoming a regular, helped by the regular injuries to Craig Bellamy, and he knows that Alan Shearer has himself said that he's going to retire at the end of next season, so he has something to aim for. But Steve Harper has the most thankless task of all. Here he is, the best homegrown North-East goalkeeper for a generation, and he's restricted to occasional Cup matches. At least the outfield players get a run-out as a sub for twenty minutes or so now and then, but a goalkeeper doesn't even get that chance. The risk is obviously too high that if the sub goalie gets injured, then the original goalie can't come back on. Mind, that could be a good innovation for UEFA to think about: to allow the subbed goalie to come back on if the sub is injured.

As for Breda, they had a couple of players called Seedorf and Stam but their play, while not to be sneezed at, didn't do much to persuade us that they were related to their more famous namesakes. Our section was just to the left and behind the goal that we were attacking in the second half, and so ideally placed to see Laurent Robert's close-range goal from a clever through pass by JJ just before the end. That was one of the few incidents worthy of mention in the match, which was very much a lacklustre affair, given that we were so far ahead after the first leg. Lua Lua came on as a substitute towards the end and he at least tried to liven things up a bit, and managed a glaring miss of almost Ryan Giggs and Ronnie Rosenthal proportions. I suppose we'd saved Breda's honour by not whacking them again, but maybe this was taking it too far.

It's just a small ground, the MyCom Stadium, though modern and well put together, as Dutch grounds invariably are, including even some of the smaller ones like Helmond Sport who'd hosted our pre-season training games. Breda are another one of those European teams whose fans have a call-and-response chant which one end of the ground starts, then the other end replies, then they echo it back and forth. I like it – if you're one of the privileged ones sitting at the halfway line, it must be great hearing it in stereo. We should do it at St. James's. Can you imagine it? Gallowgate: 'Toon Toon', Leazes: 'Black and White Army', repeated *ad infinitum*.

The Breda crowd also had another song which went on for minutes on end that demonstrated, if any further proof were needed, that the Dutch and Geordie languages are blood brothers. You couldn't make out what it really was, but it went 'Whey yer knaaaaa, whey yer knaaaaa' in a long plaintive call, lingering on the 'knaaaaa'. Not ones to pass up on an offering of brotherly and mutual appreciation, the Toon Army joined in with gusto, and the whole ground resounded to the refrain. At the end of the match, as Breda bade a farewell to European football, the call went up again as the ground slowly cleared, and, whey yer knaa, it was geet good. We still don't know what it meant, and we haven't heard it anywhere else in Holland, so it must be Breda's own unique homage to their team. And as we filtered down the steps of the terracing, one lone Geordie stood in reverie as he contemplated the emptying stadium, murmuring 'Whey yer knaa, whey yer knaa' to himself, no doubt moved by the confluence of the two languages.

The spell was broken when we got down to the front of the terrace just as Big Al came out onto the pitch with the rest of the subs to jog and stretch their legs, and a round of 'Shearuhherrr, Shearuhherrr' echoed around the now almost empty stadium.

The car park after the match was in absolute gridlock, and with our black and white stripes we were granted no quarter – if they couldn't play us off the park, they could at least block us in the car park. There was nothing for it: Don got out of the car and, adopting his best impression of Monty Python-era P.C. Michael Palin stopping the traffic on Westminster Bridge, he started directing the traffic and got us and a few other Toon cars out and on our way. As we chugged along, we heard that Man City had scraped past

Lokeren, whom we had obliterated in an earlier Intertoto competition, and then we listened to Blackburn being knocked out by an unpronounceable Turkish team; too bad. There were big jams on the motorway so we didn't get back until after one, and then after three hours' sleep, we were up again so that I could run Don down to Charleroi airport for the check-in for his fistfull-of-euros Ryanair flight back to Stanstead. It turned out to be one of the last flights out, as not long after, Ryanair stopped the route after a dispute with their competitors who had complained about allegedly unfair advantages given to Ryanair by the city council.

Your journey back was even worse though, wasn't it, Pete?

Too right it was! The other NAC car park where I had parked had also been jammed solid and there was no P.C. Don on points duty, so it took me a good hour to get clear. But after that it was plain sailing as far as the Brussels ring. I was heading for the E411, which by day is a lovely scenic sweep through the Ardennes (Battle of the Bulge country). Came to a grinding halt, however, near the Tervuren exit on account of night-time resurfacing work. The halt lasted a good hour and a half and it was about one-thirty in the morning before I was clear of Brussels with the prospect of a further three hours before getting home to Trier. I realised it had been a very bad idea not to take at least the next morning off and spend the night in Breda. So now I planned to stop over at the first hotel/motel. Unfortunately the next one was not until Arlon (in Flemish it's Aarlen), which was a good hour and a half away. And I didn't fancy driving off into the Ardennes, i.e. out into the sticks, on the off chance of finding something somewhere. By the time I reached Arlon (that is the place where that bastard Dutroux went on trial, by the way – may he roast slowly in hell), I reckoned I might as well press on, and finally got home and into bed about four-thirty. The alarm went at six-thirty and I had to get ready and take my daughter Tina to school in Luxembourg. Such is life.

Didn't get a lot of work done that day. But we were in the next round...

So we'd NAC'd them and we were through round one. The Champignons League it certainly wasn't; in their parallel matches, our conquerors in that mushrooming competition, Partizan Belgrade, had been battling it out with past champions Real Madrid, future champions Porto, and our later nemesis Marseille. On the same night as we completed our six-nil aggregate victory, Malatyaspor had gone out to a 'silver goal' in extra time to Basel, who were to be drawn out as our next-round opponents. The draw was made the next day, the seventeenth of October. Over at UEFA Headquarters in Nyon, we were in the seeded half of the draw in Pot Four, with potential opponents lined up as Basel, Hearts, Teplice, which is somewhere in Yugoslavia, Gençlerbirligi, the Turkish team who had just knocked out Blackburn while we were stuck in the Breda car park, Hajduk Split on the Yugoslavian Riviera, or Torpedo Moscow. Out of that lot, I think we were quite lucky to get Basel, from the point of view of it being a good place for a trip. Though footballing-wise they represented quite a step up in standard, as - like us - they had been in the Champignons League the year before when they had beaten Deportivo and matched Liverpool and Valencia at home.

The tale of Basel (nothing fawlty about this trip!)

When the draw for the second round decreed we'd be in Switzerland on the sixth of November, the Toon Army was naturally hoping for some cross-bow fireworks. And as wor Sir Uncle Bobby might have put it: we had hit the apple right on the head...

It was delightful to listen to the sing-song Swiss-German accent of the receptionist when I rang the Merian Hotel in Basel to book rooms overlooking the Rhine and the old town on the far bank. Plus, I was informed that the number fourteen tram that went to the *Sankt Jakob* stadium stopped right outside the hotel's main entrance. That was the accommodation sorted.

Chris and Sarah were once again unable to travel because of work commitments, but Harvey was up for it and we'd be meeting up with Don and co. So it was all systems go.

On the logistics front, Barry was going to get the train from Brussels to Luxembourg, arriving about twelve-thirty on the day of the match, and we would take my motor for the four-hour-or-so drive south. The train all the way to Basel would also have been a viable option as the connections from what is probably the best run Grand Duchy in the world are very good (there are a couple of direct trains from Brussels through Luxembourg to Basel every day, and they helpfully go on to other possible UEFA venues such as Zürich and Milano). On the other hand it can be a very pleasant drive through Lorraine and Alsace, passing by or through picture-postcard 'Alsatian' villages right the way down to the Swiss border. Bloater and Gloater might like to take a detour that way themselves and look at their brand of dogs!

As regards tickets, it was to be the usual belt and braces job, with all possible avenues being pursued and no stone left unturned (mental note to self: remember to turn all stones when next walking down any avenues). Barry's brother Ian put in his usual application to the club for two tickets based on the season tickets Ian has with his colleague Michael, and Brighton-based season ticket holder Don was super-confident that he could produce the goods as well. We reckoned that, as usual, we would be well able to get shot of any spares.

A propos of getting shot of spares, I had conveniently forgotten about the Bolton game on the eve of the 2003 Great North Run (for the record, our time was a pathetic two hours forty-five, but that included a break for an ice-cream on the John Reid Road and for a beer about a mile and a half from the finish, when some kind souls shouted out 'last beer before the finish' - well, I ask you, who could turn down an offer like that?). Anyway, I had ordered two tickets, one for me and one for wor Scon. Unfortunately, he had to work a half shift that day and couldn't get across to the Toon. The usual meeting place on these occasions is Bar Oz, and in the past I had got rid of spare tickets within about five minutes of entering the place. This time it was just impossible, and after asking Barry the Bouncer, the bar staff and several clusters of drinkers I gave up. We had got off to a completely shite start and were eighteenth in the table with just two points from four games, having lost the first two home league games to boot (Man U. and Birmingham having put the boot in). Plus, of course, we had gone out of the Champignons League at the hands of Partizan Belgrade. The Red Star had beaten the Blue Star Boys again! In short, the mood was not one of unadulterated optimism that we were going to set the Premiership alight this season. Nor was demand for spare tickets at an all-time high. On the way to the match I thought I'd try my luck in the doorway of the Trent House – no joy there, either. But while I had been inside Chris had asked the young programme seller positioned outside whether he was interested. He was!

'Much ye askin'?'

'Just the price on the ticket.'

'Much is that?'

'Thirty-five quid'

'Cannit afford that much!'

'Much can ye afford?'

'A fiva'

'That'll dee'

Should have been a car salesman, shouldn't I? Still, I thought, the ticket had gone to a deserving home. The lad took his seat next to me just in time for kick-off. Half-way through the second half of a goal-less draw that bored the collective arse off 52,014 paying spectators, I was on the point of apologising to him and giving him the fiver back. We were SHITE and now deservedly nineteenth in the table.

But this was the UEFA Cup and selling any spare tickets would be a doddle, wouldn't it?

Ian's application was successful and Barry duly arrived in Luxembourg armed with two tickets. Don would be waiting for us in Basel with another three. Harvey had to cancel at short notice due to an unexpected business trip. Equals three spare tickets. Piece of cake, we thought. Or, as we were off to a German-speaking city: *Ein Stück Kuchen*. The Germans don't say that at all, of course, except when ordering a piece of cake. And the difference between *Kuchen* and *Torte* escapes me to this day, as do the rules of *Skat*. On the other hand, no German I have ever met understands the rules of cricket, so I guess that evens things up. Not that my native turf has ever been a hot-bed of cricket, mind you! Until the Ashington Express, Steve Harmison, steamed in.

Although Basel is very definitely in the German-speaking part of Switzerland, it is usually referred to in English as *Basle* (roughly pronounced Baal), which is its name in Frogspeak. This is more than a little curious, I find. But such was the influence of France and the French culture and language in Europe for a couple of hundred years that traces are still to be found even in the English designations of German(!!) place names. This is the case with Cologne (*Köln* in German – so *Eau de Cologne* should really be 'Köln water', and *Eau de toilette* should really be netty water, or *vaux* beer).

By the way, when in Cologne go to my favourite Kraut boozer. It is called *Früh am Dom* and is located just yards away from the Cathedral. It is a down-to-earth sort of place whose labyrinthine interior features a series of rustic - nay, Gothic - wooden-tabled beer halls where wholesome nosh of the basic German variety and goodly beer is on offer. The beer in question is actually brewed on the premises. It is a top-fermented ale known as *Kölsch* and it tastes a bit like keg Ex. It is served in quaint tube-like glasses that hold about a thimble-full, so just tell the waiter (*Köbbes*) to keep on bringing you a fresh one every five minutes (the technical term is a 'standing order'). It is the kind of place where you would be forgiven for expecting to be served by buxom German wenches clad in *dirndls* overflowing with busty substances. Alas, this is not so. Still, can't have everything.

On the other hand, Munich, the scene of our Intertoto Cup triumph over 1860 and highlighted by Nobby Solano's best ever goal for the Toon, definitely *is* the kind of place where you are likely to be served beer (in properly dimensioned glasses) by buxom *Fräuleins* clad in *dirndls* full to the brim and beyond with busty substances. And Munich is another example of the Froggy name for a German town finding its way into the English language and staying there. In German, the name is of course *München* (as in *Bayern München* – about which club most people in Deutschland feel pretty much the way we feel about Man. U. or Chelsea, i.e. they HATE them, often referring to them as Hollywood FC). So you can imagine what kind of split-personality feelings ran through my mind when Bayern München played Man. U in the Champignons League final in beautiful Barcelona. One team I hated in my host country playing another that it is my birthright and duty to hate. I was still hoping they would both still get disqualified somehow even at that somewhat late stage in the competition. I didn't know whether to laugh or cry when one had it snatched away by the other in the dying minutes. As Neville's Chinese marra so aptly put it in the Cuban AWP series, it was 'a jammy end to a jammy season'.

Not that many years ago, the German town of *Braunschweig* was regularly called Brunswick in English, *Mainz* was called Mayence, while my current place of abode, Trier, was referred to, believe it or not, as *Treves*. The river that flows through Trier is called the *Mosel*, but we use its French name, the *Moselle*. Okay, I suppose there is justification for that one, as the Moselle starts off in the Vosges mountains in Alsace and then meanders along through Lorraine into Germany.

On our trip to Basel/Basle we would be following the Moselle upstream in the general direction of its source before veering eastish into Tobleroneland. And as you drive down through Lorraine and Alsace (*Lothringen* and *Elsass*), the name game comes into its own. When you read place names on the road signs you would certainly be forgiven for thinking you were sausage- rather than frog-side. Yet, historically speaking, Alsace-Lorraine is truly as French as *sauerkraut* itself! You pass all sorts of places with out-and-out German-sounding names, such as Metz, and a host of others that have been Frenchified, but without losing their undeniably German character. Villages whose German names originally ended in –*weiler* (which literally means 'hamlet') were rechristened -*willer,* e.g. Neuwiller, Uhlwiller, Bouxwiller; and others ending in –*dorf* (= village) became – stroff.

A particularly striking example of the latter phenomenon is to be found right on the border between Germany's Saarland region and Lorraine. A village originally called *Blittersdorf* literally straddles the border, which at this point is the river Saar. The smaller bit of the village lies on the German side, where it is called *Kleinblittersdorf*, while the larger part on the French side is called *Grossblitterstroff.*

And it is not just the names of places in Alsace-Lorraine that bear witness to the region's German past. Look at the names of shop and garage owners, or leaf through a local phone book, and you'll find no shortage of *Mullers, Schmidts* and maybe one or two *von Klinckerhoffens* etc. In Lorraine, German is still widely understood in rural areas, though you will not hear it spoken much, except possibly by German tourists. In Alsace, on the other hand, it is still very much a living language of the region, especially in the more rural parts. The version of German that is spoken there is a very distinct dialect, called *elsässisch* (or Alsatian – woof, woof). And as you'd expect, it is thoroughly peppered (plus plenty of garlic) with French words. In much the same way, Welsh speakers will inevitably resort to English words or expressions when they wish to express a degree of subtlety that cannot be conveyed in their native Welsh, e.g. *f**** off you English bastard*, or *another pint of Double Diamond, isn't it please, Taffy*. Where would the world and Craig Bellamy be without such poetic Anglo-Saxon renderings? With fewer yellow and red cards, that's where. Thus it is, *mutatis mutandis*, with Alsatian German.

Barry's train arrived bang on time at twelve thirty – we're talking European not English trains here, remember. I'd been able to work that morning, thus saving a valuable half a day in leave for later rounds. Fifteen minutes later we were on the motorway speeding towards *la belle France.*

The bit of France you enter on the motorway from Luxembourg isn't really all that *belle* at all, as you soon pass a decidedly grotty steelworks and drive right smack bang through the middle of the somewhat grotty town of Thionville (formerly Diedenhofen). But never mind - you have no time to take in these wonderful sights: because you are travelling on the A31 between the Luxo border and Metz – one of the most dangerous stretches of motorway there is, and you have no attention to spare. At this point the A31 is toll-free. In France this is always the case in the immediate vicinity of big cities. The traffic is too much to bring to a halt at tollbooths. So the urban motorways are free, like the national health, and that is a good comparison because they are equally crap and full of potholes. On we went beyond

Metz towards Nancy. After Nancy things get more countrified and before long we were stopping at the tollbooth to take a ticket. You cough up when you exit from the *autoroute*.

Pretty soon you leave Lorraine and enter Alsace. The scenery gets very nice: rolling countryside dotted with little villages nestled against the hillsides, the half-timbered houses clustered around the church. We could have stayed on the motorway as far as Strasbourg (where they brew *Kronenbourg* and *Kanterbrau [la grande bière du maître Kanter]* – supporting my theory that the best French beers are Alsatian – so it would be quite legitimate to order a bottle of Dog), but our map-reading skills told us we could lop a good few kilometres off our journey by turning off and taking a *Route Nationale* and joining the motorway again well to the south of Strasbourg.

This took us past a little village called Marmoutier, a quintessentially French name hand-picked especially to destroy my theory that all Alsatian villages have got German names. Nevertheless, we decided it would be a suitable venue for a late lunch (it was about half two already). Marmoutier turned out to be an idyllic if slumbering Alsatian village (let sleeping dogs lie, that's what I say). Had it not been for its French name and signs like *Boulangerie* and *Patisserie*, plus of course the French number plates on the parked cars, this could equally have been somewhere in the Black Forest (only about a hundred km away as the usually black crow flies). Suitably attired in our black and white stripes, we entered what appeared to be the only *bar-restaurant* in the village. The landlady of *La Couronne* was very apologetic, but they had just stopped serving lunches and the cook was just clearing up in the kitchen. But *she* assured us *he* would be happy to rustle up some sarnies. The locals took a keen interest in the colours, and one clued-up chappy asked, in French, if we were on our way to Basel. Then, in Alsatian German, he gave his marra his opinion on the likely outcome. The chatter in the bar was a strange mixture of the two languages. The pictures and pennants on the wall suggested the good people of these parts followed Racing Strasbourg.

The cook duly emerged from the kitchen with two French loaves each filled with a shank's worth of ham and recommended, in a form of German, that we wash them down with some Kronenbourg. He too followed Strasbourg, and we followed his recommendation. He wished the Toon well and we were soon on our way again through the Alsatian countryside. Before long, we rejoined the motorway and headed more or less due south, travelling roughly parallel with the Rhine, i.e. the German border. To our right, a dozen or so miles away, were the foothills of the Vosges mountains. Perched on the hilltops here and there were medieval-looking castles, though I think one or two were built as rich peoples' 'follies' in the nineteenth century (à la Bamburgh castle). A particularly famous one is in Haut Koenigsbourg, between Strasbourg and Colmar. You get a picture-postcard view of it from the motorway, or *autoroute*. The original castle was built in the 12th century, but when Kaiser Wilhelm II got his hands on it in 1899 he had it rebuilt in the style of the 15th century.

Pretty soon, Basel airport was signposted. The interesting thing about the airport belonging to the Swiss city of Basel is that it isn't in Switzerland at all. It's in France. This must surely be of interest to Ryanair, as they are into landing in countries that don't include your destination. Fly with them to Copenhagen and they drop you off in Sweden. Though if you have too much luggage, they may not let you on in the first place, the bums-on-seats airline! On the other hand, Basel railway station – which definitely *is* in Switzerland – has a section that belongs to the French railways, SNCF. Some years ago, Swiss time was an hour ahead of the French (now both countries have the same time) so there were two separate time zones within the same station complex! Europe is good at throwing up such strange quirks. One such quirk is the fact that Berwick Rangers play in the Scottish league.

Both Gateshead and South Shields have applied for membership in the past. In my heart of hearts, I wish the Toon played in the Scottish league as well. That way we might finally win something. No, what am I saying? We would regularly go out of the Scottish Cup to teams like Hamilton Academicals and Stenhousemuir (and Berwick Rangers, of course).

Another fifteen minutes or so and we were at the Swiss border. Two people in black and white shirts in a German registered car were a bit of a curious sight for the border guards, so they asked us a few questions in their quaint Swiss accents. A few years earlier I had been stopped at the same border checkpoint on my way to the game in Zurich. On that occasion the border guard had got straight to the point: *'Haben Sie Schweizer Franken?'* ('Do you have Swiss francs on you?'), he asked without so much as a 'by your leave', or a *Guten Tag* for that matter. I had been tempted to tell him how much I was turned on by the 'crisp antiseptic sting of the newly minted Swiss franc', but I thought the better of it and coughed up the twenty-five francs he charged me for a motorway sticker.

It really pisses me off that the Swiss have the gall to charge an annual motorway fee even if you just want to use their motorways on two consecutive days and never again that year. Still, NUFC had once tried to sell me a season ticket when all I wanted was to watch them play Wolves on Boxing Day! But on the other hand, they are pretty good motorways, which is more than can be said of some of the seats at SJP, especially for people with fat arses like mine. In fact, everything in Switzerland seems to be spot on – from their watches and other precision products to their numbered bank accounts and their Toblerone. They seem to be getting just about everything right. Like securing all the benefits from being in the heart of Europe without paying to join it. Or like making loads of dosh in World War II without having to join in that either.

After crossing the Franco-Swiss border, we were in Basel in no time at all, at all, as the city is nicely nestléd (Nestlé, get it?) in the *Dreiländereck* (or three-country corner) of Switzerland, Germany and France. Driving from the centre of Basel, you can be in France or Germany easily within twenty minutes. The overwhelming impression you get when driving, walking or jogging through the streets of Basel (or of any Swiss city for that matter, and Zurich in particular) is one of extreme wealth. Switzerland is all about money, and the Swiss have plenty of that particular commodity. That's basically what they do: make money. They're doing all right, thank you very much (*danke schön, merci, grazzie* and whatever the Romansch is for thank you). In fact, they are pretty much on a (Swiss) roll and in no hurry at all to join the EU or the euro. A bit like Norway in fact, and that is a good comparison. The cities and overall infrastructures of both countries simply exude prosperity. They kind of jump up at you and grab you by the throat, yelling: 'This is a seriously rich country, so spend some money here, you pathetic git, and go back home. We don't need you.' Or words to that effect. And, of course, they're dead right.

You can see Swiss quality and attention to detail absolutely everywhere. In every public and private building, restaurant, shop, hotel room, motorway services' bogs, you name it – everything is top quality, and with prices to match, of course. And you just don't see any litter on the streets. In short, they may strike you as being more German than the Germans in terms of being hard-working and ultra-efficient. Just like the Norwegians.

Mind, they seem to have some strange views now and then (well, nobody's perfect). As a nation, they appear somewhat obsessed with the fear that someone is about to invade them, presumably to steal all their Toblerones. As a result, everyone has to do compulsory national service, and when they are finished they stay in the armed forces reserve for just about forever and get to keep their reservist gun or cross-bow at home. And just about every weekend they have to tootle off on exercise somewhere in the mountains, where the Swiss have no doubt built some huge bunkers housing vast supplies of munitions and Toblerones. I am not certain, but I think Switzerland has a Troll-exchange scheme with Norway to pool tunnelling expertise.

Sunday evening is not a good time to use the Swiss railways, as every carriage will be stowed out with reservist squaddies. And going first class won't help you either because the seats will be taken by officers of the reserve all homeward bound after a weekend's exercise spent trying out Switzerland's *wunderwaffe*, the Helvetic nuclear snowball. Yes, the trains are full of reservists on their way *heim* to a supper of *rösti* and *raqulette* followed by Toblerone for their pud. And the blocks of flats that are home to the city dwellers among them must all, by law, have a nuclear-bomb-proof cellar, no kidding! No wonder the best psychiatrists have a central European accent.

Incidentally, it is also not a good idea to walk around in Switzerland with an apple on your head, even in jest, as some clever shite is liable to whip out his reservist cross-bow and take a pot shot at you or your apple while whistling the William Tell overture. An interesting people, to be sure, and they make remarkably good chocolate.

Ever wondered why the international car sticker for Switzerland is CH? Well it stands for the Frog words *Confédération Hélvétique*, or the Helvetic Confederation. The Romans called what is now Switzerland *Helvetia*, a land then populated by a Celtic tribe that Caesar and co. knew as the *Helvetii. Helvetia* was part of (unoccupied) Gaul, until around 50 BC, when the *Helvetii* reckoned that the land they lived in did not offer them enough room, or *Lebensraum*. They decided they would move through Roman-occupied Gaul (present-day South of France) in search of pastures new. Julius Caesar, who was in charge of Roman Gaul, was having none of it and gave the *Helvetii* a good scudding. Having acquired a taste for Gaul-bashing he decided to conquer the whole of present-day France and south-west Germany as far as the Rhine, and, for good measure, had a couple of sorties into the South-East of England (he's welcome to it), laying the foundation for the later Roman occupation. In a very real sense, therefore, the history of modern Western Europe started in Switzerland. If the *Helvetii* had stayed put, Rome might never have pushed northwards, and we would all be speaking Gaelic.

The tribe of the *Helvetii* actually had a kind of vote about upping sticks. They voted in favour and burned their townships so as to ensure they had an incentive to find something new elsewhere. This is a 'democratic' tradition that the present-day inhabitants of the Helvetic lands would appear to have inherited. Because the Swiss have had more referenda than most of us have had hot dinners. You name it, the Swiss will hold a referendum on it.

'Please Miss, can I go to the *Toilettli*, I need a *pipili*.'

'*Aber Burscheli*, vi must häv a *referendumli* firstly. Can you hang on a month or so?'

This makes Switzerland a true democracy. If three quarters of the population are against something, well that something just doesn't happen – which admittedly can be a bit of a bummer if all you are asking for is permission to go for a slash!

Without even having recourse to a map, let alone a referendum, we managed to home in on the Merian Hotel without any great difficulty. We knew it overlooked the Rhine, so all we had to do was keep going until we reached the river and then stop and ask the way. Driving through town, we passed a few groups of Toon wallahs and a few other vehicles with black and white scarves hanging out the window, like ours.

As soon as we'd parked up and checked in, Barry gave Don a bell on the mobile. Zurich-based(!) Don and his mates had successfully accomplished a reconnaissance mission and located the team *Hotel-li*, a five-star affair (as one would expect), only a few blocks away from our humble abode-*li*. Thither we betook ourselves...

'How much, bonny lad?' – this wasn't a scene from the Likely Lads, this was reality. I don't think I have ever paid that much for six beers, even in a hotel bar. Still, it keeps the riff-raff out...

'Aye well, cheers lads' as we sat down and squared up with Don for the three spare tickets. We'd have no bother getting shot of them. There were at least a dozen Geordies in the bar area, and there were even a few Brits hanging around, so we asked if anybody needed a ticket. It turned out most of them had spares as well, and the general message was that there were plenty available throughout Basel. Couple of team photos in the bar, and then somebody spots Shay Given sipping an orange juice in the reception area. Over Barry and I go for an autograph. And to my 'keep them oot' Shay replies that he'll do his best. Can't ask for more than that. Through the window behind Shay we could see what was obviously the team coach waiting in the hotel's courtyard. We tappy-lappied over to the reception desk and asked the *concierge*, in German, if we could wait for the team in the corridor leading to the courtyard. In a distinct Swiss-German accent he replied that that would be fine. When Barry and I then exchanged a few words in English, the *concierge* asked if we were Geordies. And he told us that he was from Manchester!! So it goes!

So we waited in the corridor for about ten minutes and then the team started to trickle through to the waiting coach. Alan Shearer kindly gave us his autograph, as did Kieron Dyer, Olivier Bernard and Laurent Robert, whom we asked for *au moins un but*, and later that evening he duly obliged. We remembered about an Italian colleague who had asked his Portuguese boss, in French, whether he could go on a business trip to *l'Île de Réunion*, where Laurent Robert hails from (it's in the Indian Ocean, by the way). His boss, whose French was less than brilliant, said '*Oui, pas de problème*, just fill out a trip form and I'll authorise it.' But when the boss saw it written out he called him in and said 'What's all this about? You told me you were just going up the road to *Lille* for a meeting (*une réunion*). No chance, son.'

Then came the moment of a lifetime. At the far end of the corridor we spotted the silver hair of Wor Sir Uncle Bobby. He was struggling with what looked like quite a heavy holdall, but like many a seventy-year-old he wasn't going to accept help from anyone. When he got level with us, he kindly put the bag down and signed his autograph, and when we asked him if he would pose for a photo with us he immediately agreed and said he would plonk the bag in the bus and come back out. We were as excited as little kids. Ultimately, the players are just assets out there on the pitch. They are there as our representatives, to give expression to our pride in the Geordie nation. We can rightly expect them to give everything, and more, because it is we who pay their hyper-inflated wages. And if they are not good enough or do not give of their best, well they must be replaced. Just like the Gladiators of Roman (or Greek) times. Wor Sir Bobby earns mega-bucks as well, of course, but the big difference in my eyes is that he doesn't need them. He doesn't need to be there. He could be enjoying a well-earned retirement on some Mediterranean island far from the madding (and mad) crowd. Or in Tynemouth. Or Ipswich. But he *is* there, and doing his very best for the Toon Army. And he is doing it clearly because, like us, he loves Newcastle United and is a part of it.

He is also getting on a bit, and when he got on the coach, he leaned his head against the window, forgot all about Barry and me, and drifted off, no doubt masterminding his match tactics. Or perhaps dreaming about retirement in Mallorca or Tynemouth. To say we were disappointed would be a bit of an understatement. We were gutted. I was prepared to accept our lot, but Barry to his eternal credit had a word with Sir Bobby's personal assistant and made a case for our defence of which O.J. Simpson's lawyers would have been proud. She boarded the bus, and out came Bobby. Lost for anything sensible to say, I managed: 'Very sorry, Sir Bobby, but we didn't mean to get you off the bus.' 'Well you have,' came the rather tetchy reply! But as the three of us posed for our photos, he was all smiles and the perfect PR professional! Thanks, Sir Bobby. You made this the perfect day for two life-long Newcastle United supporters. Mind, I did wonder when he told me that I should put myself about a bit in their penalty area whenever we got a corner!

Thanks to the wonders of digital technology, Barry reproduced the photo in a dozen variants. You get the picture (ha ha): one with the three of us; one with Barry's hand on Sir Bobby's shoulder; one with just Sir Bobby and Barry minus the hand; then just Sir Bobby and me; the three of us without the bus in the background; one with Julie Andrews lying naked in front of the three of us (sorry but I've had a crush on her ever since first seeing Mary Poppins at the age of six), etc., etc. Or was it Mae West, not Julie Andrews? I always get the pair mixed up. Then we e-mailed the photos to our respective families of course (except the one with J.A. and/or M.W., that is). A couple of days later my Mam was showing off a picture of her son with Sir Bobby Robson to the other residents at her sheltered accommodation scheme in Wallsend. We got the photos printed out while on a trip to Canterbury, picking up some pilgrim credits on the way, and sent a bumper sized print off to Sir Bobby - on the assumption that he would probably like to have it framed and put up in his office. Imagine our surprise when it came back in the post a few days later signed 'Best wishes – Bobby Robson' accompanied by a thank-you letter. Posing with supporters like that means a lot to them and their families, especially where the supporters concerned are middle-aged gits like us who revert to a mental age of about fourteen in all matters relating to Newcastle United, so thanks once again, Sir Bobby!

The coach revved up and left, which suggested it was about time we did the same. Also in the corridor collecting autographs were two Swiss lads who were about thirty-five years younger than us. In terms of mental age, however, they were probably five years our senior, and so did not have as good an excuse for collecting autographs as we did. We asked them if they wanted to buy tickets for the match, in the Toon End, for no extra money than the price of the ticket. They had nothing like that kind of money on them!! So they made a couple of mobile calls and arranged to nip home and borrow the cash. At this point we thought 'sod it' and made their day by giving them the tickets. What the hell! These lads were keen and couldn't afford the price of the tickets. We had lost a few quid but maybe done something for the Toon's reputation. That still left us with one ticket.

There was some kind of fun-fair going on in various parts of Basel and we passed some fairground attractions and candy-floss-eating burgers (Swiss citizens, that is) as we made our way to the tram stop. When we got on there were still a few seats, but a couple of stops later it was heaving, and the Geordies were definitely in the majority. As it wended its way through the streets of Basel, the carriages resounded to the words of the Blaydon Races, much to the amusement of the Basel supporters, who were clearly enjoying the occasion as much as we were. I believe that Einstein hit upon his theory of relativity while observing a Swiss tram, but no such inspiration was forthcoming to us on this occasion. We found ourselves sitting next to a Brit, who like the *concierge* at the hotel hailed from Manchester. I can understand people leaving Manchester, but how come they home in on Basel? He was only marginally interested in the match but was willing to cough up twenty quid for our remaining spare ticket. Okay, that was less than we had paid for it, but – as I'm sure Einstein would have agreed – all things are relative, especially on Swiss trams.

When the tram stopped just outside the ground there was still time for another pint (or can) in the crisp air of this already dark November evening. Actually, there were no crisps, but was that roasting chestnuts we could smell? There was also time to discuss the merits of Einstein's famous formula, so famous I cannot remember it, but it includes an 'm' and an 'e' and something squared, I think. And so we sang: 'with an M and an E and something squared C, etc., etc., ...this is the relativity [half a quaver pause] theory! 'm' 'e', 'm' 'e' ... Or was it 'with an N and an E and wubbleyou C...?' Toon wallahs were thronging around the beer and sausage stands and mingling in with the Swiss fans, not a hint of bother, and why should there ever be? Looking across the tramlines to the stadium, it appeared that one side of the ground was, in fact, a block of flats. As we were commenting on this, one Swiss standing next to us informed us that it was an old people's home! But their rooms did not afford a view of the pitch, presumably lest a penalty shoot-out cause a collective heart attack. It is amazing what can be integrated into a footie ground, isn't it? If my memory serves me well, one side on the outside of PSV's ground is given over to a toyshop! Back in the old days at St James's, students in the hall of residence in Leazes Terrace (pull it down, build a bigger East Stand) could get a free view of the match, and on big occasions people would even climb onto the roof behind the Popular.

[Intervention by Barry at this point: 'Hey, watch what you're saying! My mother lived at number eighteen, Leazes Terrace through the War years and later, and she used to be able to see into the ground from the attic windows. Joe Harvey, Jimmy Scoular and the rest used to whistle after her as she walked past. It would be my ideal place to retire in the Toon, even if half of it is full of students now.']

In the ground the atmosphere among the Toon Army was buzzing. Bumped briefly into Alan from Gateshead, again. There was a bit of a pre-match run on the bogs, which resulted quite literally in an overspill into the Ladies!! One urinal, one toilet and two sinks-cum-urinals proved slightly less than enough to cater for three thousand Geordies. Couldn't they have let us use the bogs in the nuclear bunker no doubt installed under the pitch? Never mind, order was restored by kick-off time, and we were all set for another night of European adventure.

It looked like we were going to be in for a tough match even just judging by the height of most of their players. They towered over most of our lads. And when their midfielder Cantaluppi had a screamer of a shot from way outside the box, it looked as if our fears were going to be realised. But we'd hardly settled down from their goal when Robert took off like an express train down the left towards their penalty area and steered a shot beyond the reach of their keeper. We were still celebrating when they went and scored again as a result of us not managing to clear the ball from our area. Basel had a couple of very good players in the Yakin brothers, with the marvellously named Hakan Yakin in particular causing us quite a bit of trouble. But from a Robert corner the ball bounced around and came out to Titus Bramble who slammed it through the crowd into the goal. After half time we got better and better and eventually we got the winner through Shola, who with a hint of a dummy and a fortuitous break brought the ball back under control and stroked it under the goalkeeper. We deserved the win.

One of the best moments of the match was just after Shola scored when the cry went up: 'You're not yodelling any more!' and 'You only yodel when you're winning!' I remembered that in Zurich we had sung 'Where were you in World War Two' – to which the Swiss could justifiably have replied: 'Right here of course, making money, lots of it!'

On the same row of terracing as us there was a young family with a couple of kids. One lassie was fast asleep. We took a photo and offered to send them a copy by e-mail. Imagine how much it must cost to deck out a whole family in all the black and white regalia, and then the cost of travel, hotels and match tickets. And then one of them goes to sleep! I know the feeling, I've had mine eating a picnic and playing with toys in the middle of games.

A three-two away win against a good team like Basel gave us some hope that we were getting back on track after we'd been knocked out of the League Cup the week before by West Brom. We were brought back down to earth with five thumps the following weekend, however, when we travelled to Chelsea.

After the match, Don and co. had no time to spare as they had to get back to Zurich and return the gnomes which they had borrowed and painted black and white. There were huge queues for the trams, but we were in no such hurry so we decided to wander around the ground in the hope of getting another glimpse of the team. About an hour after the final whistle, we were chatting to a couple of the stewards looking out onto the still floodlit pitch and taking a couple of photos when the NUFC party started boarding their coach. We had a bit crack with Laurent Robert, whom we thanked for answering our request before the match to score us a goal, and Olivier Bernard, who very kindly agreed to talk to Chris in London, whom I had quickly rung on the mobile. Since then Chris always talks of 'my friend, Olivier Bernard', in much the same way as I always talk of 'Wor Sir Uncle Bobby'. What a great trip this had been.

On the way back to the hotel, Barry and I decided we had to have something typically Swiss to eat. So we ended up at a Tunisian place. The Swiss must go to bed really early because all of their eateries were shut for the night. Still, at least the Tunisian Swiss were still up and gave us something fried that included cheese inside, possibly Tunisian Emmenthal.

The next morning we went for a jog along the bank of the Rhine and across a bridge and through the old town. After breakfast there was time for a little walk and some shopping for presents before setting off at exactly mid-day. We bumped into the family whose bairn had fallen asleep during the match. The presents for wor lass and the girls were the Basel speciality of *Läkerli*, a kind of hard gingerbread (I think) in a wrapper bearing the Basel city colours, which are... black and white! The drive back to Luxoland took exactly three hours (there was just zero traffic that Friday). We passed the journey chatting about our Swiss experience and speculating over where the next port of call on this UEFA pilgrimage might be. We were still going to be in the seeded half of the draw, so if we were lucky we could end up in some welcoming haven with a weak yet entertaining team.

The UEFA winter break

After our November trip, there was going to be a long break until the next round in February. Even the draw had to wait until the twelfth of December, when the Champignons League first round was finished, to see who were the third-placed teams parachuting down (or should that by now have been up?) into the UEFA Cup. As usual we tuned in to the uefa.com website and learned we were in Pot Four and would be playing either Vålerenga of Norway, Gazantiepspor of Turkey, Auxerre in France, or Spartak Moscow. We hadn't got a clue where Vålerenga or Gazantiepspor were, so a quick scan of the Internet was called for. We trawled up the information that Vålerenga was in Oslo and so a very welcoming place to go, while Gazantiepspor was even closer to Syria than Malatyaspor had been; scarcely fifteen miles from the border. Hey, maybe 'Spor' means 'Syrian border' and 'Malatya' and 'Gazantiep' mean 'close to' and 'even closer to' respectively, who knows? We were very happy to be given a nice trip to Oslo in view of the alternatives. We'd be able to occupy ourselves during the winter break by remembering some tales from earlier pilgrimages. With Switzerland fresh in our mind, our thoughts first went back to F.C. Zurich.

The Gnomes' tale

The Zurich trip was a great outing. For the record, this was the second round of the 1999-2000 UEFA Cup, and we beat Zurich two-one Toblerone-side and three-one Stottie-side, only to go out to AS Roma in the next round, more of which anon. If I were looking for a slogan for Zurich airport (which I'm not), I'd be torn between 'around us only gnomes' and 'above us only Toblerones'.

I stayed at a rustic hotel with a monastic name (Hotel Franziskaner) in the Niederdorfstrasse right in the middle of town, and on my way from the multi-storey car park to the hotel I walked through the pedestrian zone, where the Toon Army were omnipresent and in great form. There must have been about six hundred spread over a handful of bars, lots of them sitting outside as it was a sunny afternoon. I checked in and got straight back to the congregation of the faithful. On this trip I was travelling on my own as none of the usual suspects could make it. But one of the great things about being a Geordie is that you are always made welcome by other Geordies on their travels. It suffices to say 'Y'aal reet?' and you'll get a 'wheyaye man' in reply, and you are part of the company.

On the way to the hotel I had asked a bunch of lads for directions, including one who introduced himself as Alan from Gateshead (my Uncle Tom used to call it 'Piggy's Waistc't') and when I walked back there for a pint, I joined them. The crack and the singing were grand as always. James Joyce would have enjoyed it if he'd still been around the bars of Zurich writing his own odyssey. We were loud of course but that's just the way we are. The Zurich police were out in force and keeping a watchful eye on us. Then a potentially dodgy situation arose. A big lad (and I mean 'big' in the North-East sense of the word) had been standing next to his seated mates in front of one café, the plastic seats belonging to which were green. He decided to take a vacant (red) plastic seat from the café next door and plonk it down next to his mates. The waiter from the red café was understandably a wee bit upset about this and tried to persuade the big lad, who had had a few (as you would expect), that this was not on. Unfortunately there was a major language barrier in operation here and the messages from both sides just weren't getting through. It wasn't that the Swiss waiter couldn't speak English, mind. From his perspective it was, er, sort of the other way around. The language that the big lad spoke was a new one on the waiter, who rather naively asked the lad if *he* spoke English... thus the situation was threatening to get out of hand. I felt it was time to step in to defuse this minor diplomatic incident. And I started by asking the waiter if *he* spoke German. I then explained that our variety of English was at least as different from the standard variety as Swiss was from *Hochdeutsch* (standard German). The lad kept his red seat, the waiter sold him a few of the beers that went with the seat and everyone was happy again.

Switzerland, with its population of around seven million (that's only about seven times as many as live on Tyneside) actually has four official languages: Kraut, Frog, Eye-tiddlie-eye-tie and a creature known as Romansch, which is a kind of mixture between Italian and French. German is by far the dominant tongue, spoken in nineteen of the twenty-six cantons, with French being spoken in six others including the Swiss Newcastle, *Neuchâtel*. Italian is spoken in Ticino, and Romansch in parts of a region known as the Grisons (meaning 'pigs', I do believe; though being Swiss they will doubtless be spotlessly clean ones).

Swiss German in its more extreme forms is as far removed from *Hochdeutsch* as Geordie can be from so-called Oxford English. So much so that on German telly subtitles are used when people are speaking *Schwyzerdytsch*, as Swiss German proper is called. As with Geordie and other regional dialects, you have to distinguish between the dialect itself and the 'standard' language spoken with a distinct regional accent. When we know the person we are talking to won't understand broad Geordie, we tend to speak a bit more slowly and use standard English words. They certainly wouldn't understand 'wor lass', for example, and so we might, exceptionally, use the term 'my wife'. Come to think of it, I certainly don't understand wor lass, and I don't see how any sane person possibly could. But she doesn't understand me either, so there you have it (only kidding)!

Thus in Switzerland, or rather in the German-speaking bit of it, you have your out-and-out *Schwyzerdytsch*, which for your average German is pretty close to absolute gibberish, and then you have your very heavy Swiss accent, using more or less recognisably German words. To get the idea, imagine

Rab C. Nesbitt speaking in his usual Glaswegian, of which we understand slightly less than half. And now, by contrast, imagine him speaking in the same twang but using words that we understand. That comparison roughly corresponds to the difference between Swiss German (Toblerone-speak) and German spoken with a pronounced Swiss accent, which sounds very quaint and is extremely sing-songy and guttural in nature.

By the way, I wish there were subtitles for Rab. C. Nesbitt! And I imagine non-Geordies feel much the same way about Oz, Denis, and Neville in *Aufwiedersehen Pet*. In Swiss German, they don't say *Aufwiedersehen* at all, by the way; they say something like *Aufwiederlugen*. And you will even find this word on hotel, petrol station and restaurant receipts and the like. *Lugen* is an old German (actually Middle High German) word that is still to be found in some regional dialects, including that of the Saarland, which is not much more than a goal kick away from where I live. It came into English as 'look' (dead easy, this comparative linguistics lark, isn't it?).

As far as Swiss French is concerned, it is a joy for the foreigner to listen to, because they speak so clearly and so much more slowly than the French themselves do. In fact, the situation is exactly the opposite to that of Swiss German! Plus, Swiss speakers of French, like Belgian Francophones and Luxembourgers use the words '*septante*' and '*nonante*' for 'seventy' and 'ninety', respectively. For this we should be grateful. Because the French themselves, bless 'em, say '*soixante-dix*' (= sixty-ten) and '*quatre-vingt-dix* ' (= four-twenty-ten, or four score and ten!). That is bad enough, but when you get into the high seventies or nineties in standard French, things get completely out of hand. For example, seventy-eight is *soixante-dix-huit* (literally: sixty-ten-eight) and ninety-nine is *quatre-vingt-dix-neuf* (literally: four-score-ten-nine). Try writing down a telephone number dictated to you in French!! They don't just say the numbers one digit at a time like we do; no, they have to do pairs at a time: seventy-eight ninety-two thirty-six. You start writing a six for sixty but then they say sixty-ten-eight and you have to scrub out the six and put a seven, then the eight becomes a nine if it's four-score-ten-something... it's just a nightmare. Come on, I ask you, is that any way to run a brothel? So thank you, Switzerland, Belgium and Luxoland, for saying *septante-huit* and *nonante-neuf.* (For the record, sixty-nine is *soixante-neuf* throughout the French-speaking world.) If you try out *nonante* and *septante* in Québec you only meet with blank stares!

The tale of two Toons

Isn't it amazing how many Newcastles there are dotted around the globe, including the equivalent in other languages? Neuchâtel in Switzerland, Neufchâteau in Belgium, no doubt a few identically named towns in France, Neuerburg in Germany, there must be a Nowy Zamek somewhere in Poland (if not, there should be), etc. Perhaps these continental cousins weren't named directly after the Toon. But Newcastle in New Brunswick (or should it be Neu Braunschweig? It actually was at one stage) definitely was! New Brunswick is the Canadian Province wedged between Québec and Maine (in the good old US of A). I was in Canada for the Québec City marathon and thought, rather naively that I'd be the only lunatic dressed in a Newcastle United strip: but of course I was wrong. There standing opposite me at the start was Don K. from Geordieland (that's a different Don, not our Brighton-based marra, by the way) dressed in the same Broon Ale logo top. We started off together and the locals were shouting '*Allez les arbitres*' (Howay the refs!) – they associated black and white stripes with umpires at ice hockey games! However, there were some better informed people who got it absolutely right, and others who came close and thought it was Juventus (well, close from the North American perspective).

Geordieland-based Don sped ahead after a few miles as we followed the bank of the Saint Lawrence from Lévis (opposite Québec City) but I overtook him on the long, long and August-hot ascent to the *Pont de Québec* bridge. He was having problems with his leg and was about to drop out (though I have to add immediately that he is a million times fitter and a lot leaner than I am). I managed to struggle home within the allotted six hours through the excruciating heat. Don had told me that his teenage daughter would be waiting in the stand at the finish, so I assumed she would recognise my NUFC strip and say hello and ask if I had seen her Dad. No such thing. Then it dawned on me that she had, of course, been brought up on Tyneside, where it was completely normal for just about everyone to go around dressed like that, and no doubt she thought it was simply the same the world over. So there was another NUFC shirt, so what?...

I had seen on the map that there was a place called Newcastle in the province of New Brunswick, only a few hundred miles away from Québec City. So I had to go and check it out, didn't I? By the way, although Québec sounds so quintessentially French, it is in fact a corruption of a native American (Red Indian) word meaning 'place where the river is narrow'. That's a joke! Even there, the Saint Lawrence is about five times as wide as the Tyne. Further down, it is as wide as the English Channel (literally!!!!!), but they still call it a river. Everything is on a different scale in Québec and Canada. The French-speaking province of Québec alone is five times the size of France, with a population of only around six million, and if it ever becomes independent it'll still be the eighth biggest country on the planet by surface area!

Off I set for Newcastle, New Brunswick. I learned at the local tourist office that it was in the county of Northumberland! So there is no doubt it was founded, a couple of hundred years ago, by a bunch of home-sick Geordies. Doubt if they ever got hyem again! I asked where the local branch of the supporters club was, but the lassie couldn't relate to that question. Never mind, I cruised through the toon a bit and slammed the brakes on when I spotted the Newcastle United Baptist Church. This was obviously where the faithful congregated! I asked a friendly local resident, who happened to be digging a hole in the road (and why not?) to take a photo of me in the colours standing in front of the sign, and it was printed in the Mag (what a brilliant institution that is!).

New Brunswick is the only officially bilingual province in Canada. In other words, the English speakers there are bending over backwards to be nice to the French speakers, who are very definitely in the minority and seem to hug (and hog) the shoreline. In Québec, on the other hand, the French-speaking majority seem to go out of their way to be nasty to the ten per cent English-speaking minority, because the province is officially monolingual and there are even language laws to keep it that way. That means no advertising in English, not even shop signs (but I'm not sure about churches – hey, maybe there's an *Église Baptiste de Neufchâteau Uni*). As a result, more and more English speakers are leaving the province each year. Newcomers have to send their kids to French schools, which is a bit of a disincentive to many! And the French they speak takes a bit of getting used to as well. It is the Geordie of the French language!!

Tarry on up the Tiber tale

Our win over F.C. Zürich in the previous round was rewarded with a very tough draw against A.S. Roma, captained by the laughably named Totti. He it was who would put us out of round three of the 1999/00 UEFA Cup with his, to say the least, disputed goal in the first leg in Rome. So he had the last laugh! That was a great trip (in both senses of the word), though but. It was November, but November in the Eternal City can be like spring on Tyneside. We were staying in a small hotel literally around the corner from the Colosseum, and appropriately enough it was called *Il Coliseo*. It was so small it didn't even have a breakfast room, so you got vouchers for a café a couple of doors along, and there we would sit outside (November, remember!).

No-one can possibly fail to be impressed by Rome. It is history pure. You can stroll through the Forum (presumably named after that shopping precinct on Wallsend High Street which they had to build a detour in the Wall to accommodate) past the very spot where Julius Caesar did his famous *'et tu, Brute'* bit. We actually had our photos taken with a JC lookalike outside the Colosseum (no doubt named after the old cinema in Whitley Bay). For a fee, of course. Standing on the actual terraces of the Colosseum is just awesome. You kind of transport yourself back to Roman times imagining the gladiator fights and the sheer carnage that went on in that arena. In Latin, *arena* simply meant sand, and that was a pretty useful material to use in the Colosseum, as it is good at absorbing blood.

Not far from the Forum is a huge great map of the Roman Empire, and it brings it home to you just how much of a super-power the Romans were. From North Africa to North Shields, they pretty well ruled the roost. On the subject of maps, we were finding our way around with the aid of a pocket-sized one that we had picked up at a tourist-information-type office. Dressed in the colours of course, we were instantly recognised by a bunch of young Geordies who were, let's say, not quite with it, not quite wired up:

'Ye gorra map?'

'Yeah'

'What, of Rome like?'

'Yeah'

'Can ye get them like'

'Yeah'

'Wheraboots?'

'At the tourist information office'

'Hey, mevies we should get one!'

They were beginning to get the idea. On we marched through Rome and decided a trip to the Vatican would be a good idea, so as to cover all eventualities like. In we steamed into Saint Peter's Cathedral and fortunately there was a Mass going on so we probably had our colours blessed. We were taking no chances. Bad timing dictated that Polish Paul was not presiding over this one, otherwise Pete could have tried out his pathetically poor Polish on him; he'd probably have been happy to hear a bit of his own lilting lingo instead of the endless Latin litany (*Dominic have the biscuits come? Yes, and the spirits, too!*). We had a bit of a discussion between ourselves and then with some of the faithful over whether the Sistine Chapel was here or in Florence, and we concluded that we were all pretty sure it's in Florence. It turns out it's here so we missed our chance, but the queues were too long anyway (it's like that at the Lenin mausoleum in Moscow, too!). If it had been a queue to get tickets for an audience with Sir Bobby on the other hand …

You have to be on your toes in Rome because there are pickpockets everywhere, and on the metro from the main *Termini* station to the stop near the Spanish Steps a group of people rushed into the crowded carriage, barging their way through. A very friendly older lady opposite us made it clear, including with hand gestures, that these gits were up to no good, so we held onto our wallets and passports. They got nothing. We milled around the Spanish Steps area for a while and just about everybody wanted to exchange strips. Pete had already given yet another NUFC woollen hat away as a tip at a Pizzeria the night before and wanted to hang on to what colours he had left.

Soon it was time to head to the Villa Borghesi, which had been chosen as the marshalling point for the Toon Army. It turned out to be a dark, spooky park with a sweet shop incongruously sited in the middle of it, on top of one of the seven hills of Rome. From there we were bussed, sardine-style, across the city in a seemingly endless convoy. A bit like the way the ancient Romans paraded their prisoners of war through the streets on the way to the Colosseum to be crucified or fed to the lions. Here we were, prisoners from the *Votadini* tribe from the far-off province of Britannia.

Barbarians from the North. We were suitably taunted on all sides by the locals doing their after-work shopping or making their way to the match themselves, but we out-sang them as our *carabinieri* outriders' sirens helped them slice their way through the traffic chaos.

Inside Rome's Olympic stadium we found that the ranks of the Toon Army were swollen by a Peruvian regiment of our Foreign Legion. Turned out they worked for the Peruvian embassy in Rome and had come along to cheer us on because of Nobby Solano. (I will never understand why he had to leave). There were also a couple of young lads who looked very Italian. They were Italo-Geordies and they were able to taunt the Roma fans not only in their own language but also using their own gestures, many of which we did not understand. That really got some Roma fans upset! The Toon Army was in great voice, especially in the second half when 'We are the Geordies' started up, got louder and louder, and was sustained right through to the final whistle.

Also in the stadium we bumped into Alan from Gateshead again. It's great how these little reunions occur. You can hear it all around you. 'Didn't we bump into each other in Feyenoord' 'Nah, that was Lokeren', etc. One big happy family.

The Toon played pretty well as far as we could judge. But it wasn't easy to judge because the pitch was a million miles away. But there were giant screens at both ends of the ground to show highlights. Although of course they tended to show their own highlights. At half time they showed shots of the crowd, including some of the bigger lads amongst us who had taken their shirts off on this most sultry of November nights. Wonder what the Italians watching at home made of that, especially if they had wide-screen tellies!

After the game we were kept in for detention as usual, and when we finally got out the authorities' plan was to bus us back to the city centre. Pete and I managed to slip through the net and decided to walk back instead, following the course of the Tiber, even if it did start chafing with its banks. Accoutred as we were, we had no intention of plunging in...

Unfortunately, the Tiber also tends to meander a bit, never mind chafe. And what we thought would be a thirty-minute stroll was soon into its second hour. So we stopped for some liquid refreshment. We found ourselves in the company of some charming German girls. It turned out they were from Essen, Pete's former stomping ground, and before long they were singing some *Rot-Weiss Essen* songs. Now RWE have never really set the footballing world alight, and live very much in the shadow of their big neighbours *Schalke 04* and *Borussia Dortmund* (*Borussia*, in case you ever wondered, is Latin for 'Prussia'). However, *Rot-Weiss* (which unfortunately means red and white) were the very first club to represent Germany in a European competition back in the fifties, which when you think about it was an awesome responsibility. It's funny how some 'lesser' clubs managed to achieve the feat of being the first to represent their countries in Europe. In Scotland, it was Hibs, I believe. No disrespect, Hibs fans, but the wider world was surely expecting one of the Old Firm.

Suitably refreshed, we continued on our way, via more *Bar Italias* full of Toon stragglers, and got back to the hotel in the early hours. Next morning, at *Termini* station, we were making our way, still suitably accoutred, to the airport train when a slightly dazed Toon wallah came up to us and informed us:

'Cannit get nee train tickets heeya ye knaa.'

'How come?'

'Nee ticket office, 'av lucked aal ower.'

'There is, it's over there.'

'Nah, it dizint say noot aboot tickets neewhere.'

'Yeah, but it says *bigletti*. That's Eytie for tickets, man'

'Ah, reet, so why'z it in Eyetie, like?'

'Coz this is Italy.'

'Cheers!'

Isn't it amazing how some people cannot come to terms with, or accept, the fact that things (such as signs, for example) can be different abroad? And it is usually such differences that make travelling so much fun! It had been a terrific Roman holiday.

The Antwerp tale

As irony would have it, I had been on a trip home and ended up having to listen to the match while driving along the A69 from Carlisle over to the Toon. The closest we had ever got in a competitive match to where I now lived, and there I was back in Newcastle instead! But I wasn't the only one who'd not seen the match, because Don's friend Kevin missed just about all of it too, even though he spent all ninety minutes plus half time at the match. The Antwerp ground was in notoriously bad shape and it was a surprise that they were allowed to stage the game in the first place, and he fell victim to the crumbling stairs and ended up in a heap with a couple of near-broken legs. So instead of watching Rob Lee's hat-trick of headers, he spent his match in the First Aid tent. But you were there Pete, tell us about it.

Yes, I certainly was. This was the first game in the 1994/95 UEFA Cup campaign. Our first European outing following the dark days that had set in not long after going out to Bastia (the bastiards) in the 1977/78 season. It was our first trip across the North Sea with Super K. at the helm. To say that expectations were sky high would be to set a new benchmark for understatement. Since the Second Coming, the mood on Tyneside and throughout the diaspora had approached levels of self-delusion that hadn't been witnessed since the Supermac era.

The effect that Keegan's miracle had on me is reflected, though sadly inadequately, in a letter I recently came across in a dusty old file appropriately marked 'Dusty Old Letters'. Dated September 1992, it was addressed to the Ticket Office at St James' Park. Before reading it, please put on some suitably pathetic violin music just to capture the atmosphere:

'Dear Sirs,

Please consider a heart-felt plea from a Geordie exile who is a life-long Newcastle United supporter and who can usually manage to spend only every other Christmas at home. When I am in the North-East over the festive season, however, I never miss a Newcastle United home game. As football at St James' Park enters a new dimension whose boundaries have yet to be defined, the inevitable tidal wave of enthusiasm has swept across the North Sea and made its way undiminished down the Ruhr valley. It is clear in the present circumstances that the Newcastle vs Wolves game on Boxing Day will be an all-ticket match. It is equally clear that it will be a sell-out. As I can hardly expect my ageing parents to stand queuing in the cold and wet, I turn to you in desperation. Is it in any way conceivable that you could sell me a ticket by post for whatever part of the ground such a ticket might be available? I would be more than happy to pay in advance by Eurocheque, or, if that is not acceptable, to ask my father to call in at your office and collect the ticket for cash. Could such an arrangement also be made in respect of a ticket for the FA Cup third round if Newcastle have a home tie? Before replying in the negative, please consider how you yourself would feel in my position. How would you like your Christmas ruined?

Yours in blind faith,

Peter'

Hope you also had your Kleenex at the ready. Maybe I should have signed it *Tiny Tim* – that would have fitted in well with the Christmas theme. Come on, it was tugging at your heartstrings, wasn't it? Howay man, this was my best shot. A few years earlier it would have been enough to coax a tear out of the eye Lord Westwood no longer had. He'd have turfed his own grandmother out of her executive box seat and given it to me, wouldn't he? Wouldn't he?

So what do you reckon the reply was, then? Read on...

'Dear Sir

Due to the fact that all of our seats have now been sold as season tickets, I am sorry to inform you that we are unable to provide you with the individual match tickets that you have requested and I therefore return your application herewith.

Please note that season tickets for standing in the Milburn 'B' Paddock and Gallowgate 'M' sections are still available, priced £ 99.00 adult and £ 49 juvenile.

If you wish to purchase a season ticket you are advised to make application as quickly as possible enclosing the correct remittance with your application.

Individuals purchasing season tickets for standing areas this year will be given priority booking in respect of any season tickets which may become available in future seasons.

Yours faithfully,'

Heartwarming, isn't it? There I am living in Germany, and they tell me that all I have to do in order to see a couple of games over Christmas is buy a season ticket. If Newcastle United were looking for a slogan, what do you think it should be?

The club that cares? Or maybe: *The club with its heart in the right place?* Or what about *The club that puts its supporters first?*

Or then again, based on this and other self-confessed examples, what about *The club that knows you'll go on coughing up the money no matter what?* Or *The club run by sad-minded, self-confessed money-grabbers?* I have not taken out a copyright on either of these last two slogans, so the club can feel free to use them if it wishes!

Two years further down the line and the team were going great guns under Kev. Never mind that we regularly let in three – we just as regularly netted five. This was the swash-buckling stuff of which was made the fifties legend handed down by our fathers. The stuff our dreams were made of.

And it looked as though our dreams could finally connect with reality (fat chance!!)...

I was trying to keep my feet on the ground, and I knew it would be a waste of breath asking Newcastle United for tickets for the Antwerp game in Belgium. So I got in touch directly with Royal Antwerp, and in my very best Dutch begged them to sell me some tickets. And guess what, the reply was: 'how many would you like, Sir?'

The local (Flemish/Dutch) name for Antwerp is *Antwerpen*, but the official title of the club is the English designation 'Royal Antwerp'. This is because the club was founded by a bunch of Brits working in the city's docks.

There were four of us in the market for tickets. Only two of us were true Mags – myself and Rob from work in Essen. We were joined by a mackem colleague, Dave, and my mate Mike, who was working in Duisburg and whom I have known since we started studying German and French together in the Toon back in 1974. Two things had struck Mike immediately when he arrived on Tyneside from his native Leicester. The first was that the Chronicle sellers made a strange wailing sound that came across as some kind of Red Indian war (or wor) cry. The second was that people queued to get into pubs. He had not previously encountered either of those phenomena.

Armed with our tickets we set off from Essen, Germany, in my clapped-out Opel and were soon crossing through Holland at a spanking pace. Somewhere between Eindhoven and the Belgian border, we were overtaken by a Mini with BAOR (British Army of the Rhine) plates and decorated like ours with black and white scarves flapping in the wind. Exchanged toots of the horns until they were out of sight ahead of us. 'Toot, Toot, British Rhine Army.'

After a two-hour-and-a-bit drive, we turned off the motorway a couple of exits before Antwerp city centre and into the, in some parts, leafy suburb of Veurne. A lot of those leaves were already on the pavements of the long boulevard that took us towards the ground. We parked up at the side of the road, as others were doing, about a kilometre or so from the stadium and joined the ranks of the other pilgrims. Parked nearer the match were rows of coaches from the Holy Land... Wallsend, Jarrow, North Shields; all of these sacred sites were represented. It is always great when you have lived away for so long suddenly to be immersed in a sea of Geordie patter. Music to the ex-pat's ears, I can tell you. We easily had time for a couple of jars in their supporters' club bar, which is integrated into the back of their main stand. There was a great mix of Geordies and locals and the crack was grand. There was a Tyne-Tees camera team knocking around, so we introduced ourselves hoping we'd get interviewed, but they had already been talking to a bunch who had come from Germany (probably those squaddies who had overtaken us on the motorway), so they had already covered the Geordie-exiles angle.

Time to take our seats in their main stand, and of course half of the seats were filled by Geordies. Sitting next to us were a few Flemings (or should that be Phlegmings?), however, and when we started singing 'New-cass-ell, New-cass-ell, New-cass-ell' to the tune of 'here we go, here we go, here we go', they asked what we were singing!!!!!

The match was magic, of course, and they were all heroes. The Prince (everyone knows his name) was clearly lapping it all up, and the local telly people rushed over to him after the game before he could leave the pitch.

My enduring memories of that night, however, relate as much to the goings-on off the pitch as to those on it. The Antwerp ground struck me immediately as resembling one of those velodromes with really steep sides where the terracing was. The end behind the goal to our right at first sight looked a bit like a block of flats in which people were sitting in their glass-fronted living rooms. These were clearly expensive corporate hospitality boxes incongruously taking the place of a Leazes-type end. In the Popular-type side towards the far corner abutting the boxes was a good-sized Toon contingent who like us in the stand were in good voice.

At one point we thought some fighting must have started as people seemed to be falling forward (one of them being the aforementioned Kevin). And at half time the police moved all of them to the hitherto empty (and unsafe-looking) terracing behind the goal to our left, which happily saw our two second-half goals, crowning a memorable five-nil continental victory. It turned out that the terracing where they had originally been standing had started to crumble away. And this in the country which had seen the Heysel disaster a decade or so earlier.

It is hard to believe, isn't it? Had the Belgian football authorities learnt absolutely nothing? At the time, all the blame for Heysel was heaped upon the Liverpool supporters. But on the telly, all you could see were *tifosi* throwing things and dancing around making menacing gestures while the police seemed only to be looking on. And maybe the wall that gave way on that tragic night in Brussels was as dilapidated as the terracing in Antwerp? At all events, we should be very cautious when apportioning blame. Quite often in life, things are not what they seem to be.

A tale of two cities in Belgium

It was too bad that you missed the Antwerp game, Barry, but tell us about some of the other games around Belgium that you've seen.

Well, Pete, let's start down in the South four years ago. With living in Belgium, I thought I'd see if it would be possible to volunteer to help UEFA at the Euro 2000 championships, which were jointly staged by Belgium and the Netherlands. I was lucky enough to be offered a post as a volunteer at their official Press Centre in Charleroi, the southern Belgian town which became the scene of the confrontation between 'We've got a water cannon and we're gonna use it' riot police and followers of England and Germany. Pro-active shouldn't be the watchword for police, but it certainly was there. No-one can deny it, there were some troublemakers in the café-lined square that you'll remember from the blanket coverage, chanting inflammatory songs and just asking for a good dousing of their misplaced ardour. It's just a crying shame that they bring down trouble on everyone else who has the misfortune to be around them. The Dutch policing is applied with a light touch – it's sophisticated and watertight, whereas in Charleroi it was a ham-fisted water fight.

Even though the Press Centre was only a few minutes' walk from the riot square, we heard nothing at all about it while it was happening. Which is, to say the least, ironic – you had a building full of hundreds of journalists drinking coffee, all blissfully unaware of a major story going on under their noses! But are these stories maybe just engineered in the first place?

Come to think of it, maybe the Eindhoven railway tunnel bridge straight into the away end was invented specially for the England fans who were in Eindhoven for their first Euro 2000 game? I wouldn't be surprised, because I don't recall it being there when Dalglish brought his depleted team (Ian Rush replacing Tino in attack – i.e. attack, but no further than the half-way line) a couple of years earlier. Mind, I've heard there's far more trouble with hooligans in Holland than in England now – they're stuck in an eighties time warp – especially between the big three teams Ajax, PSV and Feyenoord, so I actually think the tunnel bridge must have been built in their honour.

Anyway I'd taken five days off work spread out over the couple of weeks the UEFA circus was in town and helped out with the journalists for all the Charleroi games, including England v Germany – Shearer's last goal for England in the one-nil win – and v Romania – his last match for England. It certainly takes a lot of organising behind the scenes. As an example, the press photographers have complex technical requirements for direct lines to transmit their streams of high-resolution digital photos straight to their newspapers, and getting everyone sorted out took some doing. Then there's the question of allocating the limited number of press seats to the hordes of sports reporters who turn up for the big matches. They have the same problem as us! There aren't enough places for all of them, so they're given in order of priority to the top papers from each country, then to the lesser papers from the countries playing the match, and then they're shared out to the rest. The lesser journalists have to turn up earlier in the day and put in a request to go on the waiting list.

At a set time a couple of hours before the game, the names on the list are sent over to the UEFA HQ, which for Euro 2000 was in Amsterdam, not in Switzerland. UEFA then make a decision on which reporters will be the lucky ones to get a press seat and send back the marked-up list. Matches don't come bigger than England v Germany, so demand was high and a lot of them missed out. And quite a lot of them got pretty angry! In fact there was a near-riot as there was such a long delay in getting the list back and handing out the few tickets that there was hardly time to get up to the ground before kick-off, even for the lucky ones, while the unfavoured ones went bananas. Not surprising, as how were they going to explain to their editors who'd paid their travel expenses that they hadn't actually managed to get in? Maybe this explains why sometimes when you read a match report, you wonder whether it really was the same game you witnessed? Probably it was reporters too frightened to admit they didn't get in, so they made it up and wired it in. The big names have no trouble in getting seats; they just stroll in and pick them up; it's the ones from the Hicksville Herald who miss out and start jumping up and down. Anyway, isn't it nice to know that it isn't just we humble supporters who can't always get in!

Still, it was interesting to meet some of the big names like Hugh McIlvanney and Patrick Barclay, and, to be parochial, Neil Farrington of the Sunday Sun, which used to be a good paper thirty years ago before sadly plummeting down-market, and John Gibson of The Journal. John Gibson is well up in the pecking order of journalists, even if he's from a regional newspaper, as I witnessed at the press conferences held by Kevin Keegan. Not many journalists were allowed to ask a question, but he was.

It certainly was quite an experience and great fun, mucking in with all the other volunteers. There were about two or three hundred of us, doing different jobs such as press centre helpers like me, photographers' runners (who stand with the old-style film camera photographers and each time they finish a film they literally run it over from the stadium to the film processing centre), official car drivers (doomed to drive Hyundais), ground stewards, hostesses, security people, caterers, and so on. They were mostly from Charleroi, including some who could speak the languages of the visiting teams, including a Romanian chef, a Yugoslavian table tennis champion, and a Colombian teacher (who could take care of the South American contingent of journalists), and others such as one of the organisers of the Anderlecht Supporters Club.

One of the perks, which I'd been half-hoping for but wasn't at all part of the deal, was that I got to go to the matches to help out with keeping the journalists supplied with team sheets and match data. It's amazingly efficient the speed with which the details of the game, scorers, yellow and red cards, background information on players and so on is relayed to the journalists. There's a constant stream of flyers of match updates to distribute. And I found out that you don't need to be too impressed when the television and radio commentators always get the players' names right, and seem to know all kinds of anecdotes about the history between the two sides, the players, the manager, the venue, and on and on. I stood behind them and I can tell you they have two monitor screens each, one showing the close-ups and action replays, and the other churning out all the information on who's got the ball, and background such as 'it's seventy-nine games since he scored a goal with his left foot', 'his granny was a fishmonger in Cullercoats', and so on. By the way, have you ever noticed that there aren't many mongers in the world? It seems you can only get iron-, fish-, rumour- and warmongers, and none of them have much to do with each other, so how do they all come to be mongers? God knows! 'Make iron and fish, not war, you monger!'

Being in the press section at the England v Germany match gave me the chance to meet a few personalities. Sparkly-eyed Katy Hill out of Blue Peter (where's she gone now?), John Motson (whose wife hails from Fenham, I believe), and also the duumvirate (a new word to you and me too; I didn't think it would exist, but it does! Sounds good, eh?) of John Barnes, ex-Newcastle maestro, and Glenn Hoddle, both there as expert summarisers for the television. The ground was bouncing after the goal; you could see the lights and shadows on the pitch moving. The floodlights were connected onto the stadium structure, which is obviously not quite rigid enough to withstand an Alan Shearer goal. A bit like Old Trafford's cantilever stand was boinging up and down in the semi-final versus Spurs.

I found myself at the end of the game leaning over the barrier of the media section looking at Alan Shearer making his way off the pitch having scored the only goal of the game, and there alongside me was John Barnes, smiling quietly to himself, and thinking like me that the hard work had been done and England had a good chance to progress. On the way out of the ground afterwards, he met up again with Glenn Hoddle, as they walked down the stairs. An England fan was just behind them on his mobile phone to someone, describing how the game had gone, when he spotted his chance. He raised his voice: 'Well, if you don't believe me, ask my mate Glenn Hoddle', and tapping him on the shoulder with his phone, he said 'Here, Glenn, tell my brother what you made of the game!' Glenn took it all in great good humour, and confirmed that it had indeed been a close-fought match, and wished him all the best.

And while we're on the subject of personalities: at the quarter final, which should have been England v Italy if Romania hadn't knocked them out, you may have wondered why a small boy in a Newcastle shirt levitated into view of the window of the ITV box while Des Lynam was doing his half-time chat. Well, it was I (as George Washington put it at cherry-tree chopping time), holding up son Brian so he could see who was in with Des, and wave to his mum and sisters too.

One big reason why Charleroi should of course sound familiar to you is that it's the hometown club where 'Prince' Philippe Albert made his name, and we all know 'everyone knows his name'. He moved on to Anderlecht before signing for us after Kevin Keegan spotted him at the '94 World Cup, and he eventually returned to Charleroi on leaving us to wear the black and white stripes for the third time in his career. In common with Juventus, Notts County, Grimsby, Exeter, Salonika, Luxembourg's very own Jeunesse Esch and more, Charleroi are lucky like us to wear the most stylish choice of team colours. If he'd only ever kicked that one ball for us, he would still be assured of his place as an all-time great in the Geordie Pantheon for his chip over the head of Peter Schmeichel into the Man Utd net for our final goal in the Howay Five-Oh win.

Philippe Albert's transfer conditions included arranging a pre-season friendly at Anderlecht in summer 1996. Anderlecht is a curate's egg of a suburb in Brussels, and only a few miles by Metro from where we live. Trying to park near the ground is a dead loss, that's why I say by Metro. You might even pass through one of the world's best-named Metro stations, Kunst-Wet, but please be careful how you say it. We try to support Anderlecht, though our hearts are not really in it, but still we go along now and then, especially to their European games. Of course, there is some history between Newcastle and Anderlecht, as they knocked us out of the Fairs Cup on the away goals rule in the year we were trying to retain it (the words Paul van Himst still spring to mind, though I don't think he scored the decisive goal...).

Son Brian and I even have Anderlecht Supporters Cards, as you need one to buy a ticket to any match in Belgium, whether it's a Belgian Jupiler League or Champignons League game or an international match. The Jupiler is so weak - the league, that is, not the beer - that Anderlecht are virtually guaranteed a place in Europe every year, which means that we've seen some good teams over recent years, including Real Madrid, Bayern Munich, Lyon and Celtic. It's so easy to buy a ticket, even though the ground capacity is only about 25,000 for European games; you just go along with your Supporters Card and buy one - no rush, no queues, no risk, as long as you turn up in the first couple of days after they put them on sale. The best idea is to buy a subscription to all three Champignons League home games as it's cheaper and you get a better choice of where to sit.

Mentioning Jupiler, it's funny how everyone in the UK has heard of Stella Artois but not the other standard Belgian beers Jupiler and Maes. That's the thing: in Belgium Stella's just another almost generic normal beer, the kind you get if you just ask for *'une bière, s'il vous plait'* or *'een bier alstublieft'* without being particular which one you'd like. Whereas in the UK, the power of advertising has portrayed it as being something mega-special that is worth a price premium over the rest. Stella even used to describe itself as being 'reassuringly expensive'!!! The really special beers in Belgium are the hundred or more which originated in monasteries and little family breweries, even if they're now mostly owned by one giant company, Interbrew, based in Leuven, half an hour outside Brussels. You've also got the naturally fermented Brussels beers like *gueuze* and *lambic* which use no added yeast, just some mystery ingredient from the Brussels air. I have an idea what it might be: you can smell it if you take a walk around Brussels just after it has stopped raining (which equates to just before it starts again) – the something special is the miasma of blue-rinsed lapdog's doings. They're all over the place!

At the Lyon match, a man in front of us jumped up when Anderlecht scored. He put his cigarette down and started hugging and dancing with his neighbour. When he'd calmed himself he sat down again but he'd forgotten about his cigarette. A few seconds later, he was back up again jumping, screaming and rubbing his bum. We could see a black smouldering hole in the backside of his trousers, and a smoking butt on his seat, before and after he sat down again.

Alan Shearer made his third appearance in his first week for Newcastle at the Anderlecht friendly after his début at Lincoln and the Charity Shield four-nil débacle, which we also witnessed. He spent a long time signing autographs at the start of the match down by the wire fence. Philippe Albert of course got a great reception from all sides of the ground. We won the match two-nil with goals from Tino and Ginola, who for some reason looked a little out of sorts and seemed to want to keep the ball all for himself for long periods.

While we were watching in the warm summer evening sunshine, now and then the comparative peace and quiet was broken by someone sitting right behind us bursting into hearty solo renditions of 'With an N and an E and a Wubble-U C....' and 'Toon Toon, Black and White Army.' Who is this? We joined in to help him out, and taught the words to our friends from Chester who'd come along with us. He liked our magpie bird's head hats that we'd bought at the Charity Shield. We had a chat at half time and it turned out that we had a lot in common: exiled Geordies working on the continent for many years, following the Toon around, born within a year of each other, mothers born on the same day, you can learn a lot in fifteen minutes. This accidental meeting eventually produced this book. Meanwhile, back to Charleroi.

The post-match travel arrangements for the England fans were something to behold. Because I'd been in the Press Stand, and so wasn't held behind by the police, I first went to see the press conference given by Kevin Keegan, which took place strangely enough in a tent pitched by the side of the stadium (Colonel Gaddafi-style). There were about two hundred journalists and there was absolute dead silence when KK launched into them over Alan Shearer. Very well said. He also made a special mention at the beginning of the press conference of the tremendous atmosphere in the Charleroi stadium. He said that some of the German players had told him after the game that it was the best crowd atmosphere they had ever experienced, even if it was for the other side, as two thirds of the committed supporters were there for England. He said that the authorities had been proved wrong about moving the game elsewhere, and that Charleroi had shown itself to be the right place for a great night. Mind, no-one mentioned the afternoon riot.

I then made my own way down to the railway station to catch the train back home, and I was engulfed by German and English hordes, and just as many riot police. The organisation at the station was non-existent: all announcements were in French, none in German or English; people were getting on trains and getting off again as the rumours changed about which trains were going where; there were plenty of police but only one or two railway guards and even they were confused about which were the special football trains. After the Romania game, I managed to find one of the more sympathetic local police and showed him my Belgian resident ID and he let me skirt around the throng and catch the little local train and get off at my stop, halfway back to Brussels. But after the Germany game, everyone who was English was corralled onto one platform, and all the Germans on another. You had no choice; you were crammed onto a non-stop train headed straight for Brussels, with all protestations that I lived somewhere else brushed aside. They clearly thought that hundreds of supporters getting off by mistake half way to Brussels was going to start off a Second Battle of Waterloo. So I ended up powerless to do anything as the train trundled through my own stop and carried on slowly to Brussels. We passed the trip talking over the events of the day. No-one near me had seen the riot; they'd been in Brussels. Reports of six hundred pounds for a ticket were very exaggerated: a few had got their tickets from Brussels sprouts (touts), and people laughed when they heard someone admit he'd paid a hundred pounds. We arrived well after midnight, long after all the local trains back out to my station had stopped running. And it wasn't finished there either, because the police were all lined up waiting and they wouldn't allow you to go your own way and try and find a taxi. Instead, along with all the English fans, we were marched off along the back streets of Brussels into the worst quarter, hemmed in on both sides of the street by riot police. What a way to be treated!

On the language front, Belgium really is a fascinating country. Unfortunately, the same is not true on very many other fronts, though definitely on a few. As explained, it only came into being in 1830, when the French-speaking South (Wallonia) was taken away from France and welded together with the Flemish-speaking North which had been hacked off the Netherlands (Flemish being a dialect of Dutch as we have established earlier). Brussels, though predominantly French-speaking (or francophone) is actually in Flanders and is thus literally surrounded by Flemish-speakers, though you only have to travel a few miles to the south before you reach French-speaking Wallonia. Confused? It's hardly surprising! After the First World War, Belgium – like the other countries on Germany's borders – decided to have a bit of Deutschland, and so the eastern *cantons* are German-speaking. 'Germanophone' Belgians account for about ten per cent of the population, French-speaking Walloons about forty per cent and Flemings for, er, let me see, fifty per cent. Brussels itself is of course very much a multi-cultural place, as you would expect since it houses NATO headquarters and the European institutions. Though largely French-speaking, Brussels is officially bilingual (French/Flemish), but in reality there are probably as many Spanish, Italian, Arab and English speakers in the city as Flemings!

As you would expect with such a language structure, there is talk from time to time of the country splitting up into its component parts, and the Flemings have a particularly vigorous, and sometimes openly racist, nationalist party called the *Vlaams Blok*. But in the South of the country too there are those who would rather be part of France. And if you drive through the German-speaking bit, you will quickly notice that on bilingual road signs the French is painted over, so there is a bit of a suggestion that some of them would maybe like to be part of Germany again.

On the subject of road signs, these can be major fun everywhere in Belgium, as the name of a particular town varies as you move from one language area to another. Sometimes, as on the motorway from Brussels (Bruxelles/Brussel) to Aachen (or Aix-la-Chapelle, or Aken, if you prefer), road signs can change linguistic affiliations several times in the space of fifty km!!! While you're in a Flemish province, the sign for Liège is Luik, and that changes to Liège when you enter a French-speaking bit, and then back to Luik a few clicks further down the road. Or if you hire a car at the officially bilingual national airport at Zaventem just outside Brussels and want to head for Namur or Mons in the French-speaking South, be aware that outside the airport you are initially in Flanders and those towns will be signposted 'Namen' and 'Bergen' respectively. And if you see a sign for 'Rijssel', it is showing you the way to Lille in France, whereas a sign reading 'Lille' in northern Belgium refers to a small Flemish town called, well, Lille. Confused? That's probably the intention, because the Flemings are getting their own back on the French-speakers, who for decades had the biggest say and simply pretended that Flemish didn't exist at all. Hence Brugge came to be known internationally as Bruges. Etc., etc. It perhaps wouldn't be surprising if Belgium broke up or melted down one day and Brussels was left as a kind of autonomous European capital.

An Intertoto interlude

Before we leave Belgium, though I think we may already have crossed the border on the way to Breda, we've got to tell you about the away game at Lokeren in the 2001 Intertoto Cup and our first sightings of Craig Bellamy, Lua Lua, and the returning Robbie Elliott. Pete brought his marra Phil up from Luxembourg for a 'taste of Geordieland abroad' weekend. It was another close-run thing ticket-wise, as Pete and Phil received theirs on the very morning of the match. And what a match it was! We wrote up a report for what, in our opinion, is the best Internet NUFC BBS Discussion Forum, which used to reside on www.greenspun.com and which is now on 'NotBBC' at www.frogger.uklinux.net. It's a godsend for the many Geordie exiles in Europe and around the world, with contributors from just about any country you can think of, as well as the Promised Land of course. While we're on the subject, there's nothing to touch the www.nufc.com website for informed comment and news on the lads' latest exploits. The official site does a good job too, but you need to pay a subscription (surprise, surprise) to get access to all the best features, especially the Internet broadcasts of match commentaries, which again are a real boon for us exiles out here in the diaspora.

Here's what we wrote on the BBS Discussion Forum, while it was fresh in our minds:

'There's three of us sitting here, Barry, Phil and Pete, just back from the match, having a pint in Brussels. Got to Lokeren at four o'clock. As expected, we were stopped by the local law at a checkpoint. Water cannon, machine guns, the works. We were turned away and told to come back at six. We were in a German-registered car, but they were letting through the Belgian cars with no questions.

We should have gone in Barry's, because the evening before Barry went in his Belgian-registered car to see the team practise and there'd been no problem at all. He had been one of only two supporters there, along with the Tyne-Tees TV crew, who were intrigued to find Geordies living locally. Barry even had the luck to have a short chat with Bobby Robson after the training session was over.

So we went to the mysteriously named Donk Lake, which turns out to be a local tourist resort, despite its name. Back to the roadblock, a bit early so we had to park up. The police advised us to go get a couple of beers before coming back!! (They did, honestly: they said 'Go and wait in that pub over there.') We put on our gear and hung around until six. We took some photos with the police, and along came the Belgian TV. Pete and Phil are both translators and they speak Dutch, which made the TV people's day. We pointed out that the good people of Lokeren could sleep easily in their beds as the Geordies had nothing to do with the mindless morons who had rampaged through Charleroi the year before! So we're on Belgian TV on the Monday sports round-up. Then it was off to the ground where we parked right outside.

The Toon Army was in good voice in the local bar, indulging in lots of good-natured banter with the locals. There were about six hundred of us (they were still selling tickets for our section on the night), and maybe about one thousand locals, that's all. All the noise was coming from our section - the Lokeren fans were very subdued throughout. A vigorous first half performance saw us go in three up. Bellamy showed glimpses of his potential, especially in his persistence in getting to the goal line and angling the ball back to Quinn for the first goal. Ameobi put his gangling frame about admirably, though sadly failing to engage that elusive fifth gear. Despite his apparent lack of speed, his tenacity of purpose propelled him past the last line of defence to place the ball beyond the keeper's reach. The third goal looked as if he'd lost the ball, but somehow he spun round on it and stabbed it home.

Second half more subdued - did Uncle Bobby tell them to keep the score down to maintain interest for the second leg? Hot-air balloon went across and Pete invented a new variation on the familiar refrain: 'Toon Balloon Black and White Army', which was taken up by a large section of the crowd - for what seemed like a drop of eternity distilled. Lokeren to their credit engineered a couple of good opportunities and could have pulled one or even two back. Our glorious leader, however, had left the best till last. On came Lua Lua to replace Ameobi, who got loud applause as he left the field. Lua Lua did little or nothing for ten minutes, gave away the ball numerous times and then wallop - what happened? The ball was floating across the penalty area, defying gravity, one giant leap for Geordie-kind and the ball bulleted into the goal from an overhead scissor kick. There then followed the most spectacular goal celebration ever seen in Lokeren - a double somersault with a twisting dismount, whatever that is. We'd never seen anything like it before.

Robbie Elliot made some very good through-balls down the left to Bellamy and occasionally got into forward positions, overlapping Quinn. They seemed to work well together. Bellamy also certainly tends to the left side, and really did very well - he's enthusiastic, talks a lot to his team mates, runs around a lot, like a Gallagher replacement, and gets into good positions. He very nearly scored a couple of goals after long dribbling runs, and we can have high hopes. On the whole, the locals were very friendly and we saw no trouble at all from any of our fans or theirs. We hope they enjoy themselves in Geordieland next week - they have a couple of buses organised, leaving next Saturday at four in the morning. Headlines expected in the Belgian and UK papers tomorrow: 'Six hundred English fans Not arrested for not causing a riot'. Before closing, must mention two interesting and little known facts – firstly, there is a bar called 'Bobby's Club' just round the corner (*Nomen est omen*), and secondly: luscious local Lokeren ladies never miss a Gallowgate match, even sup in the Strawberry, get in because they know the bouncers. A great day, even the sun came out after a downpour all morning and afternoon until four o'clock.'

It's interesting to re-read this now – how right our first impressions of Craig Bellamy turned out to be!

Tellers of tales

Commentators: don't they just drive you mad? Especially the blatantly biased ones – I don't have to tell you their names, because you know them only too well. Mind you, I don't mind so much if they're biased towards Newcastle. One option you always have had with the television is to turn the sound down, and watch as if you're deaf. But that doesn't help if you're listening to the radio. Meanwhile back on the telly, the trouble with having no sound is that you lose the atmosphere somewhat, so you try it for a while but then you're tempted to turn it up again just a little bit to hear the crowd ... but then this biased idiot comes back on. However, salvation is nigh, because in the last few years there's been a fantastic step forward with the advent of the new digital television channels. It doesn't feature on all matches, but for the big ones, if you press the little red button and get into the digital set-up, you can select which audio signal you want to hear. It's a bit like selecting the Player Cam on Sky, (which by the way I find is a waste of time, because you lose orientation – what it needs is a zoom control, then it might be more interesting). Sometimes you get a choice between the standard commentary on BBC One, who might be showing the match (I know it's a rare event at the moment, because Sky seem to buy everything up, but this is just an example), or just the crowd noise with no commentary, or Radio Five or maybe Radio Wales (if it were for instance Newcastle playing Cardiff in the FA Cup). So you can switch around and either have no commentary or choose someone whose bias suits your own! It will be great when you can also get the Radio Newcastle or Metro Radio feed. In the meantime, just the crowd noise suits me fine. After all, when you go to the match, you don't have someone shouting out the names of who's got the ball and 'my word!' or 'his granny's from Cullercoats' (hey - you told us that already, but actually that's the kind of comment I don't mind, as it adds to the local colour!).

Another idea I've been musing over is why they don't make a regionalised version of 'Match of the Day' or 'The Premiership'. The way it is now, in an hour or so of programme, you get eighty per cent devoted to highlights and studio chat about two or three main matches, which by definition have to involve London teams such as Man Utd, Arsenal and Chelsea, then you get one or two minutes at half past midnight of your team – by which time you are probably too scuttled to fully appreciate it anyway. Now that they have cameras whirring away at every single game, it can't be beyond their wit to put your team on for most of the time, and show the other games for reduced time. Maybe it would cause a re-think of the studio chat sessions, but who needs them anyway?

Speaking of bias, even the worst of our commentators you can think of would blanche at the prospect of stooping to the depths of French commentary, which it is my misfortune to hear from time to time. This really is the pits – the only nation that gets close is America – remember the 1984 Los Angeles Olympics, where the camera stayed on the American, even if he was seventh in the race, and you sometimes missed the winner until the action replay? The 1994 World Cup wasn't much better. It's not real football, but not so long ago I was driving along through France while the commentary of the Rugby World Cup was on and England was in the process of demolishing South Africa. (I can't stand rugby, but it passed the time on a long journey from Bordeaux to Pau). As the score steadily mounted, it was all 'ooh la la, was zat lucky for zose bad Eengleesh playeurz', 'I steell zeenkuh zat zee Sout Afhrreecahnzur are gerweeng to ween, eetz ernly a matter of tame', and so on. It's so bad, it becomes an art form – the theatre of the absurd. The only time it's worth listening to is when the French are losing, then their commentary is absolutely fantastic entertainment. The last real, i.e. football, World Cup was a classic: no wins, no goals, steady stream of wilder and wilder excuses. Is it any wonder that *chauvinisme* is a French word? And bias too, from the French *biais*. The Marseille v Newcastle game commentary must have had decent people retching in the aisles. Funnily enough, I find the Belgians and Dutch completely different – their commentaries are invariably fair and even-handed – full marks to them.

What I'm waiting for is 3-D Virtual Reality broadcasting where you put on goggles and you're transported onto the pitch and can watch the match going on around you, or tag along with Alan Shearer and experience the match the way he sees and plays it. Now that will be really something, and it's almost feasible now. In ten or twenty years we'll have it. The thing is, it'll never replace going to the match, will it? Will it?

Ideas for UEFA

Here's something else to discuss down the pub in the long UEFA winter break. You know how you qualify for the European competitions by doing well in the domestic league and cups the year before? So there's a built-in time lag of one year between when the club is playing well and when they get the chance to get through to a European Final. And as we all know to our expense, your team can be doing great one season, but the season after you earned your qualification, you're suddenly not playing so well and you're wishing that it could be your last season's team who could be going out to play in the semi-final. Especially because in the close season the rich clubs often buy up the small teams' emerging good players. So the in-form teams are maybe in the UEFA Cup or not even in Europe at all, while the smaller Champignons League teams can often be out of form or light of their best players from last season by the time they get into it. You can easily see the examples if you look at the 2003/04 UEFA Cup finalists: Valencia had only just qualified for the UEFA Cup, but strolled through the competition on the basis of their current season Spanish League Championship-winning form, while Marseille got knocked out of the Champignons League after the first group stage and into the UEFA Cup safety net because their form had dipped badly from the standard that had qualified them from the French League the year before. Unfortunately they perked up after ditching manager Alain Perrin, who funnily enough had been in charge of Troyes when we'd played them on our earlier European odyssey in the Intertoto Cup. He had masterminded their four-four away goals 'win' over us at St James's Park, which ironically had made his name, so in some way we'd been responsible for getting him the job at Marseille. Pity he couldn't have hung around just a little bit longer and kept them in the doldrums until we'd got past them. At least the Marseillais should thank him for bringing in our nemesis Didier Drogba, when plenty of other clubs had turned their noses up at him.

Now how about changing this safety net system from Champignons League to UEFA Cup? You could still let a few of the CL drop-outs into the UEFA Cup, but why not also allow in a few of the current year's highest-placed teams, the ones who had not already qualified the previous year? With the current winter break in the UEFA competitions, this would allow the really in-form teams at the halfway point of the season to join in. And it would add a bit of interest in the middle of the domestic season.

A tale of Troyes cities

Troyes? Odyssey? Bells must have rung in many a faded schoolboy memory: not only were we heading for the Final of the Intertoto Cup, but the match was going to be played at the historic site of the wooden horse and the face that had launched a thousand ships. But how was it so far from the sea? How did they get a thousand ships up there? Why was it in France, not ancient Greece, or actually Turkey? Yes, Troyes turned out to be in the heart of champagne vineyards in the middle of France. So instead of the wine red sea of the Aegean, we were headed for the bubbly white wine lake district of France for the first leg and the steely grey sea off the North-East coast for the amazing four-four second leg.

It happened to be another great place to combine a match with a holiday. There was a huge reservoir with a beach for swimming, windsurfing and sailing, beautiful countryside, great food and wine, and even a trip to Colombey les Deux Eglises to try to see General de Gaulle's mausoleum ('six feet below us only two unfeasibly large nostrils'), but it was

94

closed. Typical: he said 'Non' to letting us Brits into Europe when he was alive, and even now he's dead he's still saying 'Non' to letting us into his last little bit of *le continent*. We stayed a few miles outside of town at the Holiday Inn, and when we got there we were surrounded by the track-suited figures of none other than the Troyes team who stay together there before big matches. The hotel also has its own golf course and they let us have a go. There was a notice in French saying dogs had to be kept on a leash on the golf course, helpfully translated for tourists into English as 'please hang your dog on the golf course'. A bit excessive we thought, but at least they have moved on from the guillotine.

Match day dawned as bright and promising as the July days preceding it, but as the hours wore on clouds started to gather forebodingly on the horizon and by late afternoon we were in the slippery grip of the kind of tropical rainstorm that we thought was only possible in Barcelona or North Shields. By the evening you could have sailed a thousand ships through the torrents in the streets. Warm wet westerly winds indeed.

This time, the whole family had decided to go to the match and when we got to the ground we found lots of other families had had the same idea. There were mums and dads, kids, grandas and grannies aplenty in the bedraggled queue for tickets. For this match, the arrangement was that you just turned up and bought your ticket at the entrance, like in the good old days. Once inside, we were first of all herded by the ridiculously over-the-top quota of riot police – they had provided nearly everyone of us with our own personal police guard - into the lower terrace which was very much exposed to the elements. Eventually the police relented when they saw the number of children and grannies getting soaked and let us up into the roofed top stand. Despite the rain, and despite the standard of the football, which it has to be admitted was not top draw, the crowd atmosphere was great, with lots of old songs from the sixties and seventies getting an airing, no doubt started up by the many grandas in the crowd: 'Sha la la la MacNamee', 'Terry, Terry Hibbitt on the wing', 'Frank Clark knows my father', 'You can stick your wooden horse...', 'Toon Monsoon Black and White Army' and many more. The Troyes fans too were very friendly and one family even passed a couple of *Allez Troyes* royal blue baseball caps through the grille to Sarah and Emilie who at the time were only three years old and who were having a fine time.

At half time I bumped into Toby from Brussels and his brother who also came up with us to both PSV games, and as we were walking down the stairs I spotted a shirt with Jonno on the back. Now I only knew Jonno as the 'handle' – if that is what you call it - of one of the contributors on the best Newcastle United Internet forum, so I took the risk of sounding stupid and asked if he'd heard of greenspun on the Internet? He had; it was Jonno, accompanied by other BBS stalwarts Screecher and Clarky. I'd never seen them before and I've never seen them since, but it was good to be able to put a few faces to the names in the BBS, which is still going strong by the way. What they liked best was that Brian, Sarah and Emilie all were wearing Toon tops with 'Brian' printed on the back. Brian had lent his cast-offs to his sisters, and it did look very funny seeing a seven year-old and two three year-olds wandering around, all with 'Brian' emblazoned across their not so broad shoulders. The BBS gang thought that somehow we'd got a job lot of 'Brian' shirts. I wish we had, because they cost a packet. But of course we 'mugs' always cough up, as we know from that never-to-be-forgotten News of the World interview. We held out for a goalless draw, but to be honest we couldn't have complained if we'd lost, and if it hadn't been for some great Shay Given saves, and some poor shooting by the Troyes forwards, we would have. It was just postponing the agony, because in the return leg we somehow managed to draw fours apiece and went out on the away goals rule. It was exciting because we made a great comeback from a ludicrous start, but ultimately disappointing. Nevertheless it was the launching pad for a great season, which saw us earning a place in the Champignons League, more than anyone could have hoped for at the beginning of the year.

Tale of another fine Metz

When I heard the draw for the third round of the 1996/97 UEFA Cup, I could not believe my luck. Metz is only sixty clicks or so away from Luxembourg City where I work. In fact plenty people working in our office building actually commute from Metz, either by train (the connections are excellent, unlike those between Luxembourg and Trier) or by car, taking France's notorious A31. *Nota bene*, the A31 between Luxembourg and Metz is one of the most dangerous stretches of motorway in the whole of Western Europe, *ergo* in the whole world: avoid it like the plague if you possibly can. I had in fact had a trip to Metz for the previous round against Wacker Innsbruck.

Innsbruck, by the way, means 'bridge across the (river) Inn'. That reminds me: Hitler was born in Braunau am Inn, so it makes you wonder which club he supported. You can picture the scene in the Berlin bunker towards the end of the war, can't you?... General von Scheissenhausen bursts in and shouts 'Bad news, mein Führer, ze Russians have crossed ze Oder und vill soon be in Berlin'. And the reply: 'Do not bozzer me wiz such trifling matters now, Dummkopf, can't you see I am to second-half commentary listening of ze third-round cup tie between Eintracht Berchtesgaden and Oberpfaffenhofen Kickers, already?' And it wasn't just the captain who got to wear an armband in this tie.

The atmosphere at Metz's St. Symphorien stadium for the Wacker game had been brilliant and I'd been suitably impressed. It is a nice compact ground without any running track to spoil things the way it does at so many continental grounds. You feel you are part of what is going on on the pitch, which is exactly how it should be. The Toon had beaten Halmstads of Sweden in the same round and we were looking pretty good.

The day after the draw I got straight onto the blower to FC Metz and a very charming lady with a very sexy voice told me there would be no problem at all getting tickets. All I had to do was turn up at the ground the next Thursday morning – tickets would go on sale at nine o'clock. How refreshing this was – if you wanted a ticket, all you had to do was go and queue for one. Season ticket holders had priority of course, but at Metz they don't account for more than around one-fifth of the ground's capacity, which is around thirty thousand. Plus it must have been blindingly (or perhaps deafeningly) obvious to the lassie on the phone that I wasn't French, but that did not seem to bother her at all. Ten out of ten to FC Metz for their attitude towards away fans!! In a perfect world, all clurbs would be able to have surch an attitude.

I had to make a few rearrangements at work (that four-letter word) and managed to get the morning off. We Geordies know a thing or two about queuing for tickets. Ask my Mam, who always put my bait up and made sure I got up in time to queue up in Leazes Terrace (pull it down, expand the East Stand, sorry Barry) for Fairs Cup tickets in those halcyon (McFaul, Craig, Clark ...) days. With this tradition instilled in my bones, I set the radio alarm clock for three o'clock and duly left Trier at three-twenty in the morning. Now there's not a lot happening at that time of day (or night) on the *autobahn* between Trier and Luxembourg. Just short of Luxembourg City you follow a long left-hand bend that gets you to the French border about a quarter of an hour later. Then straight down the A31, where traffic was getting a wee bit heavier, past Thionville and on to Metz. You follow signs for Metz *Centre Ville* (did I mention, by the way, that in French Metz is pronounced *Mess*? And the people who live there are known as *les messins* – that's a bit of a mess, if you ask me). You come to a geet big roundabout with an impressive fountain in the middle, turn right and you are at the ground in a few short minutes. It is not as centrally located as the Holy of Holies, but it is clearly an integral part of the town centre, which I like. It is also on the bank of a canal. As you skirt the canal for the last few hundred metres you pass the supporters club bar on the right, and then you turn right into the car park directly behind one of the stands.

I parked up and walked around looking for the ticket queue, expecting to see people dossing in sleeping bags and others eating the bait their *mamans* had put up for them. Well you would, wouldn't you? Nothing of the sort. There was no queue. *Nix, nada, niente* – bugger all. So I located exactly where the tickets would go on sale – this was clearly indicated at a particular turnstile behind their equivalent of the Leazes End – and marched back to my car for a bit doss. It was only a quarter to five or thereabouts, so I reckoned I could allow myself a couple of hours in the circumstances. Out I went like a light, to be awakened by the sound of a couple of good-natured Metz fans tapping on the rear windscreen. My Opel Kadett had German number plates of course, but naturally featured a couple of Toon stickers on the rear, including 'Kevin Keegan's Black and White Army'. The lads in question were dead canny and obviously tickled pink by the fact that some Geordie loony with Kraut plates had come across to buy tickets at the crack of dawn in the middle of the working week. They said the queue would be building up soon, so I had better get my arse around there. The French for 'arse', by the way, is *cul*, as in 'cul de sac', which literally means 'arse of a sack', which is a pretty fair description of what a cul de sac is, when you think about it. Except, of course, the Froggies don't call a cul de sac a *cul de sac* at all. Oh no, that would make life too simple, wouldn't it? They call it a *voie sans issue*, which means a 'way with no exit', so there! But never mind, the (Frencher than French) *Québecois,* i.e. the French-speaking Canadians of Québec, do use the term *cul de sac*. Must have nicked it from the English, I suppose – bloody typical.

As it turned out, I was number five in the queue, and number eleven a few minutes later was a Geordie lass studying French and Spanish at Sheffield University. She was spending a year in Nancy, just down the road from Metz, as an assistant English teacher at a *lycée* and wanted a few tickets for herself and a few French friends. The fact that there were two Geordies right at the front went down really well with the rapidly increasing queue and the crack was great. Metz people are a really friendly bunch. Theirs is a friendly, provincial and homely club, and – as we were about to discover - the people who run it are so provincial and homely that they could not organise the proverbial piss-up in the proverbial brewery (which is a great pity, 'coz *Kronenbourg* lager is brewed not that far away, in Strasbourg).

By half past eight, the queue had grown, I reckon, to over a thousand. At this point, some gadgy wearing a club badge came along to the front of the queue and announced (in a voice that ensured that only the first two people heard) that the tickets would not go on sale at that turnstile at all, but in an office about two hundred yards away, integrated in the stand itself. I must stress that there was no police presence whatsoever. There were no stewards, nothing, *nix, nada,* etc. The front of the queue began peeling away towards the aforesaid office and the rest of us *moutons* followed in what developed into a completely uncontrolled stampede (if that's the right word in respect of sheep). From my original position of about fifth, I had now been relegated to around fiftieth in the new, unruly and irate queue before that office. I was not a happy *lapin*.

The Geordie student lass was now in front of me, and we communicated in broad Geordie, so as to ensure no-one else understood, to the effect that she would buy two more than she needed, so that at least Barry and I would get tickets. The door to the office duly opened at around nine-twenty and the first few people stormed in. In French, by the way, *il est neuf heures* definitely does not mean it is nine o'clock. I know this to be a fact because every morning on my way to work I tune in to the twenty-four hour radio news channel *France Info*. In fact I switch over to it after hearing the top-of-the-hour beeps on Radio Four (long wave reception in the Grand Duchy is crap, by the way) plus the news headlines (the eight o'clock UK time news, of course). Having digested those, and the fact that on the continent it is already about three minutes past nine, I hear the France Info lady with the incredibly sexy voice say 'France Info. Il est neuf heures', which thus obviously does not mean 'it is nine o'clock' but rather: 'it is some indeterminate time around about nine o'clock, so stuff you if you happen to be desperate for an accurate time check'. Lots of things in France seem to be slightly different, don't they?

But back to the plot: the people entering the poky little office to buy tickets were exiting by the SAME door, tickets in hand. So the next few people squeezed (or should that be 'squoze'?) past those coming out, and so on. This was MADNESS. As I got nearer to the door, word was spreading that you could basically buy as many tickets as you wanted. Naturally, people towards the back of the queue (now a couple of thousand strong) were upset about this and were getting restless and began pushing. The word 'Hillsborough' sprang to mind. Eventually I squeezed and squoze into the office to find a desk with two elderly Frenchies behind it and a pile of tickets on it. No partition, nothing. This was as farcical as a scene from 'allo allo', except it wasn't funny. I said 'huit billets, s'il vous plaît' and got all eight without any problem. The problems started when I tried to get out of the office again.

The in-bred revolutionary spirit of the French had encouraged them to stage a second storming of the Bastille, and getting out was a bugger of a job. Now I get claustrophobic at the best of times. And this was the worst of times. Like 'The Tale of Two Cities', the Toon and Metz in this case: 'It was the best of times, it was the worst of times'. So I was shouting at the top of my voice: 'This is going to be another Hillsborough, for Christ's sake step back!' But to no avail. This was organisation at its worst.

Metz is not very far away from sections of the Maginot Line, a massive line of fortifications built on the initiative of the then defence minister Maginot after the débacle of the

First World War. They built these defences along the German border from neutral Switzerland all the way to neutral Belgium, on the wholly reasonable assumption that the Germans wouldn't be such rotters as to breach either of those two countries' neutrality (not much they wouldn't!!). In part, the Maginot line incorporated natural fortifications such as high rocks overlooking the German border. Elsewhere, as in the vicinity of Metz, the French built huge great underground complexes that included entire barracks complete with hospitals and dental facilities. They made just two teeny-weeny mistakes. One, they stopped building at the Belgian border, so the Germans literally just marched AROUND the Maginot line. And two, the guns protruding from these underground and other workings were all trained on Germany and were not designed to be, errr, swivelled around in the event of an attack from the rear, which of course could never happen. Good thinking, Monsieur Maginot!

You can still visit certain underground sections of the Maginot line, and I strongly recommend that you do. I went to the Fort Fermont near Metz with my Mam and Dad when they came over on holiday a few years ago. It was very impressive. Here's their English-language website: http://www.maginot.info/uk/. You tootle along on a little manrider-type train that was actually used at the time. The guide informs you 'you are now passing zee 'ospital area... and now we see zee officer's mess... and zee huge great facility you see to your right was used as a wine cellar... zee temperature down 'ere was just right for a 1935 *Côtes du Rhône*... of course some other wines need a slightly lower temperature, and so the French army 'igh command appointed an 'igh-ranking general to take charge of zee provision of wines throughout zee Maginot line. Teams of 'ighly qualified engineers were assigned to zee task of designing zee perfect wine cellar. Ah yes, *mes amis*, zee *Boche* 'ad not expected such French ingenuity. Our wine cellars were thus far superior to anything zee *Wehrmacht* 'ad in eets arsenal. And our gallant troops would thus be able to withstand a six-month siege weezout ever sobering up...' Ah yes, our gallant French allies...

Now I don't know exactly how much the Maginot line cost to build. But I suspect rather more than it would have cost to equip every single hospital in France with the very latest and best equipment available at the time. The government clearly knew where its priorities lay.

This tells us something about governments in general, and that is that they have a tendency to piss taxpayers' money up against the wall twenty-four hours a day, seven days a week, three hundred and sixty-five days a year. And for hundreds of years in a Europe of 'Nation States' (God help us), that's exactly what they did, financing one mindless war after another. Actually, I think the current EU (and UEFA) set-up is a rather better idea, don't you? What it costs to have a united Europe is actually just a drop in the ocean - not even in the same league as the money and lives that have been washed down the drain over the course of divided Europe's history. Surely the UEFA Cup is a much better idea as a means of settling our differences, and of having a pint or two together afterwards. By the way, if you need convincing, have yourself a little trip to the battlefields and cemeteries of Verdun (not far at all from Metz). There you will find evidence aplenty of the sheer insanity and carnage of Europe's past. Think of a megablastically high number and then multiply it by your granny's Co-op cheque number and you'll begin to get some idea of the number of poor sods who died in the mud, supposedly for their King or Kaiser. Makes you wonder how many John Lennons or Jackie Milburns were among them, doesn't it?

But how does UEFA decide where Europe ends? Somehow, it includes Israel and parts of what others might call Asia. Let's hope we never get drawn against some of them, otherwise we're going to have to give them a miss, and it's not a pilgrim's sin of omission either, as to my certain knowledge they're not in Europe, and this is a European competition.

Safely out of that poky little office, I witnessed what can only be described as an incipient riot. I offered the Geordie lass a lift to the station, and as we drove away the CRS riot police were coming around the corner with their sirens screaming. I bought the two extra tickets from her and so now had ten. Not a bad morning's work. Unfortunately I had to get back to the Grand Duchy and work that afternoon (never again would I criticise the actual organisation of ticket queues at Saint James's Park – though I will always question the fairness).

Getting shot of the extra tickets was no problem at all. Barry was driving down from Brussels and then we were off in a couple of cars to Metz. One Scots lad in the office actually lived in Metz and was keen to go to the game also. He invited us round to his place in the centre of town for an Indian takeaway pre-match, and a few Metz-supporting local friends of his would also be there. The rest of the tickets went to four other colleagues keen on footie and a couple of Luxembourg-based Geordies who had placed adverts in the local papers. It is always interesting how these things pan out.

On the day of the match, Wednesday the nineteenth of November 1996, it started snowing in Luxembourg just after lunchtime, and by late afternoon pre-match anticipation was beginning to give way to fears of a possible postponement. But never mind, Barry arrived about four and off we set. Normally, you expect to do Luxembourg-Metz in under an hour. It took us a good hour just to get to the French border. Thankfully, the A31 wasn't too bad; maybe a lot of trucks had laid up somewhere. Whatever, we were in Metz in time for some Indian nosh before the game, and the crack with the Metz supporters was great.

Suitably replete with onion bargees and lamb rogan josh, we walked to St. Symphorien and already the atmosphere was brilliant. A good few Toon wallahs were wearing Viking helmets, which were no doubt hard-won trophies from Halmstads, while others were sporting French berets and false moustaches (possibly leftovers from the Micky Quinn era, the moustaches, that is!). The local paper, *Le Républicain Lorrain*, did an eight-page special supplement on the match, which it billed as *Le Grand Défi* (literally: the big challenge). There was obviously much interest in Ginola in particular, but NUFC as a whole were described as *un monument du football européen*!!

As for the game itself, we had Shearer out injured, but in attack we still had Beardo, Tino, and Gino-la. Oh la la, what a line up! Besides them we had Prince Albert, Bes, Pav, Rob Lee, Wozzer, Batty, Gillespie, and Peacock, with Robbie Elliott, Stevie Watson and Little Lee Clark on the bench. Not bad, eh? You wouldn't think it was going to be just a few weeks until KK would quit. We went ahead when Tino was tripped and Peter Beardsley shot an expertly taken penalty into the corner of the net. But Metz had some good players, one of whom we brought to the Toon, David Terrier. Pity we chose the wrong one because we could have tried to get Robert Pires instead, then a young and upcoming winger, whose play resulted in the Metz equaliser in the second half.

At the end of the game, I listened to the announcement about the Metz supporters' arrangements for the trip to Tyneside. The price was very reasonable and I briefly toyed with the idea of joining the Metz supporters club. I sensibly realised, however, that there is only so much wor lass will stand (bless her).

A virtual tale

When you're marooned on the dark continent, but you want to keep up on the matches, the Internet is a godsend (so thanks very much for sending it, God – nice one!). We're out of range of Radio Newcastle and Metro because they broadcast on FM, which even on a good day only covers a radius down to about Wetherby as you drive south on the A1, so we can only listen to match commentaries on the rare occasions when Radio Five or the World Service choose to broadcast our match rather than London teams such as Manchester United, Arsenal, or Chelsea, or, failing those, Liverpool. Over the last few years, things have been changing because of broadcasts on the Internet, and it's still in a state of flux. Up to now, the BBC stations haven't had the rights to broadcast commentaries on the Internet, so that route has been blocked, though it may now be changing. However, most Premiership clubs' websites broadcast their match commentaries, some for free, while many including Newcastle (surprise, surprise) charge quite a hefty fee. If you're lucky and we're playing one of the teams who broadcast for free, then you can log on to the opposition commentary instead. The 'net' effect is that Toon supporters all over the world can now tune into the Internet to follow the match commentaries. So you sit by your computer in Australia or Chile or Brussels or Trier and turn up the speakers and you're transported back to the Leazes End. Since you're on the Internet, the thing to do for a bit of world-wide company is to join the virtual crowd by opening up another window and logging on to the NUFC Forum where you can discuss the progress of the match with others who are tuned in like you to the web broadcast. It's not as good as being there, but it's a good substitute when you've got no other choice, and it's something which has only become possible over the last few years.

One funny effect of the so-called streaming Internet transmission is that there is a time lag caused by buffering of the signal, which appears to vary from one computer to another. So you can be listening to your team's stream and hearing that the ball is being dribbled through the centre circle when suddenly someone puts a message on the forum telling everyone that Alan Shearer's scored. Then you hear it on your computer half a minute later. When Newcastle were playing Columbus Crew on the USA pre-season tour in 2000, the American commentators, who were very knowledgeable and absolutely professional, had even set up a system where you could e-mail them questions and comments and then they incorporated them into their match commentary, so it became a real interactive commentary. They should do this for all matches – it wouldn't be hard to do.

By the end of the game, everyone's been contributing messages to the BBS forum and you end up with a long 'match thread' giving the progress of the game and everyone's thoughts on it. If you've missed the game and you haven't heard the score and you want to relive the excitement, admittedly in some small way, you can log on to the match thread and scroll down comment by comment, goal by goal till the final whistle blows. It can have you in absolute suspense. Bob and Terry might have done this in the Likely Lads if they'd had the Internet thirty years ago, then they wouldn't have had to go and hide from Brian Glover in the church.

There's now a big community of people who regularly visit their teams' websites to exchange news and opinions, and it also provides a new way of getting information for instance from supporters of our next round European rivals about when tickets go on sale, how to get there, where to stay, and so on. Unheard of just a matter of years ago, it is certainly a global village now.

Can I just say at this moment that it's taking me a while to write this bit, because I'm being distracted by the last few minutes of the season and Newcastle are hanging on for a draw at Liverpool. It was great to see Aston Villa losing two-nil after ten minutes, and even better when Shola scored after twenty-five minutes, but then Michael Owen levelled it, and now we're hanging on, hanging on. See if I can write another sentence before the end of the match. Why does Steven Gerrard keep trying so hard? No, I can't manage it, I'll have to concentrate on biting my finger nails! Hold on … yesssss! Yet another draw, we must have beaten the most-draws-in-a-season record! Fifth on goal difference. We're back in Europe by the skin of our teeth! More trips coming up next season! Now then … where was I? Ah yes, the Geordies…

'We are the Geordies, the Geordie ...' Yes we are. But do we really have to sing 'boot boys'? Mental and mad, well maybe in some cases. But 'boot boys'? Is that really the image we want to project of ourselves? I don't think so. What about 'nation' instead? We don't particularly need a rhyme in that first line anyway, so why choose something so mind-numbingly stupid as 'boot boys'? We have a brilliant reputation, and rightly so, both at home and abroad (which for me includes everything south of the Tees). Why spoil it? Let's go on partying and providing an atmosphere that makes families want to join in, encouraging even the bairns to be part of it. Okay, that's that off my chest.

Anyway, we definitely are the Geordies, and for that reason we also happen to be something special. (Shit, is this beginning to sound a bit like F. Shepherd?) Geordies: you can argue about the origin of the term till the cows come home (or should that be till the coos gan hyem?). My preferred theory is, of course, the George Stephenson one. Hey, I was born not two miles from where his son Robert Stephenson was born in Willington Quay, and Barry went to primary school with Billy, who lived in George's old cottage in Wylam – are those steady credentials, or wat?

Living in Germany, I have never tired of telling new acquaintances there that I hail from Tyneside, adding immediately that that is where Germany's first locomotive was built, the implication unmistakably being of course that the Germans themselves could never have managed such a thing. *Der Adler*, which means 'The Eagle', was built at the Robert Stephenson locomotive works. The site, which is just next to the Central Station, is currently being preserved.

The Eagle's flight to Germany was an arduous one. For a start, it couldn't fly. And they could hardly send it by rail, as there was bugger all in the way of iron road on the continent. So they hauled it from the Toon, largely along dusty roads, down to Hull and across the North Sea to Rotterdam and then down the Rhine. When it reached its destination,

Germany's very first railway line between Nuremberg and Fürth, none of the locals could handle the new technology. So it was just as well a couple of Geordies had made the journey as well. So we not only built the Germans' first engine for them, we also showed them how to drive the bugger. The two Geordies are still buried in German soil. Won't happen to me, mind. Wor lass has the strictest instructions to hoy my ashes off the Tyne Bridge at three o'clock on a home match day (unless of course we're live on Sky, in which case it'll be four), on the reasonable assumption that they won't let her do it – scatter my ashes, that is – in the centre circle in the Holy of Holies. That's a pity, really, because my ashes would probably bring about a marked improvement to the worst pitch in the Premiership.

Anyway, back to the theories on the origin of the term 'Geordies'. Despite a busy timetable as the father of the railways, George Stephenson had a day or two to spare and went and invented a miners' safety lamp designed to ensure that there would be fewer disasters caused by gas explosions. At about the same time (a few weeks later, if you ask me), some Welshman called Sir Humphry Davy invented something similar (not only do the Welsh imitate our glorious accent and try to emulate our leek-growing prowess, but they also copy our inventions!). And how come he got to be a Sir, and George and Robert didn't? But Sir Humphry didn't get onto the back of five pound notes!! Geordieland 1 Wales 0. The pair of them filed a patent for their inventions and no doubt the lawyers had a field day. At the end of that field day, the Welsh miners would only use the 'Davy' lamp, while only the 'Geordie' lamp was good enough for the pit yackers in the Holy Land. Hence the miners in the North-East became known as the 'Geordies', while for some reason best known to themselves the taffs baulked at being called 'Humphries' – funny, that. The old wive's tale about us being Geordies because of a fierce loyalty to King George is of course a load of bullocks, and that's official! Or can you really believe that people in the North-East saw themselves as devoted subjects of their royal Britannic majesty while they were scraping around for crumbs to survive and he was sat on his fat royal arse in the smoke, not caring a monkey's bum about the likes of us?

And so we are special – we are the Geordies. And the way we speak (when we want to) is also a bit special, though but. When occasion demands, we can converse with one another in such a way as to render it virtually impossible for anyone born south of the Tees or north of the Tweed to have any idea wot wa gannin aan aboot marra.

So why is it, actually, that when we move south, some of us feel obliged to kow-tow to southerners and start modifying those wonderful vowel sounds before the train even reaches Doncaster, never mind Kings Cross, in a kind of humble apology to those with 'received pronunciation'. The Scots don't do that, do they? And I for one really admire them for it.

Surgeon Hall sets us all a fine example here, by refusing to budge an inch from his native Pitmatic, except possibly when he is having tea with Liz. Or maybe the now rusty Iron Lady. As an aside, some of those medieval bonfire and ducking-stool traditions were quite quaint, don't you think? Coming from Waalsend, not Welwyn Garden City, you tend not to be a rabid thatcherite or royalist.

For Sur Jurn, total football is in fact 'turtle furtbaal' – just the way they say it when they 'gan doon the clurb' back in Collierland. It's funny how the Northumbrian pronunciation of 'club', as in social club, has entered Tyneside Geordie almost as a loan word. Maybe because the colliers lead the field in the 'clurb' scene. Aye, the collier laad is a canny laad and aalways of gud cheor! Another guiding light to us in this respect is Lee Clark (Giz the baal on me heed, Al Fayeed).

As another aside, Kings Cross is definitely my favourite bit of London, virtually an extra-territorial slice of Geordieland, a kind of sanctuary in the smoke. Many's the time we've crossed London from Victoria Station on the way home from Deutschland for a holiday and breathed a sigh of relief upon reaching the Kings Cross concourse. A couple of pints in the Waverly bar (probably called something completely different now) soaking in the wonderful sounds of the Geordie expats, mingling with the also very welcome range of Scots accents. You could even get the Jornal and the Chronic in the station newsagents to read on the train until not long ago, but rail privatisation and the demise of Red Star (Parcels Service, not Belgrade this time) seem to have put paid to that. Shame.

There was always an atmosphere of tangible excitement, as we prepared to leave the big fat city behind and head for the fresh air of the North-East, maybe a home game the next day to look forward to and a trip down to Tynemouth on the Sunday for a walk along Long Sands and a pint in the Gib or the Sally before getting back to the smell and the taste of me Mam's Sunday Dinner – best there is.

And then the tingle you feel as the train pulls away at last and you rush through those tunnels just like in Get Carter – I can here the twang of that theme music right now! And then you wait to catch a glimpse of Highbury, so you can stick your two fingers firmly up at no-one in particular but all the Cockney clubs in general. My Mam would regard anyone from about Coventry southwards as a Cockney. I apply the term to any club in London.

Where were we? Oh yes, the abandoning of our accent sometimes. How come people do it? Is it that our accent is second-class? Do we come from a second-class region that should be ashamed of its dialect and its accent and hide them away? I don't think so.

The tale of two birthdays

The Bayer 04 Leverkusen trip in February 2003 gave us the opportunity to follow Pete's recommendation about where to go pre- and post-match. Just around the back of our hotel we found Pete's *Früh Am Dom* in Cologne (Köln) with its dark blue aproned barmen. They were FC Köln supporters and

111

were looking forward to us beating their arch rivals. It certainly was worth the visit for the cold *kölsch* beer and the huge plates of hearty German food. One dish worth mentioning is *gulaschsuppe* poured into a big hollowed out bread bun – you eat the dish to finish off. These were so good we had one before the match and another after. We ordered some *bratwurst* sausages too, but the barman only brought the soup. In our best German we reminded him, '*Entschuldigung, Herr Ober, aber wo ist unsere Wurst, bitte?*' To which he replied in his impeccable clipped tones, 'Gentleman, vee are most sorry, but ze wurst is yet to come.'

When we saw the draw for the second group stage of the 2002/03 Champignons League, it was clear that it was going to be difficult to get tickets for the away leg against Bayer Leverkusen as the ground capacity of the BayArena for European games is only seventeen thousand. We applied for tickets on the usual European Application Form but, as we feared, were duly rejected. Luckily our saviour Don came through with tickets and we were on our way.

Leverkusen is a town dominated by the giant Bayer chemical works and the football club started out as the factory team, hence its name that might be more familiar to you from bags of fertiliser, pills and plastic objects. (Chris, Pete and their Ireland-based marra Mike actually worked at the Bayer Leverkusen factory back in the glorious summer of 1974). It's as if there would be a team called ICI Middlesbrough. Of course we do have a team called Billingham Synthonia, which I suppose actually is a very good equivalent. The difference being that Billingham Synthonia hasn't ever been Champignons League runners-up. Since reaching those dizzy heights, Leverkusen had sold all their best players including Michael Ballack, so the team we were lined up to play were pale shadows of their predecessors. Sort of emasculated, as it were. By the way, they have nothing to do with Bayern München, who get their name from the German word for Bavaria.

There's another parallel between Leverkusen and Middlesbrough. If you were a Leverkusen fan travelling to play Middlesbrough and you found out that the capital city of the North was only a train ride away, you'd naturally choose to base yourself in Newcastle, wouldn't you? Well, Leverkusen is similarly overshadowed by even nearer neighbour Köln. So the choice for us was clear and we stayed in the Dom Hotel, beside the huge Köln Cathedral, or *Dom*, as they say in German (pronounced 'dome'). I am not sure why, but the hotel was fairly empty and we got a very good deal on our rooms in the best-located and most historic hotel in the city.

There was a crisp blue sky and Don, Mike from London and I decided on a walk along the banks of the mighty Rhine. We weren't the only ones who thought this was a good way to spend the morning. As Jimmy Nail or Oz only twenty-five clicks downstream at Düsseldorf might remark, it's a big river. Everyone sang 'The fog on the Rhine is all mine, all mine' later at the match. On the way, we passed by the Köln Opera House where thirty years ago Keith Jarrett performed his magical piano solo Köln concert, and further along in a little side street we took a photo standing outside the Blue Star Bar – it seemed like a good omen. As we strolled along the embankment, we spotted a large track-suited group coming towards us. They were having a very leisurely 'Jog on the Rhine, all Rhine, all Rhine'. It couldn't be better; it was the whole squad heading our way, with Sir Bobby at the centre. Of course it was a very special occasion for Sir Bobby as it was the eighteenth of February 2003, his seventieth birthday and here were we with him. We just had to go across and pass on our best wishes for his birthday. What a gentleman he is: he carefully took off his gloves to shake our hands. I suppose he probably shook hands with a few hundred people that day, but we were proud to be among that number. This really made our day. In the heat of the moment we clean forgot that it was JJ's birthday too, though he's fifty years behind Sir Bobby, and by the time we remembered he was out of sight. Still, we had a good chat with Michael Chopra and wished him the best of luck and hoped that he would get a chance to play that night; which he did, good for him. We then found ourselves in a chocolate factory museum on the very banks of the river. Wafers dipped in melting chocolate, *kölsch*, and *gulaschsuppe*: what a mixture.

It was a good night: an easy win, good goals from Shola, the crowd singing 'Happy Birthday to you' for Sir Bobby and for JJ, who wasn't forgotten after all, and we got our Happy Seventieth Birthday banner in a prominent position and on the television cameras. The short train trip out from Köln to Leverkusen had been easy for Don, Mike, Neale, who'd joined us in the afternoon, and myself but on the way back it was absolute chaos. Where was *Der Adler* when we really needed it? Not what you expect from Teutonic thoroughness and efficiency. In fact it was possibly the slowest and most squashed train ride in the history of the Deutsche Bahn and by the time we got back, Köln was closed. I suppose that was the idea. The only place that was still open was our dependable local, Früh am Dom, with its even more welcoming beer waiters now that we'd beaten Leverkusen for them.

The pilgrimage goes on

Well, we hope those heart-warming tales have helped while away those long winter nights deprived of Euro trips. Now it's back into those hiking boots for the next leg of our long pilgrimage of 2003/04.

A tale of Trolls - Back to our Viking roots in Vålerenga

The singsong nature of Geordie and loads of the words (sadly, so many have already died a death, sacrificed on the altar of the global burger non-culture) have their origins in Scandinavia and were brought to our shores by the Vikings. Just a few examples are: bairn like the Swedish *barn*, hoose/*hus (pronounced like hoose)*, wor/*vår* (pronounced wor), efter/*efter*. The list is, in fact, huge. Tune into Swedish or Norwegian radio (less so Danish, but that too) and you'll be amazed how similar it sounds to Geordie. And you will be equally amazed how easy it is to learn those languages. As a Geordie, you already have a head start in terms of pronunciation and you'll leave any southerners among your fellow students miles behind within the first few lessons (mind, that's always the case, isn't it?), because you already master at least eighty per cent of the pronunciation.

Of course it's true that, with English, you'll get by anywhere in the world (except sunderland). But hey, isn't it great to order your beer in the local lingo and pick your way through the pre-and post-match reports in their own papers? For us it makes all the difference. Go there and absorb some of the local colour (as well as the local beer). It makes us ambassadors for Geordieland and, in the case of Scandinavia it takes us back partly to our linguistic and cultural roots. So it was with Vålerenga.

When you're based on the continent, the first thing to do when the draw is made in a European competition is to get onto the Internet and find the opponent's homepage with a view to applying for a couple of tickets on the off-chance of getting lucky. When I found Vålerenga it suddenly struck me that it might be worth looking for a Norwegian branch of the NUFC supporters club. And BINGO:

'Scandinavian Magpies' is a highly professionally organised supporters club fully recognised by NUFC (so presumably they have to pay an annual fee!!). It is run by a very amiable guy called Christian. One of my guiding principles has always been 'in for an *øre*, in for a *krona'*, and so I sent off an e-mail to Christian asking him if there was any chance of a couple of tickets for the game in Oslo. And just for good measure I joined Scandinavian Magpies there and then and posted a twenty-euro note to Christian the very next day, thus establishing my *bona fide* credentials.

These 'ticket procurement' exercises are always a hitty-missy affair, and you can easily end up with none at all – or with so many that you have to give a couple away, as happened in Basel. So it was a belt and braces job again, with me trying through the ScanMags and Barry, Chris and Sarah through their respective season ticket channels. Due to an inexplicable breakdown in communications, we thought that Don wasn't going to make it Thorside, but he was beavering away in the background and subsequent post-mortems revealed that he must have been sitting (i.e. standing) only a few rows away from us lot.

In the end, it emerged that tickets were easy enough to get through the Oslo club. Had we known that, Barry's Czech-born, now Oslo-based marra Jiri could have popped along to Vålerenga in the first place. However, it turned out that tickets purchased through the ScanMags also got you into a supporters' club social event after the match in a boozer called *Tempest* in central Oslo. So we obviously all wanted to go there. Chris and Sarah had already secured their match tickets through NUFC, but Christian assured me that they would also be more than welcome at the social. I was writing to him in my dodgy Swedish and he was writing back in Norwegian – great fun.

Swedish, Norwegian and Danish are essentially variants of the same language. Of the three, Danish is the hardest to speak (unless you're Danish, of course), the main difference compared with the other two being that Danish people can't get the words out of their mouths – it's easy to read but well-nigh impossible at first to understand them talking. Reasonably intelligent and literate Danes, Swedes and

Norwegians can happily converse with each other while using their own respective languages. Icelandic is a great-grandfather of this family and is indeed closer to Old Norse (roughly what the Vikings would have been speaking when they landed in their long boats on Tynemouth Long Sands) than to anything at all in the modern world. As for the missing piece in the Scandinavian jigsaw puzzle, Finnish, well it is from another planet. Don't even think about learning it unless you want to suffer permanent brain damage. I for one won't be touching it with a bargepole. But by all means steam in there and learn one of the Viking tongues - you'll love it!

Another barge-pole type arrangement applies in respect of Hungarian, which is a distant cousin of Finnish. They may belong to the same linguistic grouping in broad terms, but I have it on good authority that Hungarian and Finnish are about as closely related to each other as, say, English and Sanskrit. 'Wow', I hear you say, 'THAT close!'

The Scandinavian countries get on famously well with one another and have, to a very meaningful degree, a common identity on the international stage. So much so, for example, that they share a common embassy in Berlin.

Sweden and Denmark are both in the European Union, remember (though sadly, like Britain, not YET in the eurozone), while Norway is not an EU Member State. Norway's national anthem apparently begins, roughly translated, with the words: 'We've got money, fish and oil to burn, so who needs Europe?' (and it's a catchy tune, too). Despite not being affiliated (or is it filleted?) to the pan-European CIU, Norway has secured all sorts of rights for its citizens in Sweden and Denmark. It's a bit like some fiercely independent social club rejecting the CIU but still getting to sell cut-price Fed Special. For example, Norwegians moving to Denmark or Sweden enjoy all the privileges in terms of residency, establishing a business, etc. And the arrangement is reciprocal.

Don't you sometimes think that if the UK had had a bit more sense, EFTA could have been a great little club to stay in? Even if Ted Heath and the southerners wanted day trips to Calais and the EU, we Geordies and the Scots and maybe even the Humphries could have stuck with the Nordics with whom we share a common Viking heritage.

Hang on a minute, I hear you say, the Welsh don't have Viking roots. Well that may be true, but have you forgotten that Wyn the Leap and Ollie Burton played in the same team as Benny Arentoft? That clearly shows they wanted their brethren to be part of the big happy Viking family. And what a family to join: hard-working and efficient, having fantastic infrastructure (at least in the populated bits), trains running on time, squeaky clean streets, low crime and - last but by no means least - stunningly, breathtakingly beautiful blonde, blue-eyed women.

Yes, we can be suitably proud of Geordie's Viking roots. Even the names of some of the weekdays serve as a daily reminder. Some are named after Viking gods: Wednesday = Wodin's day, Thursday = Thor's day (exactly the way we pronounce it), and Friday = Frya's day (Frya being a goddess). When you travel through the Norwegian mountains, you can just imagine them praying to these gods, especially Thor. 'Wor Thor', they probably said. And their idea of heaven was a bit special, too. Your average fearless Viking warrior who was struck down in battle (no doubt looking forward to a nice bit pillage somewhere around Blyth or Seaton Sluice, and maybe a couple of pints afterwards in the Astley Arms, say) would go straight to *Valhalla*. Waiting for him there was any amount of Valkyrie maidens for the rest of eternity. But in addition, to relieve the boredom that would inevitably set in after decades of endless er, physical effort, there would be an eternal feast going on with copious supplies of *Öl*, the Swedish, Norwegian and Danish word for beer, though the last two spell it Øl. It gave us the English word 'ale'. Interestingly, the German word '*Öl*' means oil – well after all we do also have the expression 'well-oiled'!

Plus, there was this little pig in *Valhalla* (called something or other that probably meant 'little pig'), who every day (just another day in Paradise, really) would be slaughtered, cooked and eaten. Yep, every day! Having been gobbled up one day, he magically reappeared to be consumed again the next, every day during eternity, which is a f.f.frightfully long time, I can tell you. You don't have to take my word for it – you'll find out for yourself soon enough. If you end up in *Valhalla*, send me a postcard, will you, you lucky bar steward!

Since it was the school half term, Barry had meanwhile decided to make a week's holiday of it for the family and stay with another of his Oslo-based friends (is this lad well-connected, or wat?), Graham from Leeds. Barry's three kids, then eleven-year-old Brian and seven-year-old identical twins Emilie and Sarah, also wanted to go to the match. Plus Jiri, his daughter Lilly and yours truly made eight tickets, which Christian easily organised and sent by post to Jiri across town.

But remember the venue farce surrounding the Vålerenga game?

Now Norway can be a cold place in February. Rumour has it that Alan Hull might just have been returning from a mini-cruise from North Shields to Norway on the Sir Winston Churchill when he wrote his Winter Song 'and your boots no longer lie about the cold around your feet when winter… comes howling in.' It can be f.f.frighteningly cold. In fact it can be so f***ing cold (short for frightening in case you're w***ing, which is short for wondering) that you wouldn't put the cat out at night, even if you are a hardy soul brought up in the far end of Percy Main and used to hiking through the snow to the Morgue in Willington Quay for a pint. THAT'S how cold it gets. Got it?

Okay, so UEFA (that Kafkaesque organisation whose secretive workings make the Vatican look like a paragon of *glasnost*) suggested to Vålerenga that it might be a good idea to come up with an alternative venue, just in case. They came up with the local sports hall (holding 6,000), or Copenhagen,

119

or... yes, Middlesbrough. Then, just a couple of weeks before the match, they settled on Trondheim, which is where Rosenborg play regularly in the Champignons League (the ground there has excellent undersoil heating and plenty of cover).

Back down here on Earth, meanwhile, we were not really amused by the goings-on on the planet Zorg, which is where football administrators attend meditative retreats before making the really big decisions affecting us mortals.

Now I don't hold a geography degree, but I do know that Trondheim is a six-hour train journey to the NORTH of Oslo, and I also have it on good authority that the further north you go in Norway in February, the colder it gets. Plus: what are we, made of money? What the shit do they think we are going to do? Arrive in Oslo, not the cheapest of things to do in the first place, with hotel reservations made, etc, only to find out that the game has been switched to a venue several hundred kilometres to the north and hop on a train in snowbound Oslo weather and go there just like that? So might we not run out of time? Not to mention money. Ever tried getting on a Norwegian main-line train without a reservation? Believe me, it ain't easy! Just who are these people who run UEFA? What is their actual qualification?

But to be fair, the Trondheim variant was several orders of magnitude better than the Smoggie one. Yes folks, don't forget that at one stage they were seriously suggesting we play our away game to Vålerenga at Middlesbrough. And don't forget the Boro had called off our match there the season before because it had been snowing two or three days earlier and sightings had been reported in Hartlepool of remnants of kids' snowmen, or were they snowmonkeys hanging around a bit longer than usual?

What were we supposed to do then? We had already invested our hard-earned cash in makie-on cloth Viking helmets, and now were apparently expected to splash out on some gas masks as well.

Middlesbrough! Think I might have given that one a miss in case it had been called off on account of a few drops of (presumably the wrong kind of) rain. Here we were in the UEFA Cup. All the exotic venues that were possible, including Oslo, and we were handed the tantalising prospect of a trip to the Tees. Thank Thor they had changed their mind and the game would at least definitely be played somewhere in Norway.

Call me Mr Pedantic, but the fact bears repeating that Trondheim is getting seriously close to the Arctic Circle. Did you catch that, UEFA, the Arctic Circle!!! (Here are some more exclamation marks for good measure: !!!!!!!!!!!!!!!!!!).

The UEFA line of argument went something like this: the Trondheim club is more used to near-Arctic conditions. Well they would be, wouldn't they? They're not a half-frozen b****ck away from the Arctic f.f.freezing circle, are they? Consequently they have the facilities to keep the pitch warm while the fans freeze their remaining b****cks off.

To which comes my swift riposte: so what were we supposed to do? Make all our arrangements, flights, hotel reservations, and so on for Olso, only to arrive there on the morning of the match and be told, er, sorry lads, we've moved it for your inconvenience a six-hour train journey nearer the Arctic Circle - the station's thataway.

In the end, a modicum of common sense prevailed and we were told it would definitely be played in Oslo, unless of course the wrong kind of snow [or *snö*] started falling, and at last we could actually start making proper arrangements. Right from the start, Jiri had told us that the word in Oslo was that it would definitely be played in the Ulleval stadium, as they had the ground covered and heated and the Norwegian Army were on standby to clear the terraces of snow and ice in case of any last minute drastic deterioration in the weather. We trusted his local knowledge all along, set against UEFA's dithering.

If you think clubs, the FA etc. stopped treating supporters like shite years ago, think again. It is still most definitely the case. And Bloater and Gloater's philosophy is still a shining example. We non-season-ticket holders are as milked dry as the rest. There is always, thankfully, a contingent of tickets available for home matches. These are sold on a first-come-first-served basis as from two weeks before the match in question. This has always meant dialling your fingers to the bone, but by lunchtime you could usually get through and obtain the worst seats in the ground, just below the inner stratosphere, for appropriately astronomical prices, breathing apparatus not included.

Then the club came up with yet another whizzo idea: we'll introduce a membership scheme that will give priority for getting home match tickets. Membership will cost twenty-five quid a year, but there will of course be no ticket guarantee, it'll all be on a first-come-first-served basis. So what happens? Every poor sod in my position signs up for themselves (and their lass as well so as to be able to get two tickets, the second one not for their lass of course but for a marra) and coughs up fifty quid a year for the privilege. The bottom line is that nothing at all has sodding well changed, except that we are fifty quid worse off and still no surer of getting a ticket. But again let's not forget it was stated in that famous interview that we are all 'mugs'. Wish we were truly owned by ourselves, like Barcelona. That day will come, my friends. *Viva la revolución.*

It's the same with the shirts – it's a rip-off, as also openly admitted from on high. Okay, so I have bought every one. Let him who hath not sinned cast the first stone. That NTL one was particularly shitty, though but. When I bought it at the SJP club shop, I said to the lassie: 'Mind, tell your boss: I'm buying it, but I'm not wearing it.' The logo is shite – why didn't they have the nous to at least incorporate the word NEWCASTLE into their abbreviation, along the lines of N ewcas T L e.' In the event, my sister-in-law covered over the NTL logo by sewing on her own Blue Star and silhouette of the Tyne Bridge, and many a time has it been admired!!! I can just about live with the 'Northern Rock' logo, with its implied

Keeping the faith in Canada - who says we haven't got a prayer?

Who'd have thought they'd open Bobby's Club just for us, in Lokeren on the Intertoto trail?

We found the Blue Star bar in Köln just before coming across Sir Bobby on his 70th birthday taking the team for a Jog by the Rhine, all mine, the Jog on the Rhine's all mine.

Früh am Dom, possibly the best bar in Köln, and certainly the only one still open when we got back after the nightmare train journey from Leverkusen.

Duelling Red Pianos pre-match at Feyenoord, the night of the famous last-gasp 3-2 win.

Time for pre-match *uitsmijters* in Breda while just round the corner the police had sealed off the town square.

At the team hotel in Basel – highlight of the year (and now of a lifetime).

Basel celebrations.

Vålerenga's big flag at the not-so-cold-after-all Ulleval stadium.

Scandinavian Mags
Supporters Club
Vålerenga post-
match do at the
Tempest Bar, Oslo.

The Mallorcan
kop end,
empty. The
prospects of a
drenching and
a hammering
made it one of
the lowest
attendances at
one of our
matches in
recent memory.

The rainstorm gave
us time to come up
with the idea of
writing this book,
as well as the rudest
match in the world.

Green sombrero'd rubber chicken hunter distracts crowd while Shearer scores v Mallorca. No-one saw the goal (except this gadgy) - we were too busy looking his way.

'Shoes off if you love the Toon', as the Mallorcan speedboat is made ready to evacuate the players in case the pitch floods, and *el gordo* plays keepy-uppy.

The bars had never been busier down at the Vieux Port but this SBM Short Bar Maid, not to be confused with Sad Bastard Mackemme, found time for a breather.

En route to the ground with Marseille's own Mrs Brady, *Madame Femme Vieille Dame.* We'd helped her onto the stowed-out metro with her shopping trolley, whether she wanted to or not, but she wouldn't sit beside us!

Match ticket pick-pocketed while swapping shirts with a Marseille fan, and this while under police escort into the ground!

Grins of sheer relief after managing to get into the ground without the pick-pocketed ticket.

In *Le Pen*, the rat run for Toon fans with (or without) Marseille tickets. Note the cheeky OM display at the far end showing the UEFA Cup and their presumed finalists' colours of red/yellow for Spain v OM blue/white - no black and white in sight.

Escape from *Le Pen*. After the first few had broken out, the guards came in and opened up the door to let everyone through.

Marseille were really on fire that night. Unfortunately the fumes of the burning plastic didn't make the OM goalkeeper dizzy enough to let in a few goals.

The Gothenburg organisers made a big effort to promote the time-honoured 'carnival' atmosphere in the city on match day. The place was stowed out. You can just spot some Celtic fans in the throng.

The last steps of our pilgrimage led to the Ullevi Stadium, Gothenburg.

contrast with 'Southern Shite', but before long we surely have to get back to the precious Newcastle Brown Ale label shirt. That is the ultimate logo.

Okay, at least we now knew where we stood. Oslo it was, and Oslo-bound we were. The possibilities from Luxembourg being somewhat limited, I booked a flight from Brussels for the very day of the match. Barry and family had set off at the weekend to see their Oslo-based friends and get acclimatised to the freezing match conditions by having a pre-match bash at skiing. Chris and Sarah also had a match-day flight, from Heathrow, arriving in Oslo only twenty minutes ahead of mine, mid-dayish that is. It was already snowing and canny caad in Brussels, so I was wondering if we were in for another Barcelona-type disappointment. Once airborne, my spirits rose as north-west Europe unfolded below me in all its snow-covered sunlit splendour. You could trace the flightpath beautifully along the Dutch and German coasts, easily picking out the ballerina-shaped German island of Sylt, which is actually just opposite Tynemouth yet is renowned as a topless haven and favoured haunt of Gemany's rich and famous!! Pity Tynemouth's not like that. Mind you, Long Sands has had its moments...

Needless to say, I had my Teach Yourself Norwegian with me, and by the time we landed in Oslo I had mastered most of the essential differences between Norsk and Svensk and was confident of my ability to make a complete fool of myself. But hey, who cares? Life's just too short to worry. So go ahead, just do it, learn Norwegian. Learn Irish. Learn what you like. Every language is a window on the world. You'll see our world through the eyes of others, you'll gain an insight into their culture. And you'll get served quicker in their pubs. You won't regret it - you'll just end up a bit mad. Madder than being part of the Toon Army? I don't think so!

The plane landed bang on time and I rang Chris on the mobile as I was on the autowalk leading up to customs. Sarah and he were waiting just beyond in the arrivals hall, so I donned my cloth Viking helmet bearing the words Toon

Vikings. I once had a fantasy football team called the Toon Luftwaffe on account of the particularly tall centre forward I'd signed – Jan Koller, I think it was. The customs officials looked somewhat bemused, but they were too busy inspecting the passports of anyone who wasn't white, or black and white, to bother me. The rendezvous was successfully completed and Chris and Sarah duly put on their silly black and white hats too. We went to get tickets for the train into town. I couldn't resist trying out my recently acquired Nordic tongue, duly made a complete fool of myself, but got the tickets.

What was it with all these planes and trains? There is a long history of sea travel between Newcastle and Norway, from the Vikings up to the present day. DFDS Ferries certainly missed a trick with both legs of the Vålerenga tie. If I'd been in charge of DFDS marketing, I'd have diverted the normal Newcastle-Kristiansand or Bergen ferry and sent it straight up the fjord to Oslo instead. Surely there were a few of us pining for the fjords! For one thing, it would have been a fantastic opportunity for publicity, and over and above that, just imagine the lost revenues on duty free sales; they could have had a shipload of Geordies for the first leg and a shipload of equally thirsty Vikings for the second.

From the moment you set foot on Norwegian soil, or snow, you cannot fail to be impressed by their infrastructure. It is just megablastically fantastic and everything is spotlessly clean – especially the snow. It should be borne in mind of course that they have Trolls (only three feet six inches tall with long pointy noses) who come out of the mountains at night and work their magic whatsits off till dawn. They are then totally knackered but manage to get into the station buffet for a pint before staggering back to the caves for a doss in the afternoon before getting up for the next nightshift. They must be on canny money, though, 'coz the beer is seriously expensive – more of which anon.

The airport train was a case in point. It is genuine class. Fast as lightning, comfy, complete with TV monitors showing

Sky News. The metro in town was equally impressive and efficient and I took the opportunity between airport-to-town express and metro to buy a local paper and start wading through the pre-match reporting even before we got to the hotel. At first I couldn't believe my eyes because it appeared that the reporter was writing very rude things about Alan Shearer's private parts. Or perhaps they were saying that Alan Shearer was a very private person and was looking forward to the part he was going to play in that evening's match. I couldn't be sure. Perhaps my newly found command of Norwegian was letting me down. I was, after all, a wee bit tired.

Got out of the metro just around the corner from our hotel, the *Bondenheim* which, roughly translated, means the 'Farmer's Rest'. Quick showers, a short lie-down and out we went for a walk in search of a watering hole. The walk lasted about fifty yards (which is enough when it's minus six degrees centigrade – sorry, don't remember what that is in old money, but it's enough to freeze-remove important body parts) when we spotted an inviting looking hostelry on the other side of the street. Rang Barry on the mobile to give our bearings. Turned out that they'd been with Jiri and Lilly to the *Lofotstua* fish restaurant (sounds like it could mean 'lots of tuna', which would be highly appropriate for a fish restaurant, but it actually means 'the Lofoten Room'). The owner-chef Kjell A. Jensen is a very engaging man who enthusiastically advises the diners on the day's fish which are brought down from the historic fishing grounds around his native Lofoten Islands in the Norwegian Arctic. In the morning they'd been to the Viking Ships Museum (Barry and the gang, that is, not the fish) and now they were making a quick visit to the National Gallery to see Edvard Munch's 'The Scream' for the kids' school project. It was only a couple of streets away and they would come along and join us with the bairns presently.

The boozer was indeed a welcoming place, and we quickly made ourselves at home, wearing our Viking hats (to blend in with the locals) plus full colours, and draping our black and white union jack (bearing the words Newcastle United in the horizontal and Geordies in the vertical) over the back of the bench Chris and Sarah were sitting on. You can see it on the cover! The barman spoke brilliant English of course but was nice enough not to mind me ordering the beers in my dodgy pseudo-Norsk. Indeed he found the whole thing quite jolly. He even wished us the best of luck against Vålerenga, whose guts he seemingly hated. He was a Trondheim fan – Trondheim is becoming something of a *Leitmotiv, n'est-ce pas?* The bar gradually filled up, including a couple of Toon wallahs and plenty of Vålerenga fans in their colours. At one point a round of drinks appeared on our table, courtesy of some of their fans opposite. Compliment returned in due course. Barry appears with the kids, all suitably attired, it goes without saying. That really livened the place up and made for a brighter atmosphere altogether, especially when we posed for a team photo to be taken by the barman, but one of the twins (can't remember which one as I can't tell them apart) steadfastly refused to be in the frame. Barry was clutching a local paper that looked vaguely familiar. He has great Danish and is well able to read the gist of Norwegian. So he was taken very seriously when he said: 'I'm not a hundred per cent sure about this, but I think it's about a guy who is a Norwegian TV comedian who rang Alan Shearer up on air and asked him if he squeezes or shakes out the last drops after he's had a pee, and Al refused to answer and now the TV station are in trouble.' The plot thickened...

Great crack all round. Couple of trips to *el boggo,* a bit struck by the garish colours. Sarah returns from a similar mission and asks in London Geordie: 'Are you lads blind?'

This was actually a re-run of that scene in an episode of the Middlesbrough transporter bridge series of Aufwiedersehen Pet, Middlesbrough being very appropriate in this case, when the lads go to see Oz's son performing (as it turns out in drag) in a club in Spennymoor...

'Wodya mean like?' Chris and I retorted as one. 'This is a GAY bar,' Sarah reliably informs us, 'the walls in the toilets are full of adverts for gay and lesbian contacts.' Slightly awkward silence as we look around the place in a manner not likely to attract much more than the maximum of attention. The kids, thankfully, were engrossed in their own little world. Well, Sarah had a point. All you could see were single-sex couples. And some of the males looked rather effeminate, and some of the females, well... you get the picture.

It was definitely time to sup up and take a metro and then a tram to the stadium, the *Ulleval*, which is in fact the national footie stadium. So how come it is not better equipped than Trondheim's ground, or the Riverside, or Ayresome Park, for that matter? Don't know about you, but I still find it difficult to come to terms with the fact that sunderland play at the stadium of shite (all our songs about them are geared to joker park) and that the smoggies are no longer at Ayresome. I find it somehow very reassuring that WE have kept our dignity and held on to our roots.

And here we were exploring our Viking roots. Alighting at the metro stop just outside the stadium we rendezvoused with Jiri and his daughter Lilly and then inside the ground with Barry and the family's host for the week, Graham of Leeds, who'd had to work in his Oslo office until just before kick-off. And of course Brighton Don was in the immediate vicinity. It was striking and refreshing to note that the police presence was virtually zero (unless they were all in plain black and white clothes). The Toon Army's well-earned reputation had obviously gone before us and they knew they were dealing with reasonable human beings interested only in enjoying the occasion. On the other hand, it was getting sodding cold.

The game was, to be honest, a wee bit disappointing from Geordieland's point of view, especially as Big Al was on the bench. Apparently there had been words spoken between Al and the Great Sir Bobby. Perhaps he had also read that article in the local paper and was at a loss as to what to do. Maybe they really did have a bust-up. Well come on, even the most wonderful relationships have their ups and downs, don't they? By now in the season, we'd been knocked out of the FA Cup by Liverpool after false hopes had been raised by the impressive Third Round win at Southampton. So the UEFA Cup was our sole remaining hope of any success; maybe Big Al had over-stated his own case for being out there on the pitch making sure that we secured ourselves a place in the next round. His absence certainly was a big disappointment to our huge Nordic following. There must have been a couple of thousand Toon fans in our end, but most of the ones I heard were either Norwegian or Swedish. All credit to the Scandinavian Magpies. Ones apiece struck me as a fair result overall and we all felt pretty confident we would get a decent result at Gallowgate, particularly with the away goal. Considering the match was being played in Vålerenga's close season, when by rights they should have been playing a pre-season warm-up game not a major European competitive game (and you sure do need warming-up in their neck of the woods), they played really well throughout the match and thoroughly deserved the draw. The goals were scored by ex-Coventry team mates Craig Bellamy and Anders Normann. From a Viana centre, Bellamy put us ahead towards the end of an uneventful first half with a shot back across the keeper and in off the post. Early in the second half, Normann got the header which brought the scores level. We European exiles got our first view of Michael Bridges in a Newcastle shirt, and he looked quite lively, as did Ambrose replacing the dearly (or rather cheaply) departed Nobby down the right wing. The home side's player-manager Kjetil Rekdal played very effectively in his role as sweeper and taker of all corners and free kicks. He's getting long in the tooth now, but back in the early nineties he scored a thirty yards free kick for Norway against England in the decider that put England out of the World Cup qualifiers and made him a national hero. 'Maggie Thatcher, Lord Nelson, Queen Victoria your boys took one hell of a beating' – remember?

We were looking forward very much to the social (or maybe stormy) evening in the *Tempest* with the Scandinavian Mags. Don't forget, the match had kicked off at five-thirty in the afternoon, so when the final whistle sounded, the night was indeed still very young. And despite all the dire warnings the temperature hadn't quite plummeted to the Arctic levels predicted, so we hadn't needed to call on the huge stock of blankets that Jiri had brought with him into the ground. Though I think I spotted a couple of lads from Wallsend wearing two layers of tee shirts – shame on them!

Jiri reckoned we should eschew the metro (which we did, the platform being completely stowed out), and opt instead for the tram. So after freezing some more for about half an hour we finally boarded a tram bound for central Oslo. As fate would have it I got on next to a German lad from Hagen, which is not far from Essen, where I used to live. This guy was a *Ground-hopper*. That's German, not for the lesser spotted duck-billed platypus (whose mating call sounds remarkably like the long, drawn out fart of a drunken mackem), but for a complete moron who spends his life clocking up as many footie grounds as he possibly can. Not that I'm knocking it, mind. Fritz (though I think in reality his name was Adolf) had come to Oslo directly from the Netherlands, where he had watched Go-Ahead Eagles play VVV. What is it about the Dutch? Did someone in the past (Jan van de Ripoff perhaps) say 'let's give all our footie clubs either stupid Mickey Mouse names or impenetrable abbreviations so that no-one from outside their hometown can even guess where the buggers are'? Actually, I do know that VVV stands for '*Voetbalvereniging Venlo*'. This I know because Venlo is just over the border from Germany, not far at all from Essen. But I'm buggered if I know where Go-Ahead Eagles are from. Maybe it's a place where the people transporting *Der Adler* stopped over for a cool Heineken or two on their way to Nuremberg (must have been a trial).

On the subject of Essen, I have an awful confession to make. It is actually twinned with sunderland. But, on a brighter note, we lived only a few hundred yards from the border with Gelsenkirchen, Newcastle's twin town. The twinning is a good one, because the North-East and that part of Germany (known as the *Ruhrgebiet*) have a lot in common: a tradition of heavy industry – iron and steel and the pits – and steady beer (I recommend *Stauder Pils*, from Essen, and *Veltins*, from a bit further afield in the *Sauerland*). People even keep pigeons. And their (the people's, though possibly also the pigeons') mentality is very similar to ours.

Gelsenkirchen is also home to Schalke 04, whose support is comparable with the Toon Army. They have built a fantastic new stadium called *Auf Schalke*. It would be a dream come true if we were to play there, or at Dortmund, just down the road. The one time we did play in that neck of the woods was a pre-season friendly against Bochum. I found out about it while on holiday back home!!! Shades of Barry's predicament when we were in Antwerp.

This means the Toon Army should by rights look first for Schalke's results when following the *Bundesliga* - though this wouldn't go down at all well with Jörg, the brother-in-law of my marra Nobby in Essen. Jörg is a *Schalker-Hasser* (a real Schalke hater) despite living on their doorstep. So much does he loathe them that, in a results forecasting sweepstake in which about twenty of his mates take part, he will never under any circumstances forecast a win or even a draw for Schalke, even if they are a sure bet. It costs him money in lost winnings, but he sticks to his guns!

Our German friend back in Oslo, meantime, was hoping (or hopping) to catch an early flight the next morning to take him to the Czech Republic to watch some Czech third-division outfit called something like Czechoshitowsky play some other lot called Czechomoreshitowska. Still, at least the beer would be great. Slowly but surely, our street car named whatever the Norwegian for desire is (*Vällust* – actually that's Swedish for desire – I couldn't find my Norwegian dictionary, but let's not quibble) wove and screeched its way, defying possibly frozen points, into Oslo city centre.

I used to have the old Teach Yourself Norwegian book, that series with the green and yellow cover. Interestingly enough, the first edition was actually written in London during the war by Norwegian exiles. And of course for about six subsequent editions they just kept churning out the same content. And running through that content is a consistent thread of anti-German sentiment. Well the buggers were occupying Norway, after all. The reading passages in Norwegian are absolutely priceless. In one of them, a German officer asks a Norwegian girl in a café if she would like to dance. The lass politely declines with an impeccable *'Nein danke, mein Herr'*. Somewhat peeved, the officer says: 'You do not vish to dance viz me because I am German, iz zat not so?' 'Not at all,' says our heroine, 'I do not wish to dance with you because I am Norwegian!'

Anyway, this tram called *Vällust* dropped us off very near the *'Tempest'*. We only had to walk a few hundred yards past an outdoor skating rink reminiscent of 'Gorky Park' but without the fatal shots, and we were there. Appropriately enough, in view of the bitter cold, the ice-rink was playing little Sarah and Emilie's favourite 'In the shadows' by the Finnish band *The Rasmus* as we walked by.

The correspondence with Christian had suggested the place would be packed out with Newcastle supporters from both sides of the North Sea, but it turned out that we were sharing it with all sorts of other fans, including Liverpool. There were telly screens everywhere, and the whole place went reverentially silent when Wor Sir Uncle Bobby spoke. And they did so again an hour later when the same interview came on again. Essentially, Bobby's message was that we hadn't played that well, that we had been surprised by how well they had played and that the players knew what they had to do in the second leg.

Don't know about you, but I always find it heart-warmingly reassuring when Sir Bobby tells us the players know what they have to do. You see, I always worry that they don't. That they don't know they are supposed to score more goals than the opposition to win the game. That maybe they think they are supposed to go out on to the pitch and practise yoga or meditate, or say the rosary... Thank goodness for Sir Bobby, who gets them to understand what they have to do. Skills like that are priceless, truly priceless.

So the social evening didn't quite live up to our expectations after all. There was a Newcastle quiz, though, and a very up-to-date quiz it was too, including questions such as 'which Newcastle player received a yellow card at tonight's game?' (Not sure, actually, think it may have been Bernard). Plus, the quiz (it was a form you had to fill in and hand back at the bar) was in Norwegian, so that did give it an added air of Nordic mystique. Anyway, a Norwegian father-and-son team on our table won an NUFC video in the end, though we did feel they had a bit of an advantage, being Norwegian and all. Barry's twins gave up on the quiz altogether and instead wrote little notes on their *Diddl* notepads, folded them up and passed them around to everyone in the bar. One of them intriguingly read 'Scribble on Daddy's bottom'. Another showed a picture of a furry animal that they said was a guinea pig, except they'd entitled it a 'Giddy Pig'.

It was getting on for ten o'clock, so Barry and Graham had to be getting back with the bairns, who by now had fallen asleep, but Sarah, Chris and myself took the eminently sensible view that we may as well go for another couple of pints. After all, we might well wake up the next morning to hear that Europe had been hit by the return of the bubonic plague. We therefore focused our considerable collective brainpower on working out where we should go. For a brief moment we thought about going back to that gay bar for a laugh. But we reckoned on balance that, while it was probably okay to stumble into one by accident there was just no excuse for going straight back there next session. So we didn't. Instead we went to a bierkeller-type place just opposite our hotel that had not yet opened that afternoon. It was filling up sharpish but we managed to get three seats at a huge wooden table where a party of five other Toon Army members were already well established.

One of them – a young lad in his early twenties – had obviously taken very seriously the hastily propagated rumour that the Norwegian brewing industry was on the brink of recession and that if we didn't all sup at least twelve pints that day hundreds of thousands of brewery workers would be made redundant, with all the appalling social consequences that would entail. In other words, this lad was seriously consumed by premature intemperance. Barely coherent when we got in, he swiftly went comatose. However, he was doing no harm and we managed to keep him concealed between us while we had a few beers. Our fellow Geordies naturally admired our Viking helmets and the crack was good.

We soon got to the 'where yee from, then?' stage, and so we did a *tour de table* tour of the North-East. When Chris said he was born in Gateshead, one of our interlocutors with a definite Cumbrian (!) accent piped up with 'That makes you a mackem!'

Now there are some things you definitely should not say to a life-long Newcastle United supporter, especially if he also happens to have a black belt in karate. One of those things is 'That makes you a mackem!'

To say that Chris was upset would be something of an understatement. To say that Chris looked on the point of bursting this guy's liver, tearing it from his steaming entrails and feeding it to the half-frozen and correspondingly ravenous Norwegian crows would equally be an understatement. Fortunately, Chris is an eminently nice and intelligent guy who knows a cretinous turd when he sees and hears one. So we all just had a laugh and agreed that Gateshead is definitely not in mackemland. The guy opposite continued to hold that view even after Chris released his vice-like grip on his b****cks. Only kidding, he did no such thing. Everything was taken in good humour.

Our Cumbrian friend had raised an important point, though. Where does mackemland begin? Does such a place even exist?? It's certainly not on the UEFA map.

I have always regarded both banks of the Tyne to be solid black and white territory, with the sole exception of South Shields, where you are liable to see people of both persuasions walking up and down the High Street dressed in their respective colours. A shining example of tolerance, if you ask me. What tolerant people we Newcastle United supporters are!

Well past midnight, the lassie who brought us our final round was getting a bit worried about our comatose marra and said he would have to go. We pointed out he was doing no harm, but she insisted, as the police would shut the place down if they came in and found him like that. So we asked her to call a taxi, and when it came we all helped him outside. Then wham, the cold air hit him and you can guess the rest, as Washington C.D.'s own Brian Ferry once crooned. All over the pavement it splattered. At least that was out of his system before he got in the taxi. Chris later told me that Sarah and he had bumped into the same, really very friendly, bunch again the next day when visiting the Viking Long Ships exhibition. And of course by then the lad had slept off the vapours of the night's debauch but was severely hung over and didn't remember a thing.

We had had our sup and it was time to head back across the road to the hotel. We said our farewells there, as I would be up at the crack of dawn to meet up with my brother Mick at Oslo central station.

Amongst other things, Mick is a railway enthusiast. Such people also refer to themselves as 'bashers'. Personally, I think 'heedbanger' would be more appropriate. Given the chance, they would spend their entire lives travelling around on trains, inspecting all possible aspects of the rail system, reading timetables and learning them off by heart, noting train movements, reading up on the history of certain lines, and walking along abandoned tracks. In short, they are totally obsessed with their subject and spend loads of money on their hobby. It goes without saying that, as a fully paid up member of the Toon Army, I can neither understand nor condone this kind of obsessive behaviour!!!!

Mick also has a good command of German, having lived in Deutschland for a time. So he combines his interest in the German language and culture with his passion for rail travel, and by now must surely be on first name terms with just about every station employee of *Deutsche Bahn*. Intriguingly, he is also into Esperanto and has been trying to convert me to this particular cause for as long as I can remember. Our respective arguments for and against have become fairly entrenched.

Esperanto is an artificial language invented by a Polish guy called Zamenoff a century and a bit ago. He felt we needed a world language and that Polish wasn't going to be it (I wouldn't argue with that). So he proceeded to invent a language based on the established Western European tongues. That kind of ignored the Asians and others, in my view, but never mind. To cut a long story short it has never really caught on as a world language, with people tending on their travels to go for tried and tested ones like English, Spanish and French. Esperanto was always going to be a minority sport.

Since the advent of the Internet, however, Esperanto has undeniably enjoyed something of a renaissance and Esperantists seem to me to form a kind of global club, visiting each other and generally doing no harm. As a translator, I don't think it will make me redundant. So on his railway bashes, Mick will stay with Esperantists throughout Germany and Scandinavia. All jolly good fun and long may it continue.

This particular time he had already been travelling around Germany on the trains for about a fortnight, having gone over to Düsseldorf with other members of a North-East Anglo-German society to enjoy the carnival, with all the boozing and *schunkeln* that entails. The festivities over, he couldn't wait to get on those rails. To my sure knowledge, my brother has given the German language at least one new word, and at the same time a new concept to the world of medicine. And that is *Eisenbahner-Arsch*, which means 'basher's arse' (if you sit on trains long enough, you get rather saddle-sore). Back in 1987, he and I went on a rail trip from Essen to Moscow and back (I was learning Russian at the time). So I can vouch for the *Eisenbahner-Arsch* phenomenon.

I am not sure I can work out his exact schedule en route to Oslo, but when I met him on the station at about seven-fifteen he had just spent the night travelling down from Trondheim, six hours to the north. So what did we do then? Well we got straight back on that same train of course and headed straight back for Trondheim! We had organised it all in advance, which is a very good idea as it is very difficult to find an unreserved seat on the mainline trains. That is because there is basically just the one main line running up and down the spine of Norway, and even that has a couple of vertebrae missing, so the gap has to be filled by a bus service. Plus, the trains are not all that frequent. People thus don't have that good a choice. So be warned, book well in advance.

It was cold outside but it was cosy warm '*hyggelig*' inside. I had bought a couple of the local papers and with my trusty Norwegian-English dictionary on the little table in front of me I was as happy as Larry while Mick was relishing every moment of being on a train again at last! We soon sped out of the Oslo suburbs and past the airport. As we got further out, the snow seemed to get proportionally deeper and soon the houses we saw were few and far between.

On we sped though solidly Troll-built mountain tunnels, passing frozen lakes on which people could occasionally be seen walking, having parked their 4x4s literally in the middle of the lake! A couple of hours later we stopped in Lillehammer, the Olympic winter sports venue, then we plunged again into a true winter wonderland. I am told that this is not the most spectacular stretch of scenery in Norway, but it was certainly good enough for me. I had read in the paper that some British squaddies on exercise had been evacuated from Norwegian mountains a couple of days earlier on account of the bitter cold, and it struck me as I gazed out onto the snow-covered mountainous wastes that you couldn't possibly last long out there.

Yet Jiri had been telling us that Norwegians would often go out to ski across the countryside equipped only with a rucksack containing essential provisions (presumably including a mobile phone!). They would ski twenty or maybe thirty kilometres from one hut to the next, where you thaw (or Thor) out in front of a log fire and safely spend the night. As long as you know what you are doing and take all the right precautions, that must be a pretty nice way to spend those winter weekends when the footie scene closes down altogether, even in Trondheim.

Talking of huts, Barry had told us about another interesting Viking word that he'd spotted in the Holmenkollen ski-jumping museum. It doesn't take a lot of linguistic knowledge to see how *Høvel* meaning 'a little wooden shack where they shelter from the snow' has entered English as hovel. Surely this is proof positive that the Vikings invaded sunderland at some time in the dark ages. Though they no doubt left pretty sharpish when they saw the disappointing prospects for pillaging in the area. Barry had given up trying to ski after getting comprehensively out-telemarked by his eleven-year-old and two seven-year olds and their five-year old Oslo-based friends, and had decided to go off the piste (or was that off on the piste?) instead. The Holmenkollen, the first ski-jump in the world, was just round the mountain from the skiing and it was an amazing sight watching them jump. Eddie the Eagle might not have won any medals but he certainly deserved a VC for bravery, because his usual landing spot up near the top of the hill was twice as steep as where the champions land. It's steeper than Level Seven.

Having exhausted the match reports, which justifiably concluded that Vålerenga still had a sporting chance to go through to the next round at our expense, I looked at my watch, which told me it was time to repair to the buffet car for a pint. We were screeching around a long craggy bend, huge icicles hanging from the sheer rock face. The Trolls who hewed out this particular cutting must have been especially hardy.

'Hur mycket kostar det?' 'How much?' I had been prepared for a shock, but this worked out at about a tenner for a can of beer. We agreed that we should savour each and every drop to the full! Still, I suppose it really does keep the riff-raff out. And there were no riff-raff on this train. It was striking that virtually no-one was talking. They all sat there, immaculately dressed, reading the paper, probably concentrating on the price of oil shares.

But as we gazed in awe at the breath-taking winter beauty of Norway (the scenery outside, that is, not the blonde sitting opposite), I couldn't help remarking that the beer may be pricey, but that you don't get this kind of scenery when you spend a couple of quid on a pint in the Printer's Pie, or whatever they call it these days. Mick agreed that was a valid point. Of course, the Printer's Pie could always operate a dual pricing system, couldn't it? Along the lines of: Newcastle Exhibition one pound seventy-five a pint in the bar downstairs; or alternatively eight pounds ninety-nine in the observation car upstairs that gives you a view of the passing Rockies.

So on the whole we were pretty content to sit there supping our ale and admiring the awesome show put on by nature especially for us.

Occasions like this tend to generate a degree or two of nostalgia and we fell to comparing this trip with our Moscow bash back in '87. This was just like old times, wasn't it? Of course it was, with the tiny difference that the Russian train we had travelled on had been total shite and smelled appropriately; the bogs were a public health hazard; the on-board catering was a pathetic joke, only the tea being drinkable. In Moscow itself we ate virtually nothing during our three-day stay apart from peanuts in the hotel bar, because anything we found in Russian establishments was just inedible. In desperation we entered a kind of snack bar. It looked like something out of the late forties in Britain maybe, but frequented by characters straight out of Dickens' London. We ordered what looked something like fried minced meat. It tasted like I imagine maggots probably taste.

Yes, apart from those minor differences this was just the same. Oh and there was also the teeny-weeny detail that the journey to and from Moscow took us through a couple of thousand miles of boring forest, punctuated only by the odd glimpse of boring plains or rivers whereas this one offered us what was sometimes a quite spectacular snow-covered mountain landscape. But apart from that.... Don't you also find that nostalgia is not what it used to be?

Back at our seats, and well into the fourth hour of our six-hour journey, Mick was beginning to worry that his travelling would soon be interrupted and he would have to spend an entire night away from a train. A thing he hadn't done for a week or so. He duly got his trusty Thomas Cook timetable out and after ten minutes of muttering to himself (possibly in Esperanto), he announced with a proud smile on his face that it was possible after all.

'What is?'

'To travel as far as Narvik and get back to Oslo airport in time for your flight on Sunday.' This was Friday, remember.

'It'll mean getting off the train and virtually straight on the plane, but it can be done.'

'Can it?'

'Yes!'

'Narvik, as in Narvik inside the Article Circle?'

'Yes, that Narvik.'

'Oh, all right then.'

'You're on.'

I must be mad to listen to him sometimes, but in for an *øre*, etc... It meant changing at Trondheim and hopping on another train an hour later that would take us in about another six hours to the back of beyond, where we would get on a bus to beyond the back of beyond. That bus boarded a ferry somewhere and then we would get a train on to Narvik. This was crazy but it was also going to be fun.

So imagine our disappointment, as they say, when our plan was thwarted at the Trondheim ticket office, where we were informed that seats were available throughout, but no sleeper berths were available for the Saturday night leg of the journey. That would have meant sitting permanently on trains and buses for the next couple of days and then getting straight on a plane to Brussels and driving the remaining two hundred and eighty kilometres to Trier. And getting up the next morning to drive to work in Luxembourg? Er, no thanks. Though if we'd already been writing this book back then, I could have had it finished by the time I got off the last train. Another time for sure, though, as I really would like to be able to say I'd been into the Arctic Circle. Maybe next year we'll get drawn against Hammerfest (the most northerly town in Europe)!

But to say I'd been to Trondheim wouldn't be bad either. I had never been that far north before. And maybe we would see a performance of the 'Trondheim hammer dance, in vich all ze old ladies of ze willage are struck about ze head viz sticks, or *knøttels*.' Don't know if the word *knøttel* even exists; but if it doesn't, it should.

I suggested we check into a hotel and have a few hours' doss before exploring the watering holes of downtown Trondheim (or at least those of them that weren't frozen over). Mick had a better idea, however: we could check in and come straight back to the station to catch the four-thirty to Storlien, which is across the mountains in Sweden. It would only take a couple of hours to get there, and it was only a five minute connection to catch the train coming straight back (another couple of hours). Okay, says I.

This was a kind of local train (in fact it's called the *Nabotåget,* which roughly means 'the neighbourhood train' or rather 'neighbourhood train the', as the Scandinavians, in common with the Bulgarians, have a frustrating habit of sticking the word 'the' after the noun it refers to). We seemed to be climbing forever and in the late afternoon it was already getting seriously dark. As we crossed the Swedish border and were pulling into Storlien we could see a huge floodlit ski run flanked by pine trees. There must have been a hundred or so people doing some Friday evening skiing. It looked great. Scandinavians know how to live, all right.

At Storlien station we just had to cross the one platform to get the train going back. It would not have left without us, as the Norwegian guard in our train from Trondheim was also the guard for the return journey. Mick was already on first-name terms with him and had gone along with him into the cab for a driver's eye view of the proceedings. He was hoping to do so again during the return leg. This was the train that the previous evening Mick had boarded in Tromsö, having come up from Germany. Mad bugger!

While *frater maximus* was in the cab up front, I was happy to read a Swedish paper, which someone had left on the seat, and sip a can of *Dortmunder Kronen* from the emergency supply which Mick had brought with him from Deutschland in case we ran out of money and could no longer afford any ale at all.

It was getting on for nine when we got back to Trondheim so we lost no time in looking for some place to eat. We wanted something typically Norwegian, so we ended up in a Greek restaurant. But at least Phil the Greek waiter accepted the order in pseudo-Swedo-Norsk.

The Best Western hotel in Trondheim is okay and is very conveniently located just a couple of hundred yards from the station, so if we left the windows open we could fall asleep to the accompaniment of shunting noises. Dream on, Mick, there are limits to brotherly love when it is freezing cold. And the restaurant wasn't much of a walk away either, which is just as well at those temperatures. The snow fell and lay deep and crisp and even, the way snow should.

This kind of weather would of course bring the British rail system to a standstill, but in Norway it is simply par for the course, and there was never any suggestion that the train would not run the next day about noon. It left bang on time of course, on another day of brilliant winter sunshine. Same scenery in reverse and we were back in Oslo early on the Saturday evening. Back to the Farmer's Rest to check in and a taxi to the Oslo equivalent of the Quayside. This was an area where all sorts of former offices and factories had been converted into pubs and eateries and it was that nice Saturday night out sensation. The main difference between here and the Quayside was that the girls here were sensibly dressed for minus ten and everything was at least three times more expensive than in the Toon.

The bill for our Indian was over a hundred quid, but most of that was the beer, so I suppose it was all right really. The Toon trip to Vålerenga had turned into a mini-tour of Northern Europe so when the plane took off the next morning I was kind of pleased with myself and very much hoping that the European adventure would go on and on.

As we all know, the Norwegians put up a tough fight in the second leg and I'd say we were flattered by the three-one result. But we were through, and in UEFA Cup terms, that was all that mattered.

Tale from a Spanish island - Mallorca

The draw was made on the fourth of March, the day after we got past Vålerenga in the home return leg, and it was pretty kind to us. We were now in the last sixteen, and this was the first round where our middling UEFA rating over the last five years put us into the un-seeded half of the draw. Not being one of the eight seeds, we were put into Group One, with our four potential opponents being heavyweight teams Valencia and Barcelona along with Bordeaux and Real Mallorca. As it was, the draw, which we watched over the Internet from uefa.com, gave us Real Mallorca, and I think we could count ourselves very lucky. The draw at this stage goes on to tell you who your opponents will be in all the remaining rounds right through to the Final. If we got past Mallorca, we were headed for PSV or Auxerre in the quarter final, and then, in our reading of probabilities, most likely Inter Milan or Liverpool in the semi-final. Not even close!

Luckily for us and our logistics, the away leg was second, so we had exactly three weeks instead of the one week until the home leg to get ourselves fixed up with planes, a hotel and match tickets.

Because of the early morning return flights, we'd booked a hotel at Ca'n Pastilla, the nearest beach resort to the airport. In February, the airport wasn't over-run with charter flights so there shouldn't have been any problems with noise, except the Guardia Civil Training Corps had taken it into their heads to do repeated loops over our hotel in an ancient plane that looked like it might have seen action at Guernica.

It's funny how hotel prices are plucked more or less randomly out of the air: Pete had thought his travel agent had got him a very good deal at about ninety euros for a big room with a sea-view balcony, while I'd rung direct and got it for seventy, as had Harvey. We tried to get Pete's price down to our level when we checked in, but despite the persuasive command of the Spanish language demonstrated by Harvey, or Javier as they had christened him in the hotel register, they wouldn't budge because he'd pre-paid through his travel agent. There'd also been a mix-up on the bookings, and while Pete was in for the duration, Javi and I only had our rooms for that night, because *los estudiantes* were coming. Ah, we thought, a bunch of students, this should liven the place up. But they turned out to be fairly mature students, because a crowd of Mallorcan pensioners were moving in, maybe for a weekend open university session on the subject of higher bingo mathematics. Pete was in for a quiet weekend, but maybe that's how this book got started....

We took a stroll down to the beach and there in front of us stood the Hotel Ánfora. That name comes from the Latin *amphora*. *Amphorae* were those geet big earthen Roman jars that were used as the multi-purpose containers of ancient Mediterranean trade. They would be used to carry wine, corn or fish paste, which was a particular Hispanic speciality of the time. Let's hope they washed them out before carrying wine again after some fish paste. Or maybe the lingering taste of fish paste gave some Roman wines that certain *je ne sais quoi*. Whatever this particular Amphora had contained, it looked a much better bet than our original hotel, but we thought we'd ask anyway, and we couldn't believe our ears when they only asked us for thirty-seven euros, which also included a great breakfast on the terrace overlooking the Mediterranean. Try it out, if you're ever there.

It started raining in the early afternoon, and got heavier and heavier, so we holed up in a beachfront café and worked our way through endless *raciones* of grilled *sardinas, gambas, jamon iberico, manchego* cheese, and the closest *tinto* to *Vega Sicilia* that we could find. Spanish heaven, and with a Toon match to look forward to in this very setting – mackems eat your hearts out! But the soggy spectre of the two Barcelonas was beginning to loom, while the *vino* kept on flowing as fast as the rain in the gutters.

Inspired by reading in the local press that one of the Real Mallorca team was called Néné, which is the exact French equivalent of 'titty', conversation turned to nominations for the world's rudest football team. Néné was their winger, as far as I remember, which means they could sing 'We've got Titty, Titty, Titty on the wing, on the wing'. Anyway, we started out trying to favour players with at least some connection to Newcastle, but this became difficult apart from one or two classics. So we widened the net and trawled up quite an impressive line-up, and you're welcome to add more of your own subs. Here goes: the commentator's nightmare, the world's rudest football match.

'And now we're going back over to the Wankdorff Stadium in Bern, Switzerland where Ruud Gullit's Rude Boys and Arsene's Wengers have been entertaining us tonight. Over to you, Bob and Charlie.' 'Welcome back, John and listeners. And you join us as the second half gets under way. Well we've had a great display of ball skills so let's hope the goals keep flowing. We've already seen a magnificent pair of Néné's, who's built a great pairing up front with Titi Camara. And Djorkaeff (pronounced like a true Geordie) has been working well with ex-Newcastle player Brian Pinas who's spraying balls all over the pitch. Oh no, he took his eye off the ball there and he's dribbled straight into Kuntz, that's Stefan of course. Not to be confused with footballing spoonerist Kenny Lunt. Rafael Scheidt's taken a quick one, and now it's with Michael Ballack. The crowd love him; just listen to that singing: 'He's only one Ballack, one Ballack, walking along, singing a song, walking in a Ballack Wonderland.' 'Now, Bob, Rafael Scheidt's quite a big name up in Glasgow, isn't he?' 'Yes, Charlie, he used to play for Celtic and his arrival was like manna from heaven for Rangers fans, who saw it as proof positive that God must be a Protestant when he gave Celtic Scheidt.' 'They're singing his name now', 'You're Scheidt and you know you are, Scheidt and you know you are'. 'And now Arsenal's Mwankwo Kanu's been chopped down by Newcastle's Michael Chopra of all people, back there defending on the edge of his box.' 'Yes, it's going to be a free kick, and the Portuguese keeper,

Quim, is organising the wall. He's got Nicky Butt and ex-mackems Oscar Arce and Bernt Haas with Kaka and Shittu squeezed in between them.' 'That's Kaka of AC Milan and Danny Shittu of QPR, of course, Charlie. But they need to be wary of the Spaniard Lopez Ufarte who's lingering unpleasantly just behind Arce.' 'We've got Totti of Roma, Frank Awanka, and Argelo Fucks all standing over the ball. Who do you think's going to take it, Bob?' 'I wouldn't be surprised if it's my mate Argelo – I first came across him in the famous newspaper headline 'Argelo Fucks off to Benfica', but hold on, it's going to be Pahars, who's come from nowhere, and he's scored. Quim didn't see him coming.' 'Yes, great goal! By the way, Charlie, maybe you don't know that Pahars sounds like it makes you blind in Spanish. In fact Mitsubishi had to change the name of their off-roader from Pajero to Montero in Spain because the Spanish couldn't look at it without bursting out laughing. No self-respecting, non self-abusing Spaniard would be seen dead or alive in a Pajero.' 'Interesting, Bob. Well, that was the last kick of the match and I can see assistant Arthur Cox and club director Mr Bates dancing in the dug-out with their victorious manager.'

The Romans apparently used Mallorca as a holiday spot themselves, a stopping-off point for a spot of R and R (and some of the local fish paste on the bread) on the way to and from the mainland, and you can see why. Now it's been colonised by the Germans – again you can see why if you take a trip across to the north-west coast of the island and see the fantastic, densely forested mountains, the dry stone walls, the gnarled old olive and eucalyptus trees, the old stone villages clinging to the hillsides, and the little fishing harbours in the bays and inlets.

As match time approached we decided it was too complicated and pouring too hard to get various buses so we ordered a taxi instead. And we were once again pleasantly surprised by how reasonable prices in Spain can be, even in such tourist-ridden places as Mallorca. We'd already got the tie in the bag after a four-one victory in the home leg after a scare when Real Mallorca had gone into the lead shortly after half time. So we were expecting a Spanish stroll, or at least a Spanish plodge into the next round. It was pretty clear what the locals thought about the combination of the rotten weather and the insurmountable first leg deficit because inside the *Son Moix* ground we outnumbered them by maybe two to one. It was almost embarrassing. The total attendance looked like it wasn't much more than about five thousand, which is pathetic when you consider the prize was a place in the quarter finals. No wonder UEFA loves to have teams like us, Celtic and Schalke in their competitions. This must have been the lowest attendance at one of our competitive matches for years.

The way their players were piss-farting around was also quite embarrassing, and our attention was distracted to a big Spanish lad (boy was he fat) who was playing keepy-up with the ball on the running track just in front of our end. Someone threw him a hot dog to keep him going. The whole first half passed by without anything worthy of report – maybe a goal from Mallorca would have livened things up, but they never looked like they were interested. The local papers said that they were gearing up for their relegation tussle with Murcia, and so would be saving themselves against us. It certainly looked that way, and maybe it was worth it because they beat Murcia at the weekend to ease their worries. At least it had stopped raining.

At half time the substitutes came out to warm up. They were down at our end of the ground and someone shouted out 'Howay, Hugo, giz the baaall.' So Hugo Viana duly obliged and kicked a massive shot from the pitch, over the athletics track, over a very smart-looking speedboat and a giant amphora (presumably full of wine or fish paste), clearing the fifteen-foot-high wall and landing in our section behind the goal. No-one could come up with a convincing explanation as to why it was necessary to have a speedboat and a giant amphora either side of the goal by the side of the pitch, but they were there, and that was that. Maybe they'd got washed up there by flooding during the afternoon storm. Or maybe it was like a golf championship where they park a car beside a par three and if you get a hole in one, the car's yours. So if Mallorca had scored, which they didn't, the lucky player might have been presented with the amphora. Or the speedboat. More balls followed up into our stand as Hugo and Michael Chopra tried to out-do each other in ever bigger blasts until the Mallorca groundsmen started to get stroppy and complained to the UEFA officials, as no-one was giving the balls back. Hugo kept on kicking and someone started up a catchy new song 'Hugo Viana, number … forty-five'. It sounded very familiar but no-one was able to tell me what the original was until by chance Biffa of nufc.com told us: it's 'Brim Full of Asha' by the Leicester band Corner Shop. You never thought you were going to read the word 'Leicester' in a book on European football, did you? Well, now you have. Once. Actually, that's being very unfair as, thanks to winning the League Cup twice under Martin O'Neill, (twice more than us, we have to admit), they had a couple of seasons in the UEFA Cup too.

The risks of the amphora or the speedboat's windscreen getting shattered were also mounting by the second, and we couldn't have that could we? Eventually the police and stewards started to climb up into the away end and the balls were thrown back, while all the subs got a bit of a ticking off from the officials. Then out came the big fat lad again, parading around on the bend of the running track in front of us, and juggling one of the retrieved footballs. He was enjoying being the centre of attention of the captive audience, and actually he was pretty good at it too. Then someone started flinging a plucked chicken around the away end, and attention moved on to that until we realised it was a rubber one.

We'd had quite a lot of chances to practise our varying levels of Spanish on the Mallorcans. If Shakespeare had been Spanish, he might have had Hamlet musing 'Ser o no estar?

Eso está la pregunta.' 'To be or not (the other) to be? That is the question.' It's a question asked by all students of Spanish at some time, because the tricky thing is that the Spanish have two different verbs for 'to be', one for saying 'I *am* Sir Bobby Robson' and the other for saying 'Where *am* I?' You use *ser* for the first (appropriately for a Sir), and you use *estar* for the second. Come to think of it, Sir Bobby might well say that when he wakes up in the morning; he's always on the go from one place to another.

The crowd was full of sombreros of all colours, though strangely no Mallorcans were wearing them. Here were we doing our best to blend in with the locals by adopting their manners and customs and they'd gone and shifted the goalposts and given up their national headdress for the day. You might think that sombreros are Mexican, but these were authentic Spanish sombreros bought in the finest tourist tat shops of the proud Kingdom of Spain itself. Unfortunately most of the ones available in Mallorca were bottle green or Blue Star blue, but I'd brought my black Barcelona one, little knowing that it would serve the same purpose in Mallorca that it had in Barcelona: to shelter from the storm not the sun. I'd added some broad white stripes to mine, and I was resigned to the prospect of the poster paint starting to run and me ending up in blotchy grey rather than black and white, though even that would have been alright because it would have matched the away strip colours that the team wore that night. As far as I'm concerned we wore the grey far too much this year. Did we ever play a team where there was a colour clash with our black and white stripes? No.

Then an equally big Geordie lad with a green sombrero scaled the scoreboard behind us to retrieve the rubber chicken, and while all our eyes were fixed on him, we scored one of our goals, but all we saw was the ball bulging the net. Such is life. The police were a bit heavy-handed the way they got him down. After all, he wasn't doing any harm; he was simply making a complete fool of himself, that was all. But maybe Spain's macho culture cannot handle people making fools of themselves. The extroverts go and skewer a few bulls instead. Anyway, we worked out that Big Al must have scored by the way he wheeled away with his arm up in salute. Just about every one around us had missed the goal too, so it took a while to find out that the goalie had passed the ball straight out to him. The Mallorca team and their crowd gave up after that. If they'd been able to, their team would surely have sloped off like their supporters, because we were more or less left to our own devices in the stadium. If someone had come across and given us a big key and asked us to lock up after we were finished, we wouldn't have been surprised. The seven-one trouncing was completed by goals from Bellamy, who raced half way down the pitch and finished in a one-on-one just the way you would love him to do every time he gets into that kind of position, and Shearer who just before the final whistle tapped in after a good run and cross from the left by Olivier Bernard. One other point of note that we hope will become something to remember when he gets really famous: we saw centre half Steven Taylor's senior début for the last ten minutes of the game. As we made our way out, the word went round that PSV had beaten Auxerre so we'd be 'gannin' Dutch' again for the quarter-final.

The police were heavy-handed not just with the fat lad on the scoreboard, but on all fronts. As we came into the ground and again when we left, they were pushing us one way and another, as if they were hoping to provoke some kind of reaction that would give them some excuse to lay into people. Of course there was no such reaction, just a chant of 'Hoo man, hey man, hoo man, hey man'. Well done the Toon Army!

Besides the *Son Moix* Stadium (which I think means 'soggy socks'), Mallorca has another, longer-established place of pilgrimage up in the forested mountain village of Valldemosa, a cool and peaceful refuge. You associate Spain with *tinto* and *iberico*, but the local delicacy of Valldemosa was hot chocolate and castor sugar coated buns about the size of doughnuts, called *cocas de patatas*. I suppose they were a bit similar to *churros y chocolate*, those deep fried, extruded curls of batter that you dip into sticky hot chocolate for breakfast in a *bar Madrileño*. Delicious, *delicioso*. One embarrassing moment: in faltering Spanish, I attempted to ask the waitress what *cocas de patatas* were, and not understanding what she'd said, I questioningly parroted back her reply, only to find that I'd unwittingly mimicked her speech impediment. Cringe. I'd done something similar a few years previously on first meeting the wife of a colleague, when I'd repeated back to her a name with a double syllable that she said we were heading for, which I'd taken to be some town in the vicinity called 'Sessenter', when actually she'd been stuttering 'centre'. Double cringe.

I later found out that quite a lot of famous people had been drawn to the area before us, including Chopin and George Sand who'd spent a miserable winter there - their fault, not Valldemosa's, I'm sure – consoling themselves by dunking their *cocas de patatas* in their mugs of hot chocolate, and Robert Graves who spent his last years just down the mountain from Valldemosa in Deia. Well, goodbye to all that mountaineering and back to the Mallorcan seaside.

Our flights back out of Mallorca were at unearthly hours of the morning, made positively extra-terrestrial by the unfortunate coincidence with putting the clocks forward for summer time, which meant that a half past four alarm call would become half past three in your dulled consciousness. It hardly seemed worth going to bed, so we didn't. We found an all-night Karaoke bar instead and crooned the early hours away to the strains of the severely limited choice of Anglo songs, Michael Bridges over Troubled Water, A Mallorcan Pie, Imagine (Above us only fog.... again) and a host of world-famous-in-Spain songs, including one called *Angel Pecador*, which for some reason stuck in my mind (it means sinful angel, so maybe it reminded me of the Angel of the North). It was great being able to change the words to something more topical, but never in the field of human concerts have so few Geordies been so comprehensively out-sung by so many Spaniards – I think they were professional singers, they were so good.

So we had beaten Real Mallorca seven-one on aggregate. Confidence was starting to build that we could win something again at long last! Bring on PSV! Let's have another crack at them!

When we turned up this year at the PSV Philips Stadium for our second visit, we had the chance to re-live Kenny Dalglish's experience of having seen it all before. Think what you like about Kenny, but he certainly has a dry sense of humour: in the moments before our Champignons League game in the '97-'98 season, Kenny was interviewed in front of the dugouts on Dutch TV. Obviously proud of their immaculate stadium and angling for a compliment, the reporter asked: 'Mr Dalglish, what is your first impression of our Philips Stadion?' 'Well ... I've been here before...' Pregnant pause... 'Errr... So what is your second impression?' What a classic. We had very good tickets in the PSV section just a couple of rows behind the dug-out and could see it all happen, and it was obvious that Kenny was enjoying himself, though we didn't know what he'd said until we watched the video the next day. Our seats were so good that we were mixing with club officials and the press – we had a bit of a chat with Alan Oliver at half time.

Well our second impression was that it was still an excellent stadium. It's even got massive Philips electric bar heaters hanging from the roof to keep you warm. And it must be the only football ground which has a Toys 'R' Us built into the side of one of the stands! And standing outside the Toys 'R' Us this year, heavy camera on shoulder and hairy microphone in hand were the cameraman and sports reporter Geoff Brown of Look North double-act with Carol Malia fame. It's a pity Carol hadn't been there instead. Unfortunately we were unable to take up their offer of a live on-camera interview because they declined to make such an offer, despite us striking up a hopeful conversation, proffering a photogenic blonde seven-year old Toon supporter for the 'ah, isn't she cute' factor, and generally hanging around. Anyway, we'd got there too late for that night's live broadcast, and they were probably just having a breather before taking their place on the touchline to grab some close-ups and pre-match pearls of wisdom from Sir Bobby and the team.

Logistics. Even the most devout pilgrim, and they don't come much more devout than us, can't get by without logistics. For logistics is everything – or should that be *are* everything? After all, logistics does/do end in 's'. Interesting word at all events: it comes from the nineteenth century French... but who cares about the nineteenth century French, or about the twenty-first century variety for that matter? That was a good one about France heightening its state of alert in the wake of terrorist threats from 'run' to 'hide', their only two higher levels of alert being 'capitulate' and 'collaborate'. Who makes these things up? I don't know.

But I digress: logistics is all about being at the right place at the right time, and above all having the tickets for the match, even in the opponents' end if that's the only avenue open. Eindhoven revisited was a case in point.

After initial wavering due to work commitments, Chris and Sarah booked with Toon Travel on a charter from Newcastle to Amsterdam and back (which was fine, except they live in London, remember). I was raring to go, as per, despite wor lass's usual rantings. Barry had elegantly sidestepped such trifling domestic issues by arranging a mini-holiday for the family, as he had for Oslo. After all, the fixture-fixers had kindly arranged the match to be the night before the Easter weekend, so it was a perfect fit. Thus, the team was set for another reunion – reunion being an operative word.

We had reached the quarter finals of the UEFA Cup and were drawn away for the first leg. Well you had to start feeling just a wee bit optimistic, hadn't you? As always, the main trouble was getting tickets, never easy when the interested parties are based in the smoke, Belgium and Deutschland. Barry as usual came up trumps. He and his brother have season tickets, and to go one better his brother has a business associate whose company has a box at St

James's. Think of that what you will - but it gets us tickets, and WE deserve them. To be on the safe side, Barry also got in touch with his friend Wim, Professor of Engineering at the Technical University of Delft, whose son is a season ticket holder at PSV.

By a remarkable quirk of appalling planning, Chris and I had tickets for an Old Boys' reunion in the shape of a gala dinner at the Old Assembly Rooms (bottom of Westgate Road) on Friday, April 2nd, perfect preparation for my planned participation in the Rotterdam marathon on the Sunday (the match was the following Thursday). The *alma mater* in question is Saint Cuthbert's Grammar (now High) School, Benwell Hill (diagonally opposite the Fox and Hounds). Naturally, they always arrange for such events to take place on a weekend when there is a home game (in this case Everton). So for me it was flights from Luxembourg to Amsterdam and from there to the Toon on the Thursday. Chris drove up from the smoke on the Friday morning and he and I met up for a pre pre-dinner-drink drink with our now Ireland-based marra Mike in the Printer's Pie (now the Fleet Street something or other - why the Hell can't they leave pub names alone?). But whatever the boozer's name I am a firm believer in such pre-prandial tinctures, as it is definitely not a good idea to eat on an empty stomach.

As just mentioned, Mike is now based in Ireland. And guess what – he's teetotal, has been for the past million years (he's in the market for sainthood if you ask me). So he did what he had to while Chris and I had a couple of jars. Mind, the Printer's Pie has changed a bit since our O Level celebrations there back in '71, though but. Then on to the Old Assembly Rooms. The guest speaker was none other than Jack Charlton, whom I could still picture in my mind's eye jostling on our Gallowgate-end goal line with McNamee while Leeds took a corner, and scoring the same goal he got by the self-same tactic at least a dozen times back in those days. I had planned to remind him of that later that evening but was too sozzled and forgot.

It was of course brilliant to meet up with people (former pupils and even a handful of teachers, all but one of whom retired) we hadn't seen in some cases for thirty years. We met up with a group of former classmates who still kept up the good old left-footers' tradition of keeping the First Fridays. In the Anglo-Irish version of Catholicism, which was the staple for the indoctrination of our youth, you went to Mass and Communion on the first Friday of seven consecutive months (or was it nine?) and that apparently automatically got you into heaven, or got you some remission from purgatory, or something like that. It was heart-warming – nay, tear-jerkingly gratifying to see that these Old Boys were keeping up this venerable tradition. Admittedly, their version of the First Fridays is a slightly modified one. It involves meeting up at a boozer on the first Friday evening of every month for a skinfull. Still, it's the thought that counts. In the good old school days the favourite Friday night meeting place was the Durham Ox.

The speculation at our table, and I suspect throughout the three-hundred-plus gathering, was that Sting would make a surprise appearance. That most famous of Cuths Old Boys (what, even more famous than Lawrie McMenemy?) had recently brought out his autobiography - a sure sign of onsetting sentimentality, as he surely can't need the money – and it includes quite a bit about the old school. Everyone I spoke to had read it. Sting was born and raised in Wallsend (*comme moi*). His father was my middle brother's milkman, and his brother delivered the white stuff to my older brother. It's a great pity that doesn't qualify as blood, or even milk brothers! Never mind, at least there was a sting in the tale. But notwithstanding this shared cultural heritage, that autobiography nowhere contains the words 'Newcastle United', as far as I recall, which is quite amazing. Anyway, he didn't show up.

Sarah couldn't make it for the Everton game and was planning to come up a few days later for the trip to Holland. Toon Travel's package included a hotel room in Utrecht, as some of you will recall. Now call me a traditionalist - you can call me what you like for that matter, I don't care - but why in the name of shite do Newcastle fans, of all people, have to be accommodated miles away from the actual venue? Come on, we're not talking Man U or Chelsea.

Muggins had to be on the one o'clock Amsterdam flight from the Toon airport (how about 'Newcastle Sir Bobby Robson International Airport – above us only fog'?). So Chris was the only representative at the Everton game (four-two, including two crackers from Shearer). At Schiphol I met up with my entrepreneurial cousin Steve (a driven man and a fellow Wallsend wallah) and his mackem colleague/marra Marc, the latter accompanied by his charming and recently full-of-kittens mackem wife Kay. It's no problem for me mixing with mackems, not even if they are season ticket holders - like my brother's mate, Jim the mackem hanging judge.

Rendezvous accomplished, we took one of those quaint yellow Cloggie trains from Schiphol to Rotterdam Centraal. Scenes of that on-board hostage-taking in the mid-seventies sprang readily to mind and I wondered briefly if the ruud man had been playing footie at the time, before calculating that he couldn't have been all that old. We all (even those who weren't yet born) remember where we were when we heard of J.F. Kennedy's assassination. For the record, I was standing in the queue at Mrs Morton's chip shop on the corner of Howdon Lane and Tynemouth Road in High Howdon. For some reason Mr Morton always had a stock of those little fixture lists at the start of each season. They even gave South Shields' and Gateshead's games. That is entirely beside the point, however.

The same remembering-where-you-were business applies in the case of Andy Cole's transfer and Keegan's departure. Go on, I bet you *can* remember where you were on both occasions. Again, for the record, I was at work in Essen hewing away at the word face when I heard about Cole going. My boss (part of a Geordie mafia of three – it was like

Aufwiedersehen Pet, only in suits, and even the secretary was called Dagmar) came bursting into my office telling me his wife had just been on the phone and I would never guess what had happened. I knew it had to be something bad - but I had no idea it could be *that* bad. And I followed Keegan's departure on Sky in the comfort of my living room. Yeah, Special K gave us some exciting, swashbuckling stuff, but in the end he wasn't a stayer, was he?

You won't believe this, but I heard the news of Gullit's exit when I was on a boat coming from Hell. Which is most appropriate, as Hell is exactly where he had taken us. 'But it's just another game,' he had dared to say after we had been humiliated by the mackems. Actually, I was on a boat coming from the (now Polish) peninsula of Hel (but it's pronounced 'Hell', honest) during a two-week stay in Gdansk, or Danzig if you prefer, on a Polish course. (If your wooden floors or table tops need smartening up, I'm your man!) I will spare you the details of the Polish language. Suffice it to say it has lots of rz's, szcz's and other delights and basically uses the wrong alphabet altogether. Don't say this to a Pole, but they really should be using the same alphabet as the Russians, Bulgarians and others. This is the Cyrillic alphabet, and it can get across in a single letter one particular sound in Polish that takes up four letters in the Latin alphabet (szcz)!! And they are in the wrong time zone: in Gdansk, it gets dark at about eight in the evening at the height of summer.

Such was my train (ho ho) of thought while sitting in that Cloggie train to Rotterdam.

Arrived in Rotterdam, collected the starting numbers for the marathon and checked into the hotel just in time to switch on the telly and catch highlights of the Everton game. The pieces were falling nicely into place. Woke up the next morning wondering where the Hel I was.

For the record, Steve managed four and a half hours and Marc (in his mackem shirt) an equally creditable four hours fifty-five. Hopelessly overweight and still not fully recovered from the school reunion, I managed to keep ahead of the sweeper/grim reaper bus for twenty-three kilometres and was given the choice of getting on board or continuing my run on the pavement. As the pavement alternative would have meant competing for space with people taking a Sunday afternoon stroll, and facing the prospect of no more refreshment stations and no medal even if I did last the distance, the choice was simple - particularly as I knew I was only a click or so away from the hotel and some of the cool Heineken on tap in the bar.

After copious post-marathon rehydration, it was a good night's sleep and an early train to Vlissingen to join Iris and Tina at the coast. En route I rang Professor Wim on the mobile and arranged (in decidedly dodgy Dutch!!) to pick the tickets up on Wednesday. Bit of a rest at the coast for the remainder of the day and Tuesday, and then off to Delft on Wednesday mid-morning. It was getting difficult to keep a mental track of all this to-ing and fro-ing.

The Technical University of Delft is massive, and we had to park somewhere. That somewhere happened of course to be a mile away from the Institute of Engineering, where Wim had our tickets for the match. When Iris and I got to his office, Wim was still a bit bemused to hear a Geordie speaking double Dutch at him, but we quickly switched to English out of politeness vis-a-vis wor lass, who has spent at least a year of her life in the Netherlands, if you add together all the holidays we have spent at the Dutch coast. Most Brits would never think of spending their hols in Holland. A weekend in Amsterdam yeah, but a fortnight in the summer...

Well believe me, you would be pleasantly surprised, especially if you have young kids. When we lived in Essen, we took the kids to the Dutch coast just about every summer. They have lovely, and very, very clean sandy beaches complete with essential infrastructure such as showers, proper toilets and, every few hundred yards or so, pavilion-type cafés or restaurants where you can also enjoy a glass or two of the cool Heineken or Amstel. Even when the weather's a bit wet and windy in the autumn or winter it is nice to sit in such a beach pavilion looking homeward across the grey North Sea, getting happily sozzled and maybe listening to Focus playing 'Moving Waves'. I have never understood why there isn't such a place on Long Sands at Tynemouth or Blyth's South Beach!

In the summer they are great places. And yes, the lasses go topless! Plus, it is actually possible to bathe in the North Sea on the Dutch coast without freezing your whatsits off. Must be something to do with the Gulf Stream. The Dutch get some warmth out of that while on our side of the Oceanus Germanicus, we seem to get the water that melts from the icebergs further north. The first thing you notice about Dutch beaches in the summer, though, is that they are full of Germans! And when they're not on the beach themselves their towels are there keeping their places. On the Walcheren peninsula they (Germans and towels combined) often outnumber the locals. And you could be forgiven for thinking you were in a German colony. There are surely more of them there during the summer holidays nowadays than there were during the German occupation. And ninety-nine out of a hundred of them will never ever bother to learn a word of Dutch, even though they may even have a holiday home there and spend every single Easter and summer holiday there.

Dutch is so close to German that any intelligent Dutch person will understand an intelligent German who speaks clearly and slowly enough. Indeed, if we look at the main Germanic languages (English, German, Dutch/Flemish, Afrikaans, Swedish, Danish, Norwegian and Icelandic, plus Yiddish of course), we can regard German and Dutch, of which Flemish and to a large extent Afrikaans are dialects, as non-identical twin sisters, whereas Swedish, Danish and Norwegian are first cousins to German; English being a second cousin and Icelandic the great-grandfather, as noted elsewhere.

So really, we could no doubt equally well have been speaking German with Wim, though possibly not Icelandic. I am sure he would have coped without difficulty. But he teaches all the time in English to his very international mix of students, and he is clearly an Anglophile, and a big fan of the North-East to boot. He told us he had been caravanning a few times through beautiful Hadrian's Wall country. He himself hails from a village not far from Amsterdam Airport (Schiphol), but his wife is from the Eindhoven area and his son is a PSV season-ticket holder. She was obviously better at indoctrinating their son than he was – you would have expected him to be an Ajax supporter, but no. But hey, had he been so, he would not have got the Toon Army a couple of tickets for the UEFA Cup quarter final. So thank you, Mrs Professor.

Have you ever wondered why Dutch people (and I mean just about ALL Dutch people over the age of about thirteen) speak such excellent English? Well here's why: for one thing, the Cloggies watch loads of British television, which clearly helps a lot. Secondly (and from the academic's point of view more importantly) theirs is the closest language there is to English (a bit obvious, really, when you look at the geography). In a very real way, you can view English as the ultimate (western) language. Essentially Germanic with an added layer of Latin/French, it has radically simplified the complicated grammar used by some of its Germanic cousins.

For example, German has three basic words for 'the' (*der*, *die* and *das*). Dutch has just two (*de* and *het*, though it also uses *die* for emphasis), and English of course just has 'the'. You see, the Dutch are right smack bang in the middle between the Germans and the Brits, not just geographically but also linguistically, and they have profited nicely from both aspects, turning their geographical and linguistic advantages to good account, *dank U wel*.

This being 'right smack bang in the middle' is also reflected in loads of individual Dutch words. Take 'Toon', for example. No, that's not Dutch, but it is a very interesting

161

word nevertheless. There is such a thing as the second Germanic sound shift, whereby certain sounds would change as words passed from High German to Low German to Dutch to English. A common sound shift is from 'Z' (pronounced ts) in German to a straight 'T' in Dutch and English. Take *scheiss* as an example: 'You're *scheiss*, and you know you are!' Sometimes, of course, a word would undergo not only a sound shift but also a shift in meaning. For example, the German word *Zug* is really the same word as the English 'tug'. *Der Zug*, however, means 'the train'. Well they both have to do with pulling, don't they? In (very Germanic) Norwegian this word becomes *tog*, which was useful to know when getting to the Vålerenga match!

But back to the Toon. It comes from the German word *Zaun* (pronounced tsown, as in town but with an s after the t). In German this means 'fence', as in the thing that surrounds a garden, or in bygone days a whole town. In Dutch, this became *tuin* (pronounced more or less in the same way as someone from Northern Ireland might pronounce 'town'). But in Dutch, *tuin* means garden. When it reached the shores of Old Blighty, it became 'town', which the Geordies and the copy-cat Scots turned into Toon.

Amazingly (well, amazingly to me anyway), you have the same idea in the Slavonic languages. In Polish, *ogrod* means garden, whereas the Russian word for town is *gorod*, contracted in place names to *grad* (as in the former Leningrad), and in Bulgarian a fence is an *ograda*. So if the twists and turns of political and linguistic history had turned out a bit differently, we might have been shouting ' Howay the Ograda'. Isn't it amazing? Well okay, maybe not.

In the case of the Geordies, of course, 'Toon' has taken on a further meaning. It means Newcastle, but it also means Newcastle United. It means the people who are Newcastle United. No, not the players – us, you and me. Just as Gallowgate is an integral part of the very heart of Newcastle, so the football club lies in the very heart of the people, and they are the heart of the club. They are the club, the club is the Toon, the Toon is the Geordie nation. Club, city and people are inextricably intertwined. Without us there is no Newcastle United. The club would do well to remember that now and then. This relationship is special and unique. And it is precious.

The very location of St James's is also very special. How could anyone for a single moment consider moving the ground south of the river, let alone sharing a new place with the mackems? Yet this type of heresy was mooted not that long ago by men in funny suits who don't know their arses from their elbows when it comes to the Toon. I could have lived with a new stadium on Leazes Moor; that would still have been home. But maybe the local dogshit brigade and their friends (so-called friends of the Earth but no friends of mine) did us a favour in the end by putting the kybosh on that project. Gallowgate is where we belong, and in the fullness of time Leazes Terrace will disappear or be relocated brick by brick and make way for an East Stand worthy of the Toon Army. Or be built into the side of a towering new stand, like the old people's flats in the side of Basel's Sankt Jakob Stadium. Sorry Barry, but why not?

There are other Dutch words that have come across to Tyneside and loved it so much that they stayed there and simply ignored the rest of Britain. 'To go' in Dutch is *gaan*. 'To throw' is *gooien* (pronounced very like hoyin') and a hoy-in at the match is an *ingooi* (pronounced very like 'in-hoy').

Tickets for the PSV game safely pocketed - I think that's not far away from an ablative absolute, but it could do with a 'having' in it somewhere - we set off on the return journey to Zoutelande. The next morning's Dutch papers were of course full of pre-match reports, and the excitement was mounting. Sir Bobby had come over a couple of days earlier to catch up with some old friends, of which he no doubt has plenty, and he is clearly well respected by the pundits in the Dutch press. One reporter was amused by Sir Bobby's knack of getting his players' names wrong, and pointed out that at PSV he was totally at sea on the names front. And of course there's the famous story about the time when Shola Ameobi was asked what Sir Bobby called him for short. The answer was 'Carl Cort'.

I had arranged to meet Barry and family opposite the central station in Eindhoven, while Chris and Sarah were en route in the rush-hour traffic between Utrecht and Eindhoven. I duly hopped into Barry's car at five o'clock and we parked up about half way between the station and the Philips stadium. It has to be said that the PSV ground is almost as centrally located as Gallowgate, with the main shops, restaurants and bars only a ten-minute walk away. And a plus-point for any of you who trail your families around with you to matches: don't forget there's that Toys'R'Us built into the side of the PSV ground (well it makes a change from the Swiss tendency to incorporate old people's homes, complete, one hopes, with a nuclear bunker). But on the other hand, the immediate surroundings are more of a concrete jungle without the soul that is palpable in Newcastle, and it is difficult to see how PSV fans on their boozer-to-ground walk could feel anything like the buzz you get in the Toon as you make your way to the ground from your favourite pre-match watering hole: 'Bar Oz' in my case - well the buggers pulled 'The Haymarket' doon, didn't they?

Don't know about you, but I suffer from 'Greggsian constipation', that means I can never pass a Greggs shop. And I always have to pop into that one by the Haymarket bus station (on the way to the match and on the way home) for a pasty or a cheese savoury stottie - magic. Mind, Carricks (now the Baker's Oven) just down from the Labour Club used to do a fine pasty and poke of chips. You were certainly spoilt for choice on Percy Street back in the old days, as half-way between, you had the pork butchers with their mouth-watering hot pork and pease pudding stotties, too.

What a boozer 'The Haymarket' was, though but. You got all sorts in there - dossers, dole wallahs, students, university lecturers, you name it. I remember once I got talking with the

Senior Lecturer in Mining Engineering at Newcastle University. Somewhat bizarrely he drank bottled McEwan's Export. Anyway, he took great pride in telling me that the acronym for his post was SLIME. That was in the bar. The lounge next door should have been called the 'Tardis'. It really was a trip back in time. Even well into the eighties you could listen to early seventies records such as Jethro Tull's 'Witch's Promise' on the Juke Box, and the place was peopled by long-haired zombies from the same era, me among them. I have it on good authority that the git at the Civic Centre who signed the ultimate demolition papers was a mackem and a joker park season-ticket holder. My brother Mick very kindly rescued a few shards of glass from the demolition site that my Dad ingeniously worked into a little replica of The Haymarket front window. It still stands on the wall unit in our living room.

With Barry's car safely parked in the same multi-storey we had used for the Champignons League game under Dalglish, whose principal tactic was to avoid scoring a goal at all cost, we made our way to the pedestrian zone. This time there were plenty of black and white shirts, and the lads and lasses were in good voice on the main square. Being creatures of habit, we opted for the same bar-restaurant again, the *Vooruitcafé*, which was absolutely heaving, mainly with PSV fans. But there wasn't even a hint of bother, just good-natured banter and a lot of loud singing.

We coped admirably with the Dutch-only menu, and the spring lamb (*voorjaarslammetje*) was jolly tasty. The poor bugger hadn't even seen Easter before getting the lamb chop. As usual, one item on the dessert list raised a smile or two. *Slagroom* is not an invitation to adjourn to some inviting and dimly lit parlour. All it means is whipped cream (no pun intended).

Right, a quick exchange of tickets and we were all set. Barry was taking little Sarah into the posh PSV seats kindly arranged by Wim. Although he was wearing his colours under his jacket, Barry was wisely taking the precaution of wearing the PSV hat he had worn when we went under cover for the Champignons League game – yeah, we should definitely have been spies. Outside the *Vooruitcafé*, we'd bought some of those souvenir scarves that are split half PSV, half Newcastle. Seeing we were making a mass purchase of four of them, we tried to get a discount but without luck; the seller, who was a Geordie, said his boss wouldn't let him sell them for less than ten euros apiece. The scarf seller talked very slowly to us. He'd got the idea that we were PSV supporters – I suppose it was the red and white PSV woolly hat. It was like listening to a Gazza interview when he's in his earnest southern-media-friendly mode, pronouncing every separate word very slowly and precisely and making every effort to taak proper.

The first PSV match had been a fun occasion as well, back in the 1997/98 season. It was in the November and I had taken the afternoon off to drive up from Luxembourg. I had booked a hotel between Eindhoven and Venlo for that night while Barry was heading straight back home to Brussels after the match. Driving into Eindhoven in my German-registered Opel Kadett of the time and wearing my colours, I was stopped at a checkpoint just outside the city centre and asked, in German, if I was going to the match. I replied in DDD (Dodgy Double Dutch) that I was, and that I was meeting a marra in town who had the tickets. The poliss was clearly just too confused by that combination and wished me a pleasant stay.

There had been next to no Toon wallahs in town that day as they were all in hotels around the Arnhem area (as in a bridge too far). I had the time to wander around a bit before Barry arrived, and so I took the precaution of buying our woollen PSV hats and also a copy of the local paper. After our meal at the *Vooruitcafé* we walked to the ground speaking snippets of Dutch to each other. It was all very cloak and dagger. The Professor had got us the tickets for that match as well, and so we would be in the Lion's den.

As it turned out, loads of other Toon supporters were near us, and none of us could resist shouting and waving when the team came out. We weren't far at all from the Toon bench and I kept on shouting advice to Dalglish but he took no notice at all. Still, we did get (sub keeper) Pav Srnicek's autograph at half time. We were complete shite, and Dalglish's marra Rush kept on retreating whenever he got near the halfway line. How had we stooped so low after the Keegan glory days? We were impressed at the time by the heaters in the ground that November evening which made us take off our coats. It was like sitting in a theatre! Well done, Philips! Behind the stand, the facilities were excellent. It was the carpeted comfort of a social club, complete with a live band. Great stuff!

But back to the 2003/04 UEFA Cup. I was taking Brian into the Toon end, but we still had to rendezvous with Chris and Sarah. The away fans at PSV are accommodated in the *spoorzijde*. This means 'railway end' and is to be understood very literally indeed. You cross the road separating the ground from the railway line, walk up the steps parallel to the track, and then across a completely enclosed bridge that takes you back over the road and into the ground. What you then enter is basically a hermetically sealed-off away-fans section. The body searches were thorough, almost insulting. Just who and what the hell do they think we are? Brian (aged eleven) was told he could take his (plastic) bottle of mineral water in with him, but not the screw-on top. To add insult to insult, there was a net between us and our view of the pitch, presumably to catch any objects or pitch invaders lobbed in the direction of the players.

This is the sad reality of the modern age, boys and girls. The likes of you and me go to these occasions, usually at considerable expense, and sacrificing a day or two of our annual holiday entitlements, in order to enjoy the match and savour the atmosphere, even in order to get to know a little bit more about the people, culture and language of our host country and city, and to rejoice in a mutually understood, almost transcendental love of the Geordie homeland.

Some other clubs, on the other hand, have a small faction that goes with the sole purpose of causing trouble. Doesn't it piss you off to constantly have to worry about mindless yobbos? It does me. Let's ostracise them completely (but check the dictionary first!).

Anyway, that was the set-up for away fans at PSV, probably as a result of bad experience with travelling Ajax and Feyenoord fans. Remember our little encounters with the latter in Rotterdam, and bizarrely in Breda?

Only ten minutes to go till kick-off and still no sign of Chris and Sarah! Panic call on the mobile – they were just outside the ground, the bus having been delayed severely by the traffic. Just outside the ground, okay, but if they were body-searching everyone... Rushed down from the stand to the tunnel exit and there they were with about two minutes to spare. Talk about just in time delivery. Thought that was a Japanese speciality, not a Dutch one! Turned out that the traffic had been just horrendous between Utrecht and Eindhoven. You need to know that the traffic between any Dutch city and any other Dutch city is ALWAYS horrendous.

Memo to Dutch clubs. Please note carefully that there is no need to treat the Toon Army like animals to be dropped off at the last possible minute before a game and picked up or herded into trains immediately afterwards as if we posed some sort of threat to law and order. We DO NOT. We are eminently nice people and well able to keep the odd idiot in order ourselves. Ask Oslo fans; ask Scousers, with whom we always get on well; ask any reasonable, thinking fans in the UK and abroad. For crying out loud, there are solicitors among us, accountants, financial advisers, successful businessmen – but also some honest people.

There were so many fans coming through the tunnel that the body searches were discontinued altogether. This was just as well for one lad sitting, i.e. standing, next to me, who was enjoying his joint and a can of the cool Heineken. He

168

kindly invited me to inhale, but I declined in view of the two-hour drive back to the coast. How was the view for you down there in the posh seats, Barry?

Well Pete, we were wondering what pitch-side paraphernalia might be in store for us. After all, we'd just been treated to the sight of a speedboat and an amphora in Real Mallorca it seemed like just a few days earlier, and our memory had gone back just a little over a year ago to another Dutch ground, De Kuyp, home of Feyenoord in Rotterdam. There we had been nonplussed by the spectacle of twin, red, duelling grand pianos rattling out jolly Dutch oompah music from down on the pitch by the halfway line before the match had begun. The pianos hadn't been there when we went with colleague and authorial inspiration Malcolm and his wife, who's from Rotterdam, for the Feyenoord pre-season game a few years before. But despite the pre-match musical psycho-torture, that Champignons League encounter had turned out to be a great night in the end - three-two in the last seconds of what was the final first-round game, with the Bellamy goal just a few yards in front of us. We were hoping for a similar result against PSV tonight, though preferably less stress-inducing. Certainly we were hopeful of getting away with a better result than the one-nil and two-nil losses we'd suffered at the hands (or rather feet) of PSV under Kenny, when injuries to Shearer and Tino had left us with a too old Rush and a too young Tomasson as strikers.

We were staying at the Carlton de Berg Hotel in Mierlo, about ten miles out of Eindhoven, which was the hotel used by the team for the Ruud Gullit pre-season training camp in July 1999, when it had still been a Holiday Inn. We had stayed there with the team back then and we had been half-hoping that they would have returned for this match, but maybe the Ruud Gullit associations had too many bad memories for them. The hotel has marvellous sports facilities: a couple of full-size pitches, other outdoor training areas, a swimming pool, a couple of huge gyms full of weights, rowing and running machines, tennis courts, squash courts, golf simulators, indoor bowling, saunas, you name it, they've got it. A lot of big clubs and international teams use the hotel for summer training camps, and you can see why.

They had a giant chessboard in the foyer and Laurent Charvet spent most evenings playing against all-comers from the hotel guests - he was better than us! We played three matches (of football, not chess) against local teams Den Bosch, where Lionel Perez played his one game in goal; SV Deurne, where Kieron Dyer made his début after his transfer was finalised half way through the tour; and Helmond Sport. Throughout the camp, Ruud Gullitt looked very remote from his players, walking around permanently tuned in to his hands-free mobile phone. Still, he was very good with the public, happily signing autographs at the hotel and at the games, as did all the players. Another thing you could sense was that the team spirit really wasn't there. Some of the new players looked very uncertain about approaching the established players. It made you feel sorry for some of them like Marcelino, who'd just joined too and who actually looked a bit lonely.

This PSV game turned into a real nail-biter. They went ahead after thirteen minutes through Kezman, who was doing his level best to impress Sir Bobby and presumably succeeded. My view is that he would certainly suit a black and white shirt (but since when has Sir Bobby ever listened to me?). PSV played the sixties Batman tune when he scored, and the bat symbol came up on the scoreboard – I suppose they got the idea because of having Robben in the team too, although luckily he was injured and never played against us. Now they're both at Chelsea (ptuh). Bit of controversy just before half time when van der Schaap went down very dramatically after being ever so slightly elbowed by Bramble in the PSV penalty area. Van der Schaap means 'of the sheep' (second Germanic sound shift again, f to p, this time: German *Schaf* becomes Dutch *schaap*, becomes English 'sheep'). Makes you wonder a bit, though, doesn't it? Well, those Frisian Islands can be lonely places on those cold winter nights, I suppose. The crowd turned a bit nasty after the elbow incident and started throwing stuff on the pitch and hissing and booing our every touch of the ball, especially when it went anywhere near Bramble. A minute later the same Cloggy stupidly gave away a free kick from which Jenas headed home – o joy.

They had another impressive forward called Hesselink of Venegoor, who put himself about to good effect. They obviously bought him to boost the sales of XXL shirts and sticky black lettering. Funnily enough, *of* in Dutch doesn't mean 'of' – it means 'or', so he has two alternative surnames. Apparently his ancestors at one time couldn't agree which surname to use when a couple got married, so they agreed to differ, and to use either one, depending on how they felt when they got up in the morning. Of course, if one had been called Robson and the other Lilliecrap, the question would not have arisen.

Despite PSV having this big-name striker, we held on with grim determination in the second half and came a step nearer the semi-final. We were all very proud of the Toon.

Kept in as usual for about twenty minutes after the game. Went back through that tunnel, which now opened on the other side straight onto a platform on which a train bound for Amsterdam was waiting. Yes, we had literally been in the 'Railway end', all right. No doubt loads of Geordies were headed back to the Dutch capital, though not the seat of government, which is The Hague, with a view to visiting the *Rijksmuseum*, the Anne Frank House or 'other sights'. Kept tight a hold of Brian's shoulders to make sure the pair of us didn't end up on a train or indeed on one of the buses waiting at the bottom of the steps. Farewell hugs and Chris and Sarah were whisked away on their coach. As they were getting on, you could here the cans of Heineken being cracked open. They later told us there had been a great party on the streets of Utrecht.

Had to talk our way past the police, who first insisted we should get on one of the buses. Some of them were heading for Denmark! Barry was waiting on the other side of the street. Said 'Hi Sarah, did you enjoy the game?' Of course he'd only switched twins in the meantime, hadn't he? Emilie was not best pleased at being mistaken for her sister and firmly instructed her Dad: 'Tell him I'm Emilie.' You just can't win, can you? We tried to signal through the windows of the Denmark-bound buses to ask why they'd come from that country. Were they our fans or theirs? There are connections on both sides. So there were two possibilities: either they were all relatives of Benny Arentoft or Jon-Dahl Tomasson, or of PSV's Danish assistant manager, Frank Arnesen.

Both cars were parked in the same car park, so there we set off in our different directions, Pete to the coast and Barry and family to the hotel.

At breakfast in the hotel the next morning, I asked Brian to go out into the foyer and bring me the local papers so we could read the match reports. He came back saying 'I couldn't find any, they're all on Iraq.'

'It doesn't matter if the headlines are on Iraq, they're bound to have a sports section at the back. Are you sure you couldn't get any?'

'No, go and see for yourself, they're all on Iraq.'

So I went out and found them – they were all hanging up on 'a rack', with a wooden slat down their spines and they were difficult to get off. Makes sense.

Meanwhile Sarah had been busy drawing a picture of the game. I asked her to write down her match report: 'I went to the football and saw Bobby and Alan Shearer and I had great fun with my daddy.' That's the spirit.

On the walk back to the car park the night before, we'd said that we'd all meet up again for the semi-final. Talk about counting your chickens all in one basket (as Sir Bobby might well say). All PSV needed at wor place was to sneak a one—goal win or draw twos apiece or upwards! In the event, the lads did us proud with a two-one victory after they had pulled level, and we were as good as on our way to Marseille.

Marseille – tales of woe

Everyone had been expecting another trip to Milan, to renew the battle with Internazionale after the previous year's two-all draw, when Newcastle had surely emerged as at least the moral victors. Preparations were being made – getting out the sou'westers, and oilskins, and rubber boots, and pith helmets to shelter from the storm of pith, sorry I mean piss, hockle, coins, razor blades, cigarette lighters, even mobile phones, which had rained down on our section from the disgusting eyeties ensconced above. How they didn't get a UEFA ban for that, God knows.

It was therefore with a mixture of some surprise and much relief that we learnt our next opponents were instead to be *l'Olympique de Marseille* – OM, with their motto of *'Droit au But'*, which unfortunately was to turn out to be sadly prophetic – 'straight to the goal'. Still, according to the inscription on my souvenir half-NUFC, half-OM scarf, their motto is *'Droit au Butt'*, which somehow sounds more like it: 'Right up yer arse'. I suppose it was intentional – it was knitted in England. There's a lot in common between Newcastle and Marseille: two post-industrial towns on the outer edges of their respective countries; a history interwoven with the sea; fanatical but fair supporters; Chris Waddle; Shearer's scored in both football grounds; the list goes on till it stops.

There are also plenty of differences: for one thing they don't need a roof on their stadium, because it doesn't rain (except when we visited, when the Barcelona effect briefly took hold), and secondly, they've won a few championships and also the European Cup in most people's living memory, whereas at the time of writing you have to be well into your second half century to have your own personal living memories of our last domestic trophy, the FA Cup in 1955. When I was a little lad, my favourite questions in a sports quiz book we had were: 'who has won the FA Cup the most times?' and 'who has appeared most times in the Final?' Certainly we were the answer for question one – six times, and I think we were just behind Aston Villa on question two. Don't bother looking now, you won't be happy with the up-to-date answers. We've notched up three more appearances in the last fifty years, if you can use the word 'appearances' to describe our performances, but no more wins.

'*Allons enfants de la patrie, le jour de gloire est arrivé*'. Those are the opening words of the French national anthem. Everyone knows the tune, of course – the Frogs pinched it from the intro to the Beatles' 'All you need is love'. Appropriately enough, the anthem is known as the '*Marseillaise*' (Marseille lass). Maybe many of us also went in search of love, who knows? But all we really needed was a goal; one lousy stinking rotten goal would see us through to the final of the UEFA Cup for the first time in thirty-five lousy stinking rotten years without a meaningful trophy to put NUFC firmly on the European footie map. Provided the *Marseillais* didn't score more than one, of course. Nowts apiece from the first leg gave us every reason to be at least hopeful, if not cheerful. Those opening words of the Frog anthem mean 'Come, children of the homeland, the day of glory has arrived.' On this particular occasion, they could equally have been rendered thus: 'Howay the lads, we can dee it!' Perhaps this was to be our day of glory, and the homeland concerned was Geordieland. We would then be on our way to Gothenburg wearing our cloth Viking helmets, riding on a 'cold wind to Valhalla!'

Now thirty-five years is a long time in anybody's book, except perhaps God's, of course. He presumably thinks in terms of eternity, set against which thirty-five years is a piddling trifle, maybe no longer than the average fart in heaven above. Imagine that, though but, farting around the place non-stop for thirty-five years – come to think of it, that's all Newcastle had been doing on the silverware front, unless of course you count the Texaco Cup. Hang on, though, we have won the Northumberland Senior Cup loads of times, and that's a trophy neither Man U nor the Arse have ever won.

'Fart', incidentally, is not unlike the German word '*Fahrt*' (or the Swedish word '*fart*' for that matter), whose pronunciation is very similar indeed but whose meaning can at best be described as being 'vaguely related': it means a journey or trip. You'll all have seen the word '*Ausfahrt*' on German motorway signs. Contrary to what any self-respecting Army of the Rhine squaddy will tell you, it is not the biggest town in Germany (it must be, it's signposted everywhere) - in fact it simply means 'exit'. One way of saying 'to fart' in German is '*einen fahren lassen*' (let one travel). So there's one to ponder next time you're thundering down the *autobahn*.

Even in the build-up to the Marseille trip, the excitement was taking its toll, and in the exchange of e-mails with Chris the pair of us were starting to take on a strangely French identity so as to ensure we would pass unnoticed on any unexpected undercover mission into the murk of the Marseille underworld. Here are some extracts from that most secret of wartime files. The exchanges plumbed their pathetic depths the day after the first leg:

'Salut Christophe

The words *putain de merde* sprang readily to mind when Ameobi should not only have burst the net, but the ball should have carried on drilling its way through the Leazes End and ended up in Leazes Park lake. Apart from that near heart attack, I stayed relatively calm thanks to the sedation I had self-prescribed: some rather charming 2001 Bergerac to get into the Frenchy flavour and some Warsteiner to remind myself that what we needed was some ruthless teutonic efficiency with a crisp antiseptic sting to it.

We can be really proud of last night's performance, though but, with Woody absolutely outstanding. I enjoyed the comment that he had also sorted his private life out, now that he is with the right club. The whole back four were rock solid and we were, and are, always going to create chances up front. We're still in it and we can bally well still win it. Have you already booked a hotel in Marseille, by the way?

Santé,

Pierre'

(If Jerry were monitoring this, he wouldn't have a clue what was going on! *Vive la résistance!*)

'Pierre,

We have booked our hotel in Marseille, but I'm not sure which one (I have people who arrange that sort of thing for me, y'know). I can find out for you if you like. That Bergerac/Warsteiner combination sounds fab - I had prescribed myself some Bar Oz Kronenbourg, but the dose was far too small because I didn't feel anywhere near sedated enough. (Note to self: double the dosage next time.) When Robert gave the ball away and handed them their best chance to score, I nearly had kittens (I have a 'special relationship' with next door's cat). I forgave him after a few minutes (Laurent, not the cat) - unlike the tit behind me who slagged him off throughout the match. The lad is a match-winner and he more than makes up for his dodgy moments with his goals and assists. I was going to explain this to the man behind, but it would have taken too long so I just head-butted him instead.

Christophe'

'Salut again Christophe,

Do not worry, mon ami, your secret concerning zee cat next door is safe with me. Mind 'ow you go and steer clear of zee Boche.

Pierre'

Fine undercover work there, Pete, I'd never have guessed. As for myself, how to travel there was easily sorted out. This time I took the opportunity to travel by the TGV high-speed train – nearly a thousand kilometres, city centre to city centre in five and a half hours – amazing. Occasionally the track runs parallel with cars in the fast lane on the motorway and they seem to be reversing back up the road as you flash past, the speed difference is so high. As the photo-montage of a man standing on the platform with his trousers round his ankles and a bog-roll in his hand showed in *Le Canard Enchaîné* (the French equivalent of Private Eye) the week the TGV (*train à grande vitesse*) started about twenty years ago, you've hardly got enough time to have a good shit before you've got to get off again. And as far as I'm concerned, it's a lot more comfortable and less stressful than a plane (and in terms of city centre to city centre times, it can be quicker, too!).

I agreed with Pete that I'd look out for a hotel. A scan of the Internet showed up a good choice at very reasonable prices, even in the vicinity of the *Vieux Port*, which was going to be the place to be, pre- and post-match. I reckoned there'd be no rush as Marseille's a big place and there were plenty of hotel rooms for a couple of thousand of us, so I set off to my meeting in Ireland thinking I'd book it while I was over there.

Kinsale is a harbour town near Cork, not as big or famous as Marseille, but more picturesque. A great place for music, food and drink, and also for spotting rainbows – the weather changes so fast that you get two or three a day. Cork Roy Keane Airport 'Above us only rainbows'. I've been told that a Dutch woman saw the potential and started up a restaurant in Kinsale around about twenty years ago when the little town was quite run down, and gradually attracted other people to open up more bars, restaurants, hotels, what have you, and now it's a boomtown (rats!). They've even got a hotel with a clock that tells you when it's high and low tide, and not many towns can boast that. Since April 2004, the Irish government have banned all smoking in bars, over fears of the staff being able to sue employers for passive-smoking-induced diseases, so you don't get stunk out. One of the rules is that if you go outside for a quick smoke, you have to stand at least ten yards away from the pub entrance. But I don't see how they can apply this law in Kinsale because if you move ten yards along from the pub door, you find yourself standing in the entrance of another bar, there are so many of them in every street. If you get a chance, go - you won't regret it. And while you're there, take a trip out to Cape Clear Island, where Gaelic is the spoken language and the land has hardly changed in hundreds of years. It's the last piece of Ireland the Titanic passengers saw before heading off towards America, except for the famous Fastnet Rock that stands about a mile out from the island. Speaking of nautical and musical disasters, you'll remember that's where Simon Le Bon's yacht sank in a storm, just as he was launching into the last chorus of that old sea shanty 'Rio' on that yuppie video. Pity Ireland doesn't have a better football team that we could go and play, though come to think of it, maybe some time Cork City might get into the first round of the UEFA Cup. Wor Jackie was manager of Linfield for a while, but it didn't have a lasting effect on their footballing prowess. Another thing they don't have is an Internet café that stays open in the evening after office hours, so I couldn't organise the Marseille hotel.

When I got back all the hotels in Marseille were full, so I made a provisional booking out at Marignane, the airport, 'above us only the lingering stigma of an early nineties football scandal', in the hope that there'd be some last-minute cancellations in town. With coming by train, it hardly made sense to have to go miles away to the airport, as we'd miss out on the atmosphere in town. I hadn't counted on Marseille having as many exiled fans all wanting to come back to their hometown for the match too, and so fill up all the hotels. It's something else they've got in common with Newcastle. When stories began to come out that a lot of Newcastle fans who'd sent in ticket applications were having their money returned, I figured there'd be some hotel cancellations, so I started phoning around again but the hotels were still jam-packed. I eventually found a *Résidence de Vacances*, which usually is a kind of apartment hotel for long stays of a week or a month, but amazingly they had places left. The *Maeva City Prado Perier* turned out to be the ideal solution – two stops along the metro line from the *Vieux Port* and one stop further to the *Stade Vélodrome*, brand new, spotlessly clean and even with its own kitchenette too if you fancied having a bash at a DIY *Bouillabaisse* fish soup, and only fifty-seven euros for a single or sixty-three euros for a double. You couldn't beat that.

So now we had our hotel and our trains, but still no tickets. We'd applied in the usual way by sending in our NUFC Box Office European Away Leg Application Forms, and we were hopeful that, with it being a 59,000-seater stadium with at least 3,000 places for away fans, we would be safe. But it was the semi-final, and in a decent place with easy travel links, so demand was high, too high for us to get tickets in any event. There was quite a furore in the local press, and on the Internet fans' sites, and quite a lot of people apparently sent complaints in to the Box Office. It would be interesting to find out how tickets really are allocated. If it's true that it is based on your last eight years' away games applications record, then it hardly seems fair to give first priority to people who book on the Club's own organised travel and match ticket package. It might be worth another letter to the Club Secretary. On the other hand, it might be worth talking to the wall.

We tried the OM route too, and were intrigued to learn that they have a different way from English clubs of handling ticket sales. You can of course buy tickets from the Box Office, but you can also purchase them from their numerous club shops around Marseille, including the OM bar in the *Vieux Port*. You can in fact even buy them directly through their Internet website, but you had to be extremely quick for the semi-final, because when we looked just a day after the draw, the online sale had already been closed. But the big difference is that the club also gives whole blocks of tickets out to be sold under the responsibility of supporters clubs – in fact all away ticket sales go through them. Marseille has quite a few supporters clubs, with blocks of tickets for different parts of the ground, which rival each other not only in the strength and number of their support, but also in selling tickets to their members. They have names like *Fanatics, Ultras, Winners, MTP, and Yankees*. It's interesting that they are trusted with ticket sales, and that there are so many different supporters clubs to choose from, all supporting the same team. They're quite advanced, these Froggies – they've leap-frogged ahead of us in this respect. The parallel history of the formation of rival sub-groups of fans in England got stuck at the more basic level of forming the LBAB Longbenton Aggro Boys and other rival boot boy gangs to have a fight with each other. Of course we now have supporters clubs based around the UK who organise coaches to matches, supporters' evenings and so on, but they haven't yet been entrusted with anything like the level of responsibility that we saw in Marseille. The nearest equivalent that we have seems to be the Scandinavian NUFC Supporters Club run by wor Christian in Oslo. In any case it's a very interesting and different way of running things and involving the supporters more in the running of the club – power to the people!

So for once, Barry's outstanding connections had failed to produce the goods, and like thousands of other faithful Geordies we were in a state of abject ticketlessness and were getting more and more desperate as the time tick(et)-tocked tantalisingly towards kick-off.

Desperate times call for desperate measures, so I got straight on to *e-bay* to chance my luck. As an *e-bay* virgin, I first had to register, which meant I had to choose a pseudonym. So I naturally opted for something Geordie. 'Bonny lad' had already been allocated, as had 'Wor lass', 'Wor bairns' and 'Haddaway and Shite' and

'HeyHinnyHoyaHammaOwaHeor'. I thought to myself 'wheyabuggama, perhaps I'm not the only Geordie to have tried this route' and chose instead one of our cats' second names. The (former) tom is called Panda Pandolowski Schlubelpludowski Kalashnikowski, while his sister is Kitty Katowska Schlubelpludowska Kalashnikowska. I was in Poland learning *polski* when Wor Lass told me on the phone that she and the bairns had got two cats. I wasn't to worry, though, as the tom was black and white and we were going to call him Panda. That was a bit of a porky, however, as he also has several shades of grey. But never mind, the pair of them are great crack and they never miss a televised Toon game.

So my e-bay pseudonym was *Pandolowski*. One or two clicks of the mouse (not the cat) and I had located a ticket for the match being offered by a Frog (that's quite a menagerie we're building up here). The bidding stood at one hundred and fifteen euros when I entered the fray. On being prompted, I immediately set my limit at two hundred euros and the system told me it would automatically keep upping the ante on my behalf till that figure was reached. So I got on with a bit graft and went back into e-bay about an hour later. On so doing, I immediately received the message that the ticket had gone for – you've guessed it – two hundred euros!! Being new to this game, I didn't know whether that meant I had got it or not. Anyway, you can click on a field to e-mail the vendor, which I did forthwith. In my very best French, I asked him (or her) whether I was the lucky one. 'Alas and alack', came the reply: 'No. But I have another two tickets available for one hundred and eighty euros apiece. Are you interested?'

'Does the Pope wear a funny hat?' I inquired. Of course I was f-flipping interested. Would I have bid two hundred euros for the first one? 'I'll pay three hundred and sixty euros for the pair, please do not sell to anyone else in the meantime!' I e-mailed back. That was late on the Tuesday afternoon/early Tuesday evening, and I couldn't hang around for a reply in the office as I had to get sausage-side sharpish to collect my daughter Tina from her jazz-dance class. As I belted down the *autobahn*, I asked myself why I hadn't had the presence of mind to give *Tigrou* (that was the Frog's e-bay pseudonym) my Kraut e-mail address.

Driving back into work from Deutschland the next morning, I was filled with trepidation: was I being taken for a ride by a Froggie tout? I was suitably nervous when I opened the mailbox, and my worst fears appeared to be borne out when reading *Tigrou's* mail sent that morning: "'ave been offered four hundred and ten euros for zee two tickets, are you prepared to offer more?' Now I hate these touts as much as the rest of you, but I really wanted to see us at Marseille. Shit, how often do we get to a European semi-final? I'll tell you how often: once every thirty-five years, that's how often! This was only the second time in my lifetime. Would I ever get another chance?

My previous e-mail to this git had been quite friendly in tone, but this time I kept it to the bare minimum: '*D'accord, quatre cents soixante euros pour les deux billets ensemble, mais c'est vraiment ma limite.*' (Okay, four hundred and sixty euros for the pair, but that is definitely my limit). I had already told him/her that I'd be arriving in Marseille dead early and could rendezvous basically anytime and anywhere. When the next e-mail suggested I should get my arse over to the Sainte Marguérite district for about eight-thirty in the morning, however, I began to get cold feet. Call me Mr Slightly Distrustful, but I had no idea what kind of district Sainte Marguérite was. Was it the Marseille equivalent of Elswick? Or was it somewhere where they wore 'for coats and nee knickers', how could I know? Had visions of myself being mugged and left for dead – this was French Connection country!

E-mailed back saying 'I'll take the first train to Marseille and I'll meet you at the station.' Sounds like I was writing a song for the Monkees. I felt, on balance, that the station would be a better bet (on the grounds that there would probably be an Edgar Wallace or two about) – that way there would be what one might call *'une sécurité optimale'* for both of us! The reply was that I should be at the entrance to platform C at half-past seven. *Tigrou* would go there on his/her way to work. I liked this 'on the way to work' bit, as it upped *Tigrou's* credibility considerably in my eyes.

I had kept Barry informed about these goings-on all along, of course, and he was – quite rightly – dead against the idea of buying from a tout as a matter of principle. But I didn't want to tell the Frog tout in advance that I was only in the market for one ticket in case he or she sold the pair in the meantime.

So that was how things stood as I sat in the train at Luxembourg station waiting for it to make its journey through the night to Marseille. I looked out of the window, wondering whether this ticket gadgy (or gadgy-ess) would even turn up. As an aside, the Bulgarian word for bloke sounds very like 'gadgy' as does, apparently, the Japanese word for 'stranger' or 'foreigner'.

My mind was filled with other disturbing thoughts too. Not least among them was: would the German beer I was drinking join forces with my chicken curry sandwich and produce a poison to rival the mustard gas in the trenches of the Great War, some of whose battlefields I would be speeding past while hopefully dossing in my sleeping compartment. This was the 19.46 from Luxembourg to Nice (*oh mein Gott*, 19.46, just one minute after the end of the second war) and it was scheduled to arrive in Marseille's St. Charles station at 5.17 the next morning (two minutes after The Who). My original plan had been to pay the extra and stop on till Nice, where it would arrive at about twenty past eight. That way I could have had a Nice lie-in, if you see what I mean. I would then have doubled back over, taking the next train from Nice to Marseille and taking in some steady views of the mountains and the Med as I had my SNCF *café et croissants*. That rather neat plan had been scuppered by the aforementioned minor inconvenience. To wit: we still didn't have any frigging tickets, did we!

I watched the former mining region of Lorraine speed past. It is, of course, the 'Lorraine' bit of 'Alsace-Lorraine', a region rich in coal and iron ore which over the centuries has been bounced back and forth between France and Germany and has seen more than its fair share of battlefield bloodshed. When the Roman Empire collapsed, Germanic tribes poured in and made it part of a German empire of sorts, off and on, until Napoleonic times. After the Congress of Vienna, it fell to France and then Bismarck seized it back after the Franco-Prussian War of 1870-71. It was German until the end of the First War, and then French till 1939. German again under Hitler till 1945, then back to France... you get the picture. All over the region, as we have already established, the people and the towns and villages have German names. Walk through a town like Metz or Strasbourg, and you could be forgiven for thinking you are in Deutschland. Metz central station is a cathedral-like celebration of German architecture and was opened by the then Kaiser himself not long after the end of the 1870-71 war.

Indeed, it was the Germans' mastery of the railways that enabled them to walk all over the French in 1870. The Krauts were ultra-efficient, whereas the Frogs were unable to organise the proverbial piss-up in a brewery. German troops were moved about the place with consummate ease, while the French railways were clogged up in a massive Froggy log jam. They had plenty of material and supplies; they just could not get them to the right place at the right time. The old logistics problem again... The Germans had it all sorted, however, and before you could say *Champs Élysées* in Del Boy's Peckham accent, Paris was under siege. At the same time, however, they were also besieging Metz and a few other fortress towns – that was the way the French organised their defences, pretty much along the lines of the Middle Ages, or Caesar's Gallic war for that matter! The Germans were nice and patient and waited till the inhabitants of the besieged towns starved. In Metz, things got so bad that they ate their horses. They must have liked the taste, because you can still order a jolly good horse steak in Metz restaurants. Neigh, I hear you say!

When you think about it, the Germans would never have mastered the railways had it not been for Geordie and Robert Stephenson, who got them started on the iron way in the first place. Without that they would never have won the Franco-Prussian war of 1870-71. One of the results of that war (German annexation of Alsace-Lorraine) was a major factor in eventually starting the First World War. One of the results of that war (France's recovery of Alsace-Lorraine plus the cession of land to Poland and Czecho) was a major factor in starting the Second World War. At the end of that, the German rocket scientist Werner von Braun was enlisted by the Americans to teach them how to make rockets. They then duly put men on the moon. ERGO: had it not been for George Stephenson and his son Robert, there would have been no such thing as the Apollo space programme. That means it was the Geordies who put man on the moon. That is probably why that boozer opposite the Central Library used to be called 'The Man in the Moon'.

About three quarters of an hour after leaving Luxembourg, the train stopped at Metz (the station opened by the Kaiser). Memories of the UEFA Cup game against Metz in the 1996-97 season came flooding back: snowbound on the autoroute, pre-match curry, young and unheard-of Pires playing for Metz, Tino tripped, Beardo pen...

The train pulled out of Metz, and I relaxed in my bunk. It was certainly jolly relaxing to watch the French countryside slide by in the setting sun. The only blemish on an otherwise perfect end to the day was the fact that I had run out of beer, so I tappy-lappied along to the end of the corridor for a slash and on the way back bought a couple of cans from the sleeping car attendant as a last nightcap before turning in. The first part of this particular French connection was well under way... zzz...

There I was on the touchline. Maybe it was that Wallsend Senior Schools cup final when my brother John was keeping goal outstandingly for Saint Aidan's at the Rising Sun footie ground, my Dad standing next to me bursting with pride. Saint Aidan's won, wor John made a couple of brilliant saves. But then I was standing on the railings at the back of the Popular right in front of Kenneth Wolstenhome's commentary position. I was hanging on to a bush so as not to lose my position. It was difficult to get a proper view of what was going on down on the pitch, but we were storming forward and Bob Moncur... the net bulged. It was heaven. I was back down at pitch level, running to keep up with the play but couldn't. Jumped up just in time to see the net bulge. It was the Marseille net this time. That was it. We had won. Must have been Shearer. Who cares? Could have been Robert. Actually, maybe it was me. Or wor lass. It was slow motion. It was like trying to swim faster but you can't. It was wading through treacle. But it doesn't get much better than this, man. We were all jumping up and down as one. Your lungs were bursting. There was just no air. You were trying to say something to your marra but couldn't. It was unreal yet it was so real. The Toon had done it. You were just floating, man, looking down at the seething mass of it all. A sea of black and white. We had done it. We were floating, that was it. Our feet just weren't touching the ground. 'Giant steps are what you take', as another Waalsend lad would say. We were no longer part of planet earth. And to cap it all, we could see on the horizon - set against a purple-haze sunset - a display of porcine aerobatics. Soaring and banking, ducking and weaving they were - and grunting 'oink' at each other. The Toon were in the UEFA Cup Final for the first time in thirty-five years. The Toon Army was in heaven. My arms were shooting up to the sky. I was floating, and reality was light years away.

A sudden air-cushioned pressure thud, and the slightly opened window rattled a bit. A flash of light as a train heading in the other direction thundered past and a dream was stripped naked for all to see. Must have been the early hours by now. Wasn't going to have a proper sleep anyway so might as well take stock. Bursting for a hit and miss... God bless SNCF: this carriage must have been sixties or even fifties stock, I guess. Very French, very SNCF and therefore very French-army green (there must have been a lot of spare paint around). The window was opened by a crank-type handle, which was steady. But the best feature of all in this sleeping compartment was the tippy-up piss-pot under the washbasin. No kidding! I must admit it took me a while to work it out, but a piss-pot it was, and a very useful facility it was too. You pull back this little flap under the washbasin, take out the pot, have a pee and place the pot back in its holder. Tilt the flap back into the upright position and the suitably angled piss-pot discharges onto the tracks – absolutely brilliant if you ask me. This convenience was very convenient but it makes you wonder a little bit, doesn't it? I remember being absolutely flabbergasted on a French campsite in the seventies by the fact that they had standy-up bogs. I mean: come on, standy-up bogs? In the 1970s? Had they not made any progress at all since Roman times? Not that I am knocking the Romans, mind, far from it!! The French call them 'Turkish' (the standy-up type bogs, that is, not the Romans). And I mean 'call', not 'called', because there are still a good few of them lurking about (including in at least one Marseille bar, as I was later to find out). Yet the only people who still use these Turkish bogs, as far as I know, are the French. Actually no, they have them in the more rural parts of Bulgaria, too. Maybe you have also come across them on your travels elsewhere? Even back in the 1970s the Turks had abandoned them – probably sold them all to French restaurants. It's revealing to note that the French say that they're going *aux toilettes* - to the toilets - while Belgians just say they're going to the toilet *à la toilette*. I suppose the French must be resigned to having to need to visit a few before they'll find a one in a clean enough state to use. Contrast that with the well preserved examples of the might of turn-of-the-century British bog engineering that we have spotted on our travels through Belgium and the Netherlands. For instance in those bars in Eindhoven and Breda. Names like Twyford, Shanks and Crapper have gone down in the an(n)als of urinal history and there's a good chance you'll see their names in any Dutch or Belgian hostelries of a certain age; Britain appears to have been the world leader in toilet technicalities in the late nineteenth and early twentieth centuries. You can flush with pride.

A bit more dozing, then semi-awake again. A full moon. We're well into the South of France by now. Well maybe it was only a 99.99% moon actually, as I think it was full the day before. It was still pretty good, though. A fitful sleep, the moon keeps waking me up. That's fine. A few more trains pass in the night, could swear I could smell lavender out there. Definitely something beginning with 'lav' anyway. Dose off again but the attendant wakes me at a quarter to five (wish I'd been staying on till Nice and doubling back – *mais les billets obligent*). Brushing of teeth etc. and a look out of the window. I had a view of the Med. In the distance I could even see that chapel, or whatever it is, perched up a height in Marseille above the *Vieux Port*. The yellow aura of the street lights shone on the red roof tiles of Marseille suburbia and mingled with that special light of a Mediterranean dawn to create a tingling early-morning glow, something special indeed. Wasn't it great to criss-cross Europe following the Toon? This was being part of something. Pity those poor mackems. Will they ever have these euro-trips?

The train pulled into Marseille St. Charles bang on time at 5.17 a.m. I had hoped that the Froggie railways would live up to their national reputation and be at least an hour late, but no such luck. The trains, it would appear, are the exception that proves the rule. What I did not realise is that St. Charles is a terminus station and the trains have to reverse out in order to embark upon their onward journeys. And that takes time, of course, uncoupling the original locomotive and setting everything up for the next loco. In other words, muggins here could probably have had an extra half an hour in bed, but as we say in English: *c'est la vie!*

As I put pen to paper again to continue this merry tale (okay, okay, so I'm hitting the keyboard again – it just doesn't have the same romantic ring to it, does it?), it is around seven minutes to ten in the evening on Wednesday, 19th May 2004. Mean anything to you? Well it should, because it's half time in the UEFA Cup Final in Gothenburg, and we should have been there. I was busy in the garden during most of the first half, taking Voltaire's sound advice and trying at the same time to take my mind off the fact that I wasn't in *Göteborg*, shouting for the Toon. As a minor aside here, why is it that UEFA sets the venue for the final even before the competition gets underway? I refuse to believe that it has got anything to do with backhanders from city councils. Okay, Sweden wouldn't have been a bad venue for the Toon v. Valencia. But Marseille v. Valencia? Fans are not made of money, and I genuinely feel sorry for the people from the shores of the Med who had to trek that far north. Why not Switzerland, or Barcelona, or Mallorca or Corsica or the Eternal City (Rome, that is, not Newcastle this time)? One thing is for sure, and that is that the fans are the last people to be given any consideration in UEFA competitions.

I came in from the garden just in time to see Barthez go mad and give away that penalty just before half time, and for good measure get sent off at the same time. One-nil to Valencia. Why couldn't the baldy French git have done something similar against us? Listened to some of Günter Netzer's pearls of wisdom at half time. The cameras then went over to a sizeable group of suitably attired Celtic supporters who had got tickets well in advance and made the trip anyway. Tried to spot Barry, Brian, Sarah and Emilie somewhere in with them. What a fantastic occasion that would have been: the Toon v. the Celts. The crack in the boozers before and after would have been fantastic, whatever the result. I'm a left-footer as my forebears came from Potatoland, so am therefore an honorary Celtic supporter of the second order (i.e. after the Toon), so there would have been a smidgen of consolation if the result had gone the wrong way. Half time was also livened up by a streaker – maybe it was a Newcastle Celt who was in such a dilemma about the colours to wear that he ended up wearing nothing at all! Who knows? Who cares? I couldn't bring myself to watch the second half, lest it should give me nightmares. Does anyone know what the result was?

So out I gets in Marseille. I had two hours and a bit to kill before the rendezvous with *Tigrou*, so my first concern was to deposit my suitcase and go for a coffee. Unfortunately, the left-luggage office did not open until seven, the café thankfully half an hour earlier. The newsagent was open, however, so I bought two of the local papers. One of them, *la Provence*, was running a semi-final special, the headline on which read *Offrez-nous la finale!* – Give us the final! It was a sentiment I could relate to.

All around me in the waiting area were (first or second generation?) Arabs. In some quarters, the city's population is in fact predominantly Arab. Marseille is sometimes referred to, not inaccurately, as one of the biggest Arab cities in the world. For the record, it is also the third biggest French-speaking city in the world, after Paris and Montréal. In terms of the Arab aspect, Marseille clearly has a lot in common with South Shields. From my visits to the partially re-constructed Roman Governor's residence in South Shields, or *Arbeia* (go, it is brilliant), and the Roman fort of *Segedunum* in Wallsend (go, it is brilliant), I know that even in Roman times there were Arabs (from present-day Iraq) in South Shields. They obviously liked it so much that they stayed on and are there to this day.

People can say what they like about Tyneside, but in one particular respect we have been very lucky. Over the centuries, immigrants have come from the four corners of the globe (they still do) and the place is a veritable melting pot. Okay, there are some rough bits all right, but generally speaking people have mixed in and in the end we are all Geordies, some of us with secondary affiliations. The pattern of immigration is still to be seen even today: the Arabs in South Shields, Scandinavians in North Shields, Catholic Irish in Jarrow and across the water in Willington Quay, Protestant Irish in Hebburn, Jews in Gateshead, Asians in the Big Lamp area, etc. And every one of them qualifies as a Newcastle United supporter, no problem!

But in Marseille, at any rate, there are loads of Arabs. Quite what so many of them were doing milling around St. Charles station at half past five on a Wednesday morning I couldn't work out. Perhaps one of them was *Tigrou* (*Abdul Mustafa Fistfulla Euros Al Tigrou*?) and the rest were his marras – I had no way of knowing. Be that as it may, you have got to be on your toes at any big station in any big city, whether you are surrounded by Geordies, Brits, nuns, you name it!

In my half-awake/half-asleep state, my mind drifted by association to the famous novel *L'étranger*, 'the stranger', by the French existentialist author Albert Camus. He actually won a Nobel literature prize for it. The novel is set in Algiers, Camus' hometown, when Algeria was regarded by the French as part of France, though the Arab Algerians did not quite agree. The main character is a selfish, self-centred git who ends up shooting someone (a complete stranger) on the beach, for no better reason than that the sun was beating down and generally making him feel uncomfortable. Two shots rang out. *Avec ces deux coups j'ai frappé sur la porte du malheur* – roughly translated: it was with these two shots that I knocked on the door of sorrow. Two shots – yeah, they knocked on the door of the Toon's sorrow with two shots later that day, that's for sure.

Went for a *café et un croissant* at half six and duly plonked the suitcase in a left-luggage locker at seven. Walked up and down a bit to 'reconnoitre the fisk', as my brother Mick says (I am sure he just made that up, the bugger – all I know is that *fisk* is Danish, Swedish and Norwegian for 'fish', which is a bit fishy to say the least) and took up my position at the head of platform C at around seven-fifteen. These were tense moments. Would *Tigrou* turn out to be some desperado hell-bent on avenging that murder in *L'étranger*? Or maybe some great hairy deserter from the French Foreign Legion? Or just an out-and-out *mafioso*, who would silently apply his stiletto knife to deadly effect and make off with my wallet?

In the event, *Tigrou* was a slightly-built seventeen or eighteen year-old who was clearly terrified, certainly not by me but by the whole situation. After all, there we were on a main-line station concourse where there were not only loads of Edgars (polisses) but also armed soldiers on terrorist alert. The dialogue was straight out of John le Carré: *'C'est Pandolowski?'* came the inquiry. Well it had to be me, really, as I was the only prat on the station concourse wearing a black and white shirt under their jacket. *'C'est Tigrou?'* came my equally puerile response. *'Oui' 'Tu as les billets?' 'Tu as l'argent?* And so on. I immediately suggested we move out of the public glare to a post box on a wall running parallel to the platform. Thankfully, I was starting to feel in control of the situation. I made it clear to my little Froggie friend that I needed to check the tickets carefully to make sure they weren't forgeries, or should that be 'froggeries'? The fact was not lost on me that, had my little Froggie friend been a big Froggie bar steward, I would have been quaking in my boots and only too willing to hand over the readies forthwith. But fate had dealt me a kinder hand than I could have dared hope for and my coffee-induced confidence was sky-high. 'These tickets', says I, 'are twenty-euro tickets for the Marseille Leazes end'. This was in the same tone as Michael Caine in the 'Italian Job' when he is released from the Scrubs and is picked up by his bird driving a Roller: 'This car' (dramatic pause for effect and don't forget you should be reading this bit in M. Caine's cockney accent) 'belongs to the Pakistani ambassador'. The point I was ever so subtly making was that I was not going to pay two hundred and thirty euros a shot. 'I have just read in the local paper that tickets are going for up to twice their face value. I'll give you four times what these tickets are worth – eighty euros each. You can take it or leave it!' Again, it's best to read that bit with the Michael Caine accent, 'coz it's a bit like that scene when they're somewhere in the middle of the Alps and the Mafia are threatening to shoot them. Michael Caine, however, reminds them that 'there are tens of thousands of Italians in Britain. Ice cream parlours, restaurants, gambling dens. In London, Manchester and Glasgow. You kill us, and Mr Bridger will make them suffer!'

What I should have said, with hindsight, was 'I am taking these tickets off you now at face value, so f*** off back home and don't let me see you here again'. Unfortunately I didn't have the benefit of hindsight. But I did have the satisfaction of sending *Tigrou* an e-mail a couple of days later congratulating Marseille on reaching the final and offering my two final tickets for nine hundred and thirty euros each, which corresponded to the mark-up he had originally expected for the semi-final tickets. Even if he had offered that, I would not have sold them to him! He didn't reply.

Later that day, we could have bought a pair of twenty-euro tickets in the Marseille Leazes end for sixty euros each – such is life! The tickets we had were printed with the title 'Fanatics', one of the supporters' club names. The ridiculously low face value of only twenty euros, about twelve pounds, led us to wonder what kind of zoo we were soon to be caged in, as it was obviously going to be the cheapest and probably rowdiest part of the ground. And maybe we'd find *Tigrou* standing there surrounded by his big brothers.

Tickets safely stashed in my wallet, safely stashed in turn in my jeans pocket (by far the safest place), I made my way through the streets of Marseille towards the *Vieux Port*, just as the city was becoming properly awake and the reassuring smell of coffee and croissants wafted out of every café you passed. Why is the smell of coffee, croissants and baguettes coming out of a French café so much more inviting than in Belgium or Luxembourg? A mystery, and a definite plus point for France.

Stopped at a street corner to send Barry a text message telling him the *Adler* had landed, as it were. 'Don't ask any questions, but we've got our tickets, bonny lad.' A twenty-minute walk later and the old port was at its picture-postcard best under the clear blue sky of an early morning in early May. The crying seagulls gave it a hint of home. There was still a wee bit nip in the air (I blame all these Japanese radios), but the excitement generated by the rush-hour bustle of a Toon match day left no room for the cold. A nice strong coffee and maybe another croissant for good measure and everything would be hunky-dory. The sight of all the luxury yachts in the harbour made me more determined than ever not to forget to put the lotto on when I got back home. Looking square onto the old port and its yachts, with only a very busy road in-between, is the OM Bar, the Marseille supporters' own boozer, complete with little souvenir shop. The nearest thing they have to the Strawberry, I suppose.

I clearly wasn't the first Geordie to have graced the hallowed precincts of *la Fraise* in the past twenty-four hours because as I was having a pre-third-coffee-of-the-day slash I read on the mirror before me the immortal words (written evidently in lipstick, mind! – and this definitely was the Gents!): 'Have you ever seen a mackem in Marseilles? Have you f**k!' With poetry like this, who needs the Sun? You can see it definitely wasn't me who wrote it, of course, as whoever did had put an 's' in 'Marseilles', which is the standard English way. Now me, I always go for local colour. For some unknown reason, the English language goes around surreptitiously sticking 's' on the names of French towns such as Marseille(s) and Lyon(s), presumably to take revenge on the French language for calling London *Londres* and Dover *Douvres*, though personally I couldn't care less if they referred to both of them as 'southern English shitholes' (note the 's' on the end).

My little exchange with the very friendly waiter, who immediately recognised my colours, confirmed what I already knew about Marseille people. Like the Geordies, they have a very pronounced accent! Unlike UK English, French French (as opposed to African or Canadian French, for example) does not really have a wide range of accents. There is basically Parisian French, which just about everyone else tries to imitate, and then there is the accent of the South of France, one variant of which is to be found in Marseille. It has something of an Italian musical twang to it. Easy on the ear, certainly, but it takes some tuning into.

The bar was equipped with several TV screens, and as I was slurping (or should that be 'sloping'?) my coffee, the morning news had reached the sports slot (or should that be spotes slurt?), which was heavily focused on what was indisputably the match of the day. They showed the highlights from the first leg, and when I saw the Ameobi-in-front-of-the-Leazes scene, albeit for at least the twentieth time, I was still as convinced as ever that the ball would burst the net, bore its way through the concrete of the Leazes End and end up in Leazes Park lake. Unfortunately that did not turn out to be the case. When I asked for the '*addition*', I also asked if it would be a good idea to come back to this bar after the match, no matter what the result. '*Pas de problème*', I was told, which struck me as being pretty steady.

It was still very early of course, not later than nine o'clock I guess, so I resisted the temptation of ordering a pint or *un demi* – that could wait another hour or so - and decided instead to go for a nice brisk walk. As I was leaving the bar, I was stopped by a chappy with a south-of-the-Tees accent who introduced himself as Paul and asked me if I would like to be interviewed by Talk Sport radio. 'Whey aye man', says I.

There they were, all set up in one corner of the terrace in front of the OM bar. There was obviously a broadcast underway, as some baldy gadgy with headphones on was jabbering away into a microphone, evidently engaged in conversation with a studio team in England. I asked Paul who the gadgy was and it turned out it was former England star Alvin Martin. I managed to subdue my incipient yawn and the burning question 'who?' But suddenly the old grey cells stepped up a gear and the words 'Trevor Brooking's old club' and 'hat-trick against us' thrust themselves to the very forefront of my by now otherwise stultified and sleep-deprived consciousness. So here was I, about to be interviewed immediately after the great Aston Martin on Talk Sport. Or was it the other way round?

There was a bit of a break in the proceedings and some other gadgy with what vaguely sounded like a diluted Scouse accent filled me in on the procedure. Piece of cake really: I would be asked a couple of questions and given the opportunity to reply. Yeah, I reckoned I could just about handle that. Making small talk, he asked what I thought about Lua Lua. Didn't get it, so he told me LL had been asked to return to the Toon in its hour of need and apparently had refused. What did I think? Well, not the sort of thing I think I could repeat in front of my mother.

Absent Martian had evidently been asked (by Alan Brazil, as I subsequently learned) whether he thought we had any chance against Marseille. The short summary of his answer is 'no'. This pissed me off just a little wee bit. But now it was my turn to answer a few questions before a live radio audience of one or two British sports fans. I suppose that, had I had a terrific night's sleep and I'd been able to focus fully on what I was doing, I would have been a bit nervous. As it happened, however, I had just listened to Alison Matron (what part of Tyneside is he from, then?) spout off some load of shite. The sun was shining, I was in Marseille, I was on a different plane anyway. My mind had drifted back to Albert Camus, who when he wasn't writing existentialist novels was actually a useful goalkeeper – such a pity he died in a car accident in Algeria in 1960, such a pity he never played for Newcastle: 'there's only one Albert Camus, one Albert Camus...' In other words I didn't give a shite and was ready for anything.

I had given the Scouse lad my basic details and so was introduced accordingly. 'And here below the blue skies of Marseilles we have just met a Geordie lad having a coffee in the OM Bar. Though he doesn't live in Geordieland anymore, tell us about it, Pete...' Blah, blah, blah. Then the first real

198

question from Alan Brazil. 'Can Newcastle do it?' 'Well, Alan, Absinthe Marlin is right when he says it'll be difficult... blah, blah, blah... but of course we can f***ing do it!!!' And then the next question: 'And how does it feel to be the last club flying the flag in Europe?' Now this type of thing really pisses me off: 'Whose flag might that be, Alan?' 'England's! The English flag! Chelsea went out last night! Newcastle are the last club left representing Eng-e-land in Europe!' 'Hang on, Alan', says I, 'this is about Geordieland, not England. This is about the Geordie nation; the only flag we are flying is black and white, not red, white and blue (especially not the red bit)! We are Geordies and from Newcastle, not England.' I think the last comment may have been a bit beyond the average Talk Sport listener whose reaction was probably: 'Do me a favour, mate. Knock it on the 'ead. Leave it out,' etc. Appreciative laughter back in the studio. But I wasn't joking. I could not give a shite about England or the English team. When Newcastle players are in the England team, my only concern is that they are not injured. I am a Geordie. I do NOT want to be associated with the mindless morons who go around singing En-ge-land, En-ge-land, etc.' My national team is Newcastle United and my patriotism does not extend much further south than Gateshead. I have to admit that I make a slight exception to this otherwise iron rule when England play Germany. That's when I genuinely want England to win. But that is only because wor lass was born sausage-side (bless her *Baumwollsöckchen*).

After the interview, I strolled about the old port area for about an hour, signing autographs (only kidding). Plenty of locals wanted to have a bit crack, though, when they saw the shirt, and the banter was very friendly. Decided it was about time for a pint and hit upon a boozer just outside the *Vieux Port* metro station called (appropriately enough) *Bar Métro*, which as chance would have it was directly behind Chris and Sarah's hotel, *la Mascotte*. That hotel is on a street called the *Canebière* (Can of beer? Aye, very canny!), which has a bit of a dodgy reputation on account of pickpockets and similar scum. In fact, the club advised supporters to avoid the district altogether. So what did they do? They all went there, of course! But quite frankly there were so many of us in the end that by midnight it was almost a district of Newcastle.

Sitting outside the *Bar Métro* was a bunch of lads from Darlington, and on the balconies of the Hotel Mascotte some Toon flags were already on display, so - all in all - Geordie could feel pretty much at home. Presently a guy wearing a Man U shirt came into the bar and wished the Toon well. He had a cockney (well, okay, Surrey) accent, as you might well expect of a Man U supporter (hanger-on?) but was a pleasant chap nonetheless. It turned out that he and their lass were on a Mediterranean cruise and the ship had had to put into Marseille because of storms!! Bad omen. (Man U supporter wishing us well, I mean!)

The crack with the Darlington lads was grand, and slowly but surely the seats in front of the café filled up with more and more Toon wallahs. A couple from Corbridge sat down at the next table to me and a baldy lad from Leicester soon joined us. His accent may have been a bit dodgy, but his credentials were second to none, his Dad having been forced to leave the Holy Land to seek work in pits te the sooth for the rest of his days. My Dad almost took a job in a car factory in Coventry in the late sixties, so I could easily have found myself in a similar position. All in all, the Midlands can to all intents and purposes be regarded as a Geordie colony, *n'est-ce pas*?

It's one of the great things about these Toon Army Trips, isn't it though but? You meet so many fundamentally nice and interesting people, all of them with a tale or two to tell. It really pisses me off when people start moaning about football hooligans, etc. I am sick of having to tell them: we are not hooligans; we are ordinary respectable people enjoying a hobby. Okay, so it does verge on religion, but where's the harm in that? Yes, there will always be a lunatic element. But with a bit of effort it can be stamped out forever, it really can!

So there we were, sitting outside the café, quaffing our Kronenbourgs, when along came a film crew from the local Marseille TV station. I wasn't in the business of pushing to the front of the queue, but honestly nobody was interested, so when the lady interviewer asked me I said 'Whey aye, bonny lass', or was it *Bien sûr, jolie fille*? Well, they asked the usual things of course – what did we think of the town, the locals, etc. Needless to say, I said I thought everything was brilliant, and I also stressed that the vast majority of Newcastle supporters were decent people who had come to Marseille to enjoy themselves and make friends, which when you think about it was nothing more than the truth! I was beginning to feel like a media junkie, mind. To round off this particular interview, the entire Toon congregation in front of the *Bar Métro* gave a stirring rendition of the Blaydon Races.

By now the midday sun was beating down good and proper (shades of Camus again) and my common sense alarm system told me it would probably be a good idea to get to the hotel and have a doss. Well done Barry on having switched our original Novotel Marseille Airport reservation to a hotel, or rather a *résidence,* only a couple of metro stops away from the old port. The value for money was just amazing: for our fifty-seven euros we had rooms easily the standard of a three- or even four-star hotel.

Had an hour's doss. Chris rang to say Sarah and he were at the airport, so we arranged to meet in the old port at half past four. I then rang Barry's mobile and he told me he was in the hotel. Which room? Number nine. That was next door! It must have been one of the world's most expensive phone calls measured in euros per metre per second, relayed from number ten room to Germany to Belgium and back to number nine room. Barry then rang Nice-based Don, presumably via telephone relay stations in Belgium and the UK, and we decided we should all converge on the old port forthwith, which we duly did. Don must have this thing about being based in a town at least a couple of hours from wherever the match is - for the Basel game he was in Zurich, remember. Maybe it's just to make it more difficult for their lass to keep tabs on him, like! Only kidding – it has a lot more to do with Ryanair's imaginative siting of their destinations.

Hey Barry, I'm getting repetitive strain injury here tapping away at this keyboard. Take over for a bit, will ya?

Nee problem, Pete. We headed back on the metro to the *Vieux Port* to breathe in, no, that's not the right expression; I mean drink in, the atmosphere. Talking of metros, what have the Paris and Marseille metros both got that the Newcastle one hasn't? I'll give you a clue: it hits you as soon as you descend the escalators into the bowels of the two French ones ... the smell. What is it that gives off that special French perfume?

There are a few possibilities. I was almost convinced by a French colleague while we travelled daily on the Paris metro to and from a conference that it was unique to Paris and that it was the smell of the catacombs. You know, where they used to stack up the slake-limed skulls and bones of past citizens. You can visit them if you're that way inclined - it's near the Châtelet - Les Halles metro interchange, where by the end of the conference I was eventually persuaded that the smell got strongest. But now when I had my first trip in the Marseille metro, here was that self-same peculiar pong again. So do they have a load of old slaked bones there too? Or maybe there's a clue in that you don't get the smell in Newcastle's metro, or even in London's tube. Could it be the fragrance of the French? Is it still true that they use less soap but more perfume than any other European nation? It was unkindly rumoured that 'Lens' Armstrong was finally disqualified from the *Tour de France* when they found, hidden in his hotel bathroom, three substances that are banned in France – toothpaste, deodorant and soap! That could explain it. Mind, Marseille are sponsored by Indesit washing machines so it's probably not that, as the power of advertising should ensure they're pretty clean by now. Someone asked whether it could be because the French put rubber tyres on their metro trams? Now there's a mystery waiting to be solved.

Speaking of shirt sponsors, which team has the most embarrassing one? Marseille and their Indesit washing machines are contenders, like Liverpool with their Candy washing machine logo of yesteryear, and so too were Real Madrid when they used to have Teka cookers on their shirts (slowed them down a bit, all that excess weight). Now they have Siemens on their shirts, so they could certainly do with putting them through an Indesit wash. Then there's Portsmouth with their Ty stuffed toys emblem – now that must come pretty near the top of anyone's list of cringe-worthily embarrassing shirts. How can anyone wear one of those without the nagging fear that someone's going to call them a teddy bear or a fluffy bunny? Of course, for a year we had Greenall Whitney, which was pretty shameful for a city that is the home of one of the most famous beers in the whole world.

Mind you, my Beer Bible by the famous Beer Hunter, Michael Jackson, informs me that Newcastle Brown Ale is not a brown ale at all but in fact something like a Viennese copper ale. Can't imagine that catching on, though: 'Bottle of Viennese Copper, please Pet.' I don't think so. Don't you just hate it the way some southerners will talk of 'Newky Brown'? Personally, I didn't realise they brewed brown ale in Newquay.

Then you have Everton with something that looks a bit Japanese called Keijan – it's not immediately funny, but what is it? Does anyone know? It might be something disgusting in Japanese. Anyway, whatever it is, whoever pays Everton is wasting their money, because the message isn't getting across if it's supposed to make you want to eat or wear or drive one. We're not immune to this kind of problem ourselves. You would think everyone would know that Northern Rock's a building society. But no, we've met people on our travels who think it must be a local rival to Broon. As in 'a pint of your finest Northern Rock, barman, kind sir!' I'm sure there'll be some fantastic ones in the lower divisions where the sponsors are usually very local firms, maybe something like 'Bogshift'll unblock your U-bend' or 'Charlie's Pile Ointment'. Off the top of my head, I can't find anything worse than Portsmouth's fluffy bunnies. Nominations please. Any ideas, Pete?

How about Vaux? Couldn't get funnier than that. Anyway, we got to Chris and Sarah's hotel ahead of schedule, so I rang them from reception in my best Inspector Clouseau accent saying 'Zees eez zee sûreté Marseillaise, pleeze to bring down zee passpor's for zee control.' Chris was having none of it, however. All he said was: 'You're not foolin' me, bonny lad!' In the meantime, Barry had been on the mobile to Don, who was in the *Bar des Arts* (or was it *Bar des Artistes*, or *Bar des Pisse-Artistes*, can't remember), not a goal-kick away from Chris and Sarah's hotel, so thither we duly tappy-lappied...

Don and co. were in thirst-quenching mode, warp factor two, when we arrived at the *Bar des Arts*. The whole *Vieux Port* was by now heaving with Toon wallahs, a veritable sea of black and white. Don was with a crowd of lads that included Bruce and Jim, a couple of old boys from Don and Barry's *alma mater*, the RGS.

Yes, Pete, we were all there at various times in the sixties and seventies. It was thanks to Bruce, who'd been in the same class as Don and my brother Ian, that we'd got our tickets for Basel. Incidentally, Brian Redhead and Roger Utley also went to our school, as well as Lord Justice Taylor, who did away with terracing after the Hillsborough and Bradford disasters. That's one of the great things about these occasions - the number of chance meetings and reunions that are thrown up. Though I never met any of those three at a Toon match. I hadn't seen Bruce for nigh-on thirty years and if it hadn't been for Don we'd never have recognised each other – the ravages of the barber's scissors since the seventies, and of time itself, I'd suppose you'd say...

At the second Barcelona game we'd bumped into Ian, another schoolmate who'd been in the same class as Don, Bruce and my brother Ian, too. He has a great story to tell about our school and the Fairs Cup Final. Ian had put his name down for the school camping trip to Ryedale, but only a couple of days later he managed to get himself a ticket for the first leg of the Final. Elated, he went straight round to cancel his place on the trip, but the school refused and said his name was on the list and he had to go. To pile insult onto injury, he had the excruciating task of selling off his ticket. Said treasure (remember they could have sold the 59,000 tickets twice over) found its way into the hands of a prefect who went on the same camping trip as Ian but, and I think you might count this as just a teensy-weensy bit unfair, he was allowed the night off to go back up to see the match. Can you believe it? Strange but true, as are other apocryphal tales from our school, including bare-arsed swimming lessons and sawn-off cricket bats to help you remember times tables. Another time, another planet almost. In some small way, history repeated itself in Barcelona where Ian was again one of the unfortunates: he had to go back straight after the match was postponed so he didn't get to see that game either.

But for the grace of a possibly left-footed deity, it could have been me at your school, Barry. So thanks again, God! I don't recall any sawn-off cricket bats or bare-arsed swimming at the Cuths, but I mind the time I had to duck sharpish to get out of the flight path of a blackboard duster hurled my way for wrong-guessing the third person plural, imperfect tense, of a second-conjugation Latin verb. Still, you know what they used to say: 'Spare the sawn-off cricket bat or board duster and you'll spoil the child'. If teachers did that sort of thing these days, they'd probably end up in Durham Jail.

Getting back to the *Vieux Port*, at one point I went to the bar to order another round in French. Quite reasonably, Jim asked 'What is the point of learning foreign languages?' This is never an easy question to answer.

I could have given the longish answer, going on about how each language is a window on the world, learning the languages of our European neighbours actually gives you a better understanding and command of our own native tongue, etc. That it opens the door to a wealth of literature, philosophy, and song, which you can enjoy best in its original beauty. Or that it helps ward off Alzheimer's by keeping the brain alert... But life's too short, so I opted for the short answer, which is 'It makes it easier to follow the Toon around Europe, AND it gets you served quicker in foreign boozers!' There was no arguing with that.

The *Vieux Port* is lined with waterside bars (as you would expect of an old port), and every bar was stowed out with fans in Black and White, with a good representation of Light Blue-bedecked OM fans too. Things went along swimmingly with great bonhomie between all concerned, with the only hiccup being that quite a few bars ran out of beer. Come to think of it, that sentence isn't really expressed too well, because there was no swimming as miraculously no-one fell in the water, and there were plenty of hiccups on the part of satisfied drinkers. According to the local papers the next day, the bar-keepers had their best single day's takings for years, far better than when Inter Milan had been in town a couple of weeks before, because all they did was sip *cappuccinos*, and also topping the Koppites who'd been there in the round before that. We'll be welcomed back with open arms.

As one bar ran out of beer, the crowds moved onto the next. At one point, we gave the local bottled beer *Bois Marseille* a try, and we can report without the slightest fear of contradiction that our own most famous bottled beer has nothing to fear from *Bois Marseille*, which had that same indefinable and unwelcome extra *je ne sais quoi* which separates the French and Newcastle metros. On the same train (ha ha) of thought, one of our party, Jimmy, succeeded in emptying a bar himself before it had run out of beer, by the simple expedient of releasing two massively disgusting silent killers. It was no big problem because the bar had a sunny terrace with fresh sea breezes to protect everyone from renewed chemical attack. And as we stood outside in the sun, a bus passed by with the name *Robert* emblazoned along the side – could this have been an omen? We hoped so.

One of the barmaids in the *Vieux Port* was so short that she could hardly see over the counter, but you could just glimpse that she was wearing an OM shirt with what looked at first glance to be the letters 'SMB' across the back, but in actual fact was 'SBM'. What immediately sprang to my mind was 'Sad Mackem Bastard', with the modification that in French you put the adjective after the noun, as in 'Sad Bastard Mackemme'. Though to be perfectly grammatical it would need to have been BSM, *Bastard Sadde Mackemme*. However this would clearly have had the aesthetic drawback of being confused with the British School of Motoring, and hence must be rejected. Clearly there was nothing for it but to take a souvenir photo with the SBM, feeling a bit like Lee Clark at Wembley. The barmaid was happy to have her portrait taken, but she couldn't quite get the hang of why we wanted her to stand facing away from the camera. It turned out that, unsurprisingly enough, SBM were her initials and her full name was something like Saria Ben Mohammed, which was too long and too expensive to fit on her shirt. However I have my suspicions that they actually stood for Short Bar Maid.

We left for the ground fairly early, which turned out later to have been a good idea because of the complications that were to follow. One of the abiding memories as we left the *Vieux Port* was of a Newcastle supporter fast asleep on a terrace outside the OM bar, where his mates had abandoned him with a traffic cone perched on his head. He made the front page of the Marseille papers the next day.

We piled off the metro, following the crowd, though not before helping a nearly blind old lady with a giant wicker basket shopping trolley on and off the tram and finding her a place where she wouldn't get crushed. It was Marseille's own version of Viz's Mrs Brady, old lady. *Madame Femme, vieille dame.* Again, and as always, spreading Geordie goodwill wherever we go. We strolled to the ground, which is in the middle of a huge Exhibition Park, aptly enough, though without the Boating Lake and without any sign of the Steam Ship Turbinia (don't tell me, I know it's been moved to Blandford Street, but they should have left it in its natural setting). Which reminds me: when my mother was a little girl, the teacher took them on a school trip to the Science Museum in Exhibition Park. This is back in the early thirties, mind, when the Turbinia was most certainly still on its original foundations, and still quite a modern, up-to-date invention, come to think of it. Well, the museum guide showed them a torpedo on display by the side of the Turbinia, and explained how it could travel at high speed through the water when launched from a ship, though not necessarily the Turbinia. After his explanations, he asked for any questions, and my mother piped up with the jaw-dropper 'But where does the man sit?'

Meanwhile back at Marseille's own Exhibition Park, a very pleasant *policier* came over with his colleague and explained that it was his job to escort us to the ground. What fantastic personal service, we exclaimed. And it was. He was very friendly, though he did insist on calling the four of us under his guard *'Les Cassosses'*. I most look up what that might mean. Obviously he'd shortened the name Newcastle and come up with his preferred nickname, which maybe was somehow to do with *'casse-os'*, bone breakers, but I'm not sure. It was no fault of his, but it was to say the least ironic that it was at this point, while under police escort, that one of our small entourage, namely Don, got robbed! Amid all the joviality and general good humour and in the bright evening sunlight, a Marseille supporter came over and insisted on swapping shirts with Don - a Marseille dark blue away shirt for a Toff's Supermac replica. Much shaking of hands and patting on the back and 'may the best team win' (*'que la meilleure équipe gagne'*), and then he was off. At the first security check a minute later, Don went to his pocket to show his ticket and it was no longer there. Luckily it wasn't the actual turnstile, and he got through this first hurdle amidst the confusion of the many other supporters arriving at the same time. Desperate searching as we were shown into a big empty warehouse, but he'd definitely no longer got his ticket. Don had made the wrong kind of French Connection, and there was no sign of Popeye Doyle anywhere to bail us out.

At least Don hadn't lost the NUFC instruction sheet that had been delivered with his ticket. Paragraph seven explained that all the away supporters would be held in a marshalling-yard operation in a hangar of a building - actually an exhibition hall, but you couldn't get a pint of Ex anywhere. The authorities clearly wanted to make sure that there wasn't any mad stampede into the ground and that everyone's tickets were in order. When we first went up to the stewards, Pete and I were in front of Don and they took a look at our tickets and, without seeing that Don had no ticket, ushered all three of us across to a group of fans who, like us, had tickets for the Marseille section. It reminded us of a lost passport incident at the Channel Tunnel French border a few years before. We'll tell you some more about that soon.

There must have been thousands of us in the hangar. The local papers reckoned that a total of eight thousand NUFC supporters would be making the trip, and only three thousand had away section tickets. The rest was up to the black market. If you had an away ticket, you passed through the turnstiles and out into the stadium. This was all happening about an hour before kick-off. We weren't sure whether the rest of us were being held before being let in, or before being sent away from the ground, or what, but the mood was optimistic. With the exception of Don and two other victims of pick-pocketing who'd linked up with us when they heard Don had the same problem as them.

We weighed up whether it was better to go across and draw attention to our missing ticket problem, or alternatively to mix in with the crowd and try to talk our way through in the general rush. Eventually we decided on the latter approach, and since this was going to involve French talking,

Pete and I stuck close by Don. By now, our numbers had swollen to about three hundred, and it was becoming apparent that we were being held just so the ground staff could gauge how many away fans there were with the wrong tickets, with the aim of working out where they could put us. It wasn't as if there were going to be too many people in the ground, as we had legitimate tickets, so it was more a question of finding a good place to put us. With about twenty minutes to go, we were all called over to the turnstiles. We tried to pick out the most sympathetic-looking and overloaded steward, and Pete and I showed our tickets first and started to explain that our friend had been robbed. The queue behind built up and started to press forward as Don showed his swapped OM away shirt and acted out the pick-pocketing incident and we did the best we could to sound convincing. After some hesitation, the steward shrugged his shoulders, Gallic-style as they say, and let us all through. As he passed through, and with Don already in, Pete tucked a folded up twenty euros note into the steward's hand just for good measure – I'd been doubtful about this tactic as I thought it might backfire, but Pete, your 'Howay man, this is France' rejoinder turned out to have been justified.

Yeah, it worked a treat didn't it, Barry? Marseille is one of the key strongholds of the *Front National*, the French National Front, whose members include some of mankind's more pestilential specimens, including *le führer* himself, Jean-Marie le Pen. This balding, aged piece of reprehensibility personified actually made it to the second round of voting in the last Presidential elections, so that socialist politicians (and in France they still are socialists) actively encouraged their own supporters to vote for right-wing Chirac to prevent the out-and-out Nazi le Pen from getting in. Thus, racist tensions are never far from the surface in Marseille, and you really have to be on your mettle at all times. We were soon to get to know another Le Pen, namely the pen into which they herded all of us Toon wallahs who had tickets for Marseille fans' areas.

We still had to wait another quarter of an hour before we finally got onto the terraces. We were let in as part of the last batch and were just relieved to be there. We were led through a tunnel taking us towards the pitch. It felt, once again, as if we were being led by the Romans as prisoners of war into the Colosseum. But my dream was about to become reality, I was convinced. We were guided down a slope right onto the pitch by the corner flag, and were then led and pushed up a cordoned-off area skirting the edge of their Leazes-type end, with an impressive line of security keeping their fans at bay. If truth be told, they hardly gave us a second look and were much more interested in cheering at their team warming up on the pitch.

We found ourselves in a rat run a few yards wide stretching diagonally from the corner flag up to the rim of the stadium. The Newcastle wedge of the ground was appropriately enough in the north-east corner, and we were right alongside. Hemmed in on all sides by fifteen-feet high, barbed-wire-topped fences, this was a buffer zone that normally should have been kept empty. (For you, Geordie, ze var is over!) The view wasn't good because of all the fence posts but anywhere was good enough as long as we were there.

This, evidently, was *Le Pen*. We were penned in, here in the heartland of the French National Front. The terracing we were standing on wasn't actually terracing at all. These were obviously steps on which seats had been arranged but had now been removed. To move down a step you had to take giant steps indeed. A couple of people fell in the process (we weren't on the moon, after all). Of course there were no facilities, as this part wasn't intended to hold any spectators, so the back wall of *Le Pen* became *Le Pissoir* and it streamed down the channels between the concrete steps.

The ground was stowed out, of course, with a seething mass of 59,000 people. The atmosphere was electric, and all credit to the Marseillais. Their 'Leazes' would chant, and their 'Galligit' would chant back, and then it would all meld into a singing unison. It was impressive. The level of noise was way above what we've experienced at SJP on recent visits, and this without a roof to enhance the acoustics. Beyond the stadium, set behind *le Gallowgate*, you could see the bare rock of the local mountains bathed in the yellow-white glow of the Mediterranean moon. This was some setting, though but.

Behind the South goal, the Marseille fans held up a giant UEFA Cup banner, flanked on the right-hand side by a mosaic of light blue and white Marseille tiles, but on the left side by another hand-held mosaic of red and yellow stripes. Why not black and white, we wondered? It wasn't till the next day when reading the local match reports that it registered that both Villarreal's and Valencia's shields feature red and yellow stripes, the Spanish national colours. What a cheek, they'd already been showing the colours of who they thought were going to be the finalists.

Everyone knows that the French can't write decent rock music, even the French. So it wasn't surprising when OM came out onto the pitch to the accompaniment of a familiar song, though it was a surprise that it was a decent one – the twenty-year-old Jump by Van Halen. It soon became obvious why it's their song. The whole crowd, and I mean the whole crowd, on all four sides and from top to bottom, jump up and down. It's like 'pogo if you love the Toon', but it goes on and on and on. And no-one ever asked them to sit down – the whole crowd all round the stadium stood right through the match. After the first goal and through to the end, the whole place was, well, jumping. You have to admit it, their fervour and stamina absolutely puts the present atmosphere at St James's to shame. The only thing that I've witnessed that came anywhere near this magnificent Marseille crowd display was the sustained springing up and down to the chant of 'Ruud Gullit's Black and White Army' that had the cantilevered Old Trafford main stand resonating and rattling on its foundations as we swept to extra-time victory over Spurs in the FA Cup semi-final. The crowd was definitely

Marseille's twelfth man. Hats off to the Marseille fans – you're great!

In the first leg back home, we'd had our chances to win, especially through Shola's early shot that Baldheadz had saved with his trailing shin; but so had Drogba, hitting the post when he was clean through. So going to Marseille at nil-nil we felt we had some chance, if we could score the away goal that had evaded Marseille. But recently we'd been faltering in the League and we were by no means confident. In the event, Newcastle didn't really perform at all that night. Okay, we were severely depleted by injuries, it is true. No Bellamy, no Dyer, no Jenas, no Woodgate. We just didn't have the strength in depth to cope with setbacks of that magnitude.

After about twenty minutes they went ahead. As in my dream, all I really saw was the net bulge at the far end. Except this time it was the wrong net. But you still had to admire Drogba's powerful run and sidestep trick that opened the way for him to take his shot. And to think that only seconds before, Barthez had been steeling himself for a Laurent Robert free kick at our end of the pitch. To celebrate, the fans put on a bonfire display for everyone behind the goal down at our end. They let off a bunch of those red distress flares the Italians and French are so keen on. One of them set fire to some junk and the fire burned merrily for five minutes, billowing acrid fumes onto the pitch and terracing. By the smell, it must have been some kind of plastic that had been set alight, and it got so bad that the referee had to stop the match until the fire was extinguished. We were hoping that the fumes would make Barthez even dizzier than normal and that he'd let a couple of goals in. It wasn't a good start, but our task had not really changed. We still just needed to score one goal and stop them from scoring again, and we were through. Piece of cake? My arse (*mon cul*)! We never really looked like scoring, and half time brought some welcome relief. Maybe Sir Bobby could psyche them up to do the business.

During the break, to the tune of 'The Great Escape', someone scaled the fence of *le Pen* and jumped over into the Newcastle section proper. More and more followed until the stewards came in, saw the state of the place, and wisely opened a gate to let people go through at will and reduce the risk of a nasty accident. This was a bit like the old days back in the Leazes End when people sneaked in from the Popular. Barry and Don went through, but as the numbers herded in *le Pen* decreased, the view improved, so I decided to stay put for the second half.

We pressed hard and Marseille were getting nervous as we had a few half-chances to score, especially when Bowyer came on. The killer blow, delivered by Drogba (who else?) came less than ten minutes from the final whistle. It was obvious that we were finished. This was the end of our UEFA Cup dream for this season. I sat down on the terracing and reflected, as so many times in the past, on what might have been. Our hopes had been sky-high. But here we were, brought back down to earth with a bang. From hope to despair in around half an hour. We hadn't lost a game in the whole UEFA Cup campaign, but we were as sure as hell losing this one. From hope to despair, we had gone the full journey. Still, as the great Mr Cleese put it in that wonderful film 'Clockwise', despair is fine. We can handle despair. It is hope that we cannot handle! How fitting that thought is for the Toon Army.

We did our bit, of course, singing our hearts out. Hang on though – how is it we always sing 'sing your hearts out for the lads?' They are out there to represent us. It's not the other way around. They embody, in a very temporal way, us: the fans, the Geordies, the Toon Army. What we should be chanting, to the same tune, is 'Play your bollocks off for us!'. On the subject of singing, isn't it about time we extended our repertoire a bit? You know that French chant *'Allez la France, Allez la France, Allez*? Well what about 'Howay the Toon, Howay the Toon, Howay..'? Don and I tried it out at Breda and again in Marseille, and it was beginning to catch on!!

And what about 'The Fog on the Tyne is all mine, all mine'?' (can you get more Geordie than that?) Or Mark Knopfler's 'Why Aye, Why Aye, Why Aye Man' from the Middlesbrough Transporter Bridge Aufwiedersehen Pet series? Plus, 'Alouette, Geordie Alouette, Alouette, She's a Geordie Lass' went down well in the Marseille boozers...

As the match drew to its end, the tannoy announced that we were going to be kept back for forty-five minutes. But when the final whistle had gone and our team had dragged themselves over for a brief salute before making swiftly for the dressing room (a wee bit disappointing, that!), it became obvious that the Marseille celebrations were going to last that long, so we'd be getting out with the OM fans anyway. They were happy to stay there for an extra half; at least they had something to do and someone to cheer, so wouldn't it have been better to let us out straight away, and keep them in for the duration instead?

Never mind the result, there were the post-match antics to look forward to, and a *Bouillabaisse* in the *Vieux Port*. When the police finally opened the gates, by all accounts they were applying heavy-handed tactics, again for no good reason at all, other than maybe in their eyes it was in keeping with their Robocop-style get-ups. We heard banging and shouting but we couldn't actually see any of it, as we were pretty much at the back of the exiting Geordies. This really is such a pity. What do they think we are going to do, for goodness' sake? We just wanted to get back into town for a couple of pints, a bite to eat and maybe a singsong.

The trudge back to the metro, empty-handed yet again, brought back memories of the same kind of feelings as when we'd shuffled down Wembley Way after the Man Utd final in the stop-start queue for the trains to go home. There was some pushing, and people were getting close to being crushed. The police tannoyed a message, 'There are going to be some delays so can we ask the Newcastle United fans please to be patient?' To which the immediate rejoinder from someone with a voice as loud as the tannoy was: 'Hoo man, wa' d'ye mean patient? Wi'v been waitin' for fowaty-three years, hoo patient d'ye want?'

Eventually we got to the metro station, where Don discovered that not only had he had his match ticket stolen, but the fiendishly felonious Froggy had also lifted his metro ticket at the same time, so he (Don) had to queue up for about twenty minutes under the gaze of the police whose *camarades* had looked on while the original felony had been perpetrated. Don had to get back to Nice for a mid-day flight so he decided to head straight back for his hotel. Sarah, Chris, Barry and Pete got off at the *Vieux Port* metro station and headed for a nice welcoming restaurant for some authentic fish soup, and very steady it was too. Thus, slurping our *Bouillabaisse*, we mulled over our loss. All in all, over the whole competition, we'd done better and lasted longer than anyone would have expected: the last surviving UK team in Europe, with the highest UEFA ranking points of all UK teams, bettered only by Valencia and Porto in all of Europe. We could be proud, even if ultimately disappointed. We reflected on how much it would dent the sales of our book! And what we should do with our four UEFA Cup Final tickets for two weeks' time?

All around the *Vieux Port*, Marseille fans were going bananas, and who can blame them? Horns were tooting, people were sitting waving flags on top of cars - all of it set against the luxurious moon-kissed backdrop of yachts bobbing up and down in the old port itself. Like Monaco, this place has plenty of 'haves' and 'have yachts'. No doubt some celebrations were going on aboard some of them. Or maybe there were other reasons for them bobbing up and down, who knows? At all events, I can honestly say we did not see a ha'porth of trouble. Toon Army and Marseille wallahs were mixing and having drinks together. Wor lot were congratulating them and rightly so. This is the way it should be.

Barry and I said our farewells to Chris and Sarah and looked for a taxi. There was an unspoken sadness that we wouldn't all be meeting up in Gothenburg. But there was always next season. Have I heard that one before? It took a while to get a taxi, but the trip through the brightly lit streets of Marseille past impressively illuminated fountains and what looked like the *hôtel de ville* made the wait worthwhile. We got back to the hotel about one-thirty. Up at nine and back to the *Vieux Port* before heading for our respective trains, mine to Luxembourg via Metz, Barry's direct to Brussels. I was really looking forward to my first TGV experience. We were headed for the OM bar, but just before reaching it Chris was shouting to us from the café next door. He had spotted us in the mirror. So we had breakfast together in what turned out to be ... a gay bar! It's called *Le Soleil* – avoid it. Shades of Oslo!

After breakfast I made my way on the metro back to St Charles station. Had a bit crack with a Marseille fan from Lyon on his way home. Wished OM the best of luck for the final. Sitting in the TGV waiting for it to head north reminded me of similar occasions at Kings Cross. It had been a great trip, but I was more than ready to be whisked north, homeward bound...

The TGV really does move. Boy does it move! The mountains slid sleekly past, and before I could say the French word for antidisestablishmentarianism, we were in Lyon, where I noticed that Marseille fan making his way down the platform. Time to leaf through the Marseille papers. Euphoric of course, but also full of praise for the Toon Army. There was a picture of the OM Bar terrace, where that Geordie who had unfortunately not made it to the match was sitting fast asleep, crowned with a traffic cone. He must have got stuck into the *pastis* (very bad idea, don't do it, stick to pasties and beer instead!) and dozed off. How was your return trip going, Barry?

Well, Pete, like you I read all the local papers and then wrote up a bit of this story while the French countryside flashed by. As we pulled into the station at Paris Charles De Gaulle Airport, 'above us only two unfeasibly large French nostrils', a thought occurred to me. Now then, Paris Saint Germain would be another great draw for the future. For a start, their team is no better than ours so we can beat them, because we keep on buying their players – look at Ginola and Domi and Robert. And of course Paris would be a great place, pre- and post-match. Like the Angel of the North, the Eiffel Tower would suit a giant black and white shirt draped over it, and the *Place de la Bastille* heaving in black and white would be a sight to see. How about chartering the Tuxedo Princess and sailing it up the Seine to moor alongside *Notre Dame*? Though we'd have to take down the Millennium Bridge first before casting off from the Quayside. Maybe we can do it next season, Pete?

Sounds good to me, Barry. At Dijon (how come the English language doesn't stick an 's' on the end of that?), my Metz-bound TGV had a technical problem, which cost twenty minutes, and at Nancy there was an announcement that a *'colis suspect'* had been found on the track between Nancy and Metz, and there would be an indefinite delay. Now had that meant a suspicious collie, I suppose the TGV could simply have ploughed on and run the stupid mutt over, but in fact it meant a suspicious parcel so I suppose these days we have to be more careful. The guard came through the carriage saying there was a local train on the platform opposite that was going directly to Luxembourg. It would not be faster, of course, but would avoid having to change at Metz. So out I gets and down through the tunnel I goes to the other platform. The local train was stowed out so I went back to the TGV knowing that would at least be more comfortable. But of course just as I approached the door it closed and the TGV sped off, leaving me to rush back and hop on the local train just in the nick of time.

Got into Luxembourg about half-ten and back home in Trier about half-eleven. That wouldn't have been so bad, but I had to get up at half past six the next morning to join a coach party that was off to ... FRANCE! More precisely, to a little place called Monétau, near Auxerre, to take part in a half-marathon on the Sunday. This was all part of the twinning arrangement between Föhren, a village near Trier, and Monétau. Life goes on, so *VIVE L'EUROPE*!!

So that was it. The end of yet another great European adventure! It was only to be hoped that we would at least make it into next season's UEFA Cup. Otherwise I would at least try to get to all the games in the smoke. We had to win our last two games (away to Southampton and the 'Pool) to get into the Champignons League. Beat Southampton away in the league? The last time we did that, Queen Victoria was on the throne of England (though I doubt she was very popular in Geordieland). All right, it's a bit of an exaggeration. But Ted Heath was PM, and that's a fact. Anyway, we didn't beat them. It was a three-all draw after we'd been leading twice and then squeezed a stunning last-minute equaliser through Darren Ambrose. Then it was away to the Pool. Villa were at home to Man. U. If the Villa won, well that was it. In the end they were beaten and we drew at Anfield, which meant… we were back in Europe. There was hope for next season, as always. (Despair is definitely a better bet!)

As for the 2003/04 season, well we hadn't achieved our goal of reaching the final in Gothenburg. But at least I was spared having to decide whether to wear a Viking helmet or a sombrero. Think I probably would have worn both – the Viking helmet on top of the sombrero!

What the hell! As on any self-respecting pilgrimage, it is the path itself that is the goal. And it is the milestones along that path which appear to bring the elusive goal ever closer and at the same time push it back over the horizon. Yet those very milestones always deserve a closer look as each one of them encapsulates a little world of its own. Yes, that's it – the path IS the goal. To which, of course, you might justifiably reply: 'BOLLOCKS! – this gadgy's a nutter! The goal is that wooden (or aluminium) frame thing with a net behind it into which you're supposed to stick the f****n' ball, and we simply didn't do that often enough!' To which I reply: O Ye of little faith!

Gothenburg tale – the end of the pilgrim trail

Journey's end, the shrine, the holy grail, the ultimate challenge in the odyssey, the last station of the pilgrimage. We had to be there. Even if the team couldn't be there with us. Though maybe that most holy and renowned of all Toon Army pilgrims, Cardinal Basil Hume, was there with us in spirit. Word is that they're going to make him a saint, which arguably will make the Toon the only team able to count a saint amongst its followers. And according to Gazza's autobiography, the Pope's favourite player was Gazza while he was at Lazio – he even had a photo of him on his desk - so that might make it two saints for us, and one for Lazio. They're both welcome to lead us on our future pilgrimages.

An odyssey describes a heroic journey through a series of challenges, some in distant lands, some on returning home. A pilgrimage is an arduous journey undertaken as an act of devotion, thanksgiving and penance. It had been all these things – especially penance. We'd overcome all the challenges that fate had put in our way: we'd seen the cities of many men and known their thoughts; we'd known the taverns well in every toun/town/toon; we'd eaten their *manchego*, *geitost* and *gorgonzola* sandwiches and drunk their *rioja*, *pils*, and burgundy - though we baulked at their inner organs of beasts and fowls; we'd been to the land of ice and snow, of the midnight sun, where the north winds blow, and our boots had no longer lied about the cold around our feet; we'd faced down the fabled *Tigrou*; we'd spoken in tongues; we'd travelled ticket-less but in true faith; we'd given surfeits of tickets away; we'd helped Mrs Bradies onto trams whether they'd wanted to board them or not; we'd been grilled on radio and television; we'd spread Geordie goodwill; we'd karaoke'd against the Spanish; we'd been robbed; and now here was the final challenge – to try to stay enthusiastic about a match when we really didn't give a monkey's bum about who won.

Three months before, I had been flicking through the Iberia in-flight magazine while heading towards Madrid on the first leg of my journey back from Mallorca, when I'd come upon an article about probably the most famous pilgrimage in the world, as Carlsberg might say, to Santiago de Compostela in north-west Spain. Mind you, if Carlsberg did pilgrimages, theirs would probably be better. I was intrigued to find that we quite literally had (a) common ground: Santiago is the Spanish way of saying Saint James and, even better, Compostela is from the Latin *Campus Stellae*, meaning the Field of Stars. Putting it all together, the pilgrimage leads to St James's Field of Stars. What better way to describe St James's Park and forge the link to the pilgrimage we had embarked upon? There must be something to this, as you have all walked the pilgrim road in Newcastle. Pilgrim Street, where the fire station is, though maybe not for much longer, was the old way into Newcastle for hundreds of years, coming over the old low stone Tyne Bridge that was washed away in the 1700s, way before any of the Nice's Five Bridges were built, through the Sandgate, round the All Saints Church and up to the high town. There was no ugly multi-storey concrete car park or Swan House roundabout in the way and you couldn't come up Dean Street and Grey Street, because back then the valley hadn't been filled in and it was still the Lort Burn running through monastery fields down to the river. Vålerenga supporters (and any obsessive linguists) amongst you will recognise *lort* as the old Viking word for shit, still used in Danish and Norwegian. You can imagine it can't have been the place for fresh air and a nice paddle, even if it had been monastically holy shit, as passed on by the bishop himself, so you were far better off on the pilgrim road.

The Iberia in-flight magazine '*Ronda*' is bilingual, and I suspect that the translators draw some amusement from slipping some private jokes into their work – translators can be like that. I spotted a couple of examples which must have been deliberate, not just mis-translations. I wonder if they put them in with the hope that someone will respond, just to prove to them that someone actually reads their work and doesn't just look at the pictures of scantily clad Iberian nymphs, or the route maps and the duty-free prices? Know which I prefer! Well, here's some feedback: the English translation of an article about a Barcelona conference on forestry conservation included a section on 'How to get wood without harming the forest' (hmm!). A few pages later, I bet it was the same translator who'd brightened his day with a survey showing that people from the Netherlands travel more outside their country than any other nationality. The Spanish headline literally read: 'People from the Low Countries move around most'; but he'd made it into 'The nether regions move around most.'

While on things literary, there's an interesting passage in 'Therapy - A Novel' by David Lodge. Inspired by the Danish philosopher Søren Kierkegaard, he gives his interpretation of a pilgrimage as 'an existential act of self-definition, a leap into the absurd'. Sounds like following the Toon, don't you think? One kind of pilgrim he calls aesthetic, mainly there to have a good time enjoying the picturesque and the pleasures of the road. Then there's the ethical kind, who sees it as a test of stamina. But the true pilgrim is religious in his irrational faith, which allows him to make the leap into the void, thousands of miles without knowing whether there will really be anything there at the end. I suppose we were a mixture of all three, with the emphasis on the aesthetic and the true. Albert Camus, the existentialist French-Algerian goalkeeper you know by now, would have subscribed to that.

As a slight aside, Kierkegaard means churchyard. You can see the similarities. But there's another interesting point about the *gaard* bit: it's pronounced more like 'gawth' meaning a yard or a farm, and it's only a small step from there to 'garth'. So if you've ever wondered why they named all those places in Killingworth 'garth', it's because it's an old Viking word which became known to our North-East forebears through the phrase, 'Out the way while we burn down your gawth. Or you can stay inside, we're not fussed.' On the basis that once you've got to a certain place and it's only a few steps further you might as well go all the way, let me point out that 'forebears' is to four bears as 'foreskins' is to four skins. Which was the miraculous name for a short-lived crappy eighties punk group comprised of four skinheads. Just so you know.

To identify themselves to one another, the pilgrims wear a scallop shell, just as we wear our colours. And like the scallop shells, our colours too were blessed, in our case under the dome of Saint Peter's in the Vatican on our trip to AS Roma a few years earlier. We collect ticket stubs and scarves along the way and they collect rubber stamps in their pilgrims' passports to exchange for a *compostela* certificate at the end.

The Santiago pilgrimage has four different starting points for four separate routes which converge in the final stages through Galicia; the UEFA Cup pilgrimage began at more than a hundred different grounds, and the attrition rate is very much higher – only two groups of UEFA followers make it to the last stage. The four longest-enduring pilgrimages in this year's UEFA Cup had begun in Newcastle, Villarreal (who'd even begun in the Intertoto Cup and so had actually had the longest journey of all), Marseille and Valencia. Now that our and Villareal's steps had faltered at the meetings of the paths in Marseille and Valencia, only the latter two had survived. Though this had not stopped followers of other faiths from completing the road to Ullevi: there must have been a few hundred or more Celtic supporters and quite a number of the Toon Army there alongside us. We're a broad church.

The Feast of St James is on the twenty-fifth of July in Santiago, but the Feast of Ullevi, honouring Ulla, the Viking God of Sport - it all fits together, don't you see? - was celebrated on the nineteenth of May at the UEFA Cup Final by the thousands who came to Gothenburg on a sunny and warm, though very windy day. And just like the *Fiesta* of Santiago, it was a time for celebration, with the parks full of entertainment laid on by UEFA, the city of Gothenburg, and the many sponsors. You had kids' football tournaments, games and competition stalls set up by UEFA and sponsors where you won a few bits and bobs, souvenir stands, and people thronging the streets and parks. There were UEFA banners and Swedish flags everywhere, streaming in the breeze. A bit like Durham Big Meetin' Day, in fact ('we listen te the speeches, and then te those brass bands, and the beer it flows like watta, so we drink aal we c'n stand!'). For a normal match, the supporters are left very much to their own devices, but here there was much more effort put in to making it a celebration that everyone could feel part of, whether they were going to the match or not, whether they were a supporter of one of the teams or another team, whether they just happened to live in the city, or were passing through.

With our usual – yes, you've guessed - belt and braces approach, we'd put ourselves down in the UEFA.COM on-line lottery for two pairs of Cup Final tickets for the neutrals section before we'd even got through the quarter-final versus PSV, on the basis that we might be lucky and at least get one pair of tickets. You can only order two tickets each and multiple requests are filtered out, so we'd both ordered a pair of tickets to be sent to our home addresses in Belgium and Germany. As it turned out, we got all four tickets, and by some amazing coincidence they were all in the same row in the same section of the ground, which was a stroke of luck. Pete couldn't face the prospect of being there without the Toon (and not even Celtic as a consolation), so we'd taken up his tickets and I was going to take Brian, Sarah and Emilie with me. Believe it or not, in a ground with a capacity of about forty-five thousand, only eleven thousand tickets were earmarked for each team's supporters, with about another quarter of the tickets going through the lottery for the neutrals section, and all the rest going to UEFA officials and celebrities, sponsors, press, and hangers-on. When you hear that, you can't complain too much about how FA Cup Final tickets are handled in comparison (well, maybe you can).

Obviously (as Beardo might say), losing in Marseille was a crushing blow, but after coming all this way and with the Final tickets already in our hands, I thought I might as well go for the complete set of matches in every round. This was the ethical pilgrim streak coming out. It was school half term too, so I decided to make a week of it and tour the exceptional Swedish west-coast scenery either side of Gothenburg with the family and then visit our friends Eric and Nina who have a lovely old summerhouse in Tisvildeleje on the north coast of Sjaelland in Denmark.

I had worked for three years near Copenhagen, with Eric as it happens, and I'd also worked for a while just south of Gothenburg (in Swedish, it's called *Göteborg*). I'd been a fair few times on the DFDS ferry between Newcastle and Gothenburg, and I'd even been to the Ullevi stadium before, so it was a bit of a trip down memory lane for me.

You know when people say 'My memory's not what it used to be'? Well, if their memory's not so good now, how do they remember what it used to be like? Maybe it was worse before. So maybe it's not what it used to be, because it's better! Or not. Nobody knows, least of all them.

On the Sunday before the Final, we collected a hire car at Kastrup Airport, south of Copenhagen ('Above us probably the world's best airport slogan'), and headed off into the town to do some sightseeing since it was a beautiful day and there was no guarantee that it would still be when we came back in five days' time. We took a trip to see the Little Mermaid down in the park by the harbour. You can spot the tourists who have never seen her before, because they are craning their necks, squinting out into the middle of the harbour looking for a big rock with the mermaid perched atop; until they see a group of people gathered around a very small rock on the shoreline, where the mermaid basks away her days. In terms of scale, the same applies *mutatis mutandis* (that is definitely an ablative absolute) to *Manneken Pis* in Brussels.

With all the travelling, we ended up having a very late lunch consisting of a couple of Danish pastries each, the kind you normally have for breakfast. Which was a very appropriate way of eating in Denmark, because they have a strange kind of time lag in their words for meals. Their word for lunch is *frokost*, which actually means breakfast, and they correspondingly postpone lunchtime to (southern English) dinnertime, which they call *middag*, which pretty clearly means mid-day, especially when you know it's pronounced 'mid-day'! You can certainly see how close some words are to English. And of course in Geordie we have our dinner at mid-day, the exact opposite. There must be some mysterious link existing between the Viking and Geordie psyches that causes us to move meals around in opposite directions. 'Ah, but what do they call breakfast?' I hear you asking. *Morgenmad*, pronounced 'mornmadth', and meaning morning food. At least that's quite understandable.

They also have a fantastically precise way of defining who's someone else's relative, especially for grandparents, aunts and uncles and the like. There's no question of not being sure if it's your grandfather on your mother's side in Danish, it's all laid down in one short word. Thus, *mormor* means 'mother's mother', *morfar* is 'mother's father', *farfar* is 'father's father' and so on. And the same goes for grandparents and great-grandparents, etc. So we all have a *farfarfarfarmor*, for example. It's obviously very important to them, and so it should be. It's like listening to Noggin the Nog, if you remember that, which was clearly based on reality. And now you know what that 'farfarfarfar' bit in Talking Heads' 'Psycho Killer' means too.

This word *far* can be a wee bit confusing in Swedish. Depending on whether or not it has a funny little circle perched thus 'å' atop the 'a', it can mean 'sheep', 'may' 'must' 'few' 'get' or 'father', and the same rules for describing grandparents apply as in Danish. Thus, 'may/must the paternal grandfather get a few sheep?' becomes *'får/får farfar får får får?'* Isn't it marvellous? If this sort of thing didn't really exist, someone would have to make it up! Maybe we just did, who knows?

We still needed to fix ourselves up with a hotel for the following Thursday when we would be returning from Gothenburg. Most hotels anywhere, not just in the Norselands, seem to believe in small families only – you're welcome with one child, two's pushing it, but three's a crowd that means an extra room and you're paying five-star prices for a two-star hotel. We'd tried booking from home, but it's even worse trying to get a good deal for a family over the phone, and we've come to the conclusion it's usually better to sort it on the spot. And if it doesn't work out, you can always do what those swarthy headscarfed itinerants of indeterminate origin do in most big Western European cities: sit outside a metro station with your bairns, look pathetic and beg. It did work out, however, because what had been impossible to book over the phone - a family room at a reasonable price at one of my all-time favourites, the Admiral Hotel – turned out to be perfectly feasible when we turned up at reception and had a good chat with the very friendly desk staff. Couldn't help thinking about Gazza's famous quip here: when he was on his way to Italy to join Lazio, a journalist asked him what he thought the reception was going to be like – so he said it would probably have a bell, a couple of phones and a computer! The Admiral's a huge old granary with massive exposed oak beams that was converted in the eighties into a hotel. My new firm put me up there for a few weeks when I first went to work in Denmark. It looks a bit like one of those big old converted warehouses towards the downstream end of our own Quayside. If you ever stay there, make sure you get a room with an even number because that means you get a harbour view of the overnight ferries coming in from Oslo and the island of Bornholm, and not just a street view. We had to splash out but it was only going to be for one night, and it was in any case a discount price because it was the start of the long weekend holiday for Ascension. I can't resist it – I wasn't going to tell you – but it's called *Kristi Himmelfart* in Danish. Christ's journey to heaven somehow doesn't have the same resonance to it. You're going to see there are quite a few *farts* in Scandinavia.

So we might as well start with one now. When I was working in Denmark, I got to find out that they have lots of jokes which are the Nordic equivalent of our 'there was this Englishman, Irishman and Scotsman' variety. A Norwegian is a Danish Irishman, if you see what I mean. Well one of my English work colleagues had a particular favourite he liked to tell when there was a good mixture of Scandinavians around, and he mixed it around so that the fall guy varied according to the audience. So: a Dane, a Norwegian and a Swede were out on a camping trip (could have been Ryedale, the night of the Fairs Cup Final) and got to arguing over who was the bravest. To settle it, Knud the Dane suggested that they should have a battle of willpower. Whoever could stay the longest in their little tent with that putrid goat over there would be the winner, and he set the example himself and managed a whole minute before he came out retching and gasping for air. 'Beat that, Bjorn', said Knud, turning to the Swede. Bjorn got to ninety seconds before he staggered out. 'It's down to you, Ole', gasped Bjorn to the Norwegian as he disappeared into the tent. Five minutes passed and the other two started to wonder what was going on when there was a big kerfuffle (I've been watching 'Little Britain'), the flap of the tent tore open, and the goat stomped out: 'You two I could just about stomach, but that Ole doesn't half stink'. It went down a storm at Scandinavian sales conferences.

Of course you can turn it into a Geordie, a smoggie and a mackem, or whoever else you prefer. It reminds me of when we went to see the summer 2002 pre-season training matches in Holland. All four matches were well attended, and at the one at Tubanters Enschede, I think it was (God knows what a *Tubanter* is – a tubemaker or tube squeezer perhaps?), we were trying to find an empty space by the barrier where we could watch the match. Despite it being two or three deep all round, we found one place where there were only a couple of people standing, with a gap either side of them, so we steamed in. As we did so, a couple of the locals pointed discreetly at the highly discrete pair and wrinkled up their noses, much as Bjorn and Knud did to the goat. They stank, and - sad to say - they were Toon supporters. I'd seen one of them at a distance at previous matches, and he'd always seemed well dressed, but maybe he wears the same togs all the time. I'd never been so close before, and haven't been since either! We retired to a safe distance and squashed in with all the rest, ending up getting a first view of Titus Bramble, who was right in front of us doing stretches pitch-side, though he never got on. Talk about barrel-chested!

With the hotel fixed up, we pointed the motor towards the majestic Öresund Bridge, which now joins Denmark to Sweden, and set off on our trip up the west coast to Varberg (Great North Runners among you will be interested to learn that there's a half-marathon across that bridge in the summer!). On longish trips like this, it's nice to be able to settle back, relax and rely on your *KonstantFartHolder* to see you through. That's Danish for cruise control (not a 'constant fart holder'), in case you're wondering. But watch out for those *FartHinders* - they can catch you out, those speed bumps. About a couple of hours after leaving Copenhagen, and having left in our wake the small town of Bastad (!!) and the River Nissan (!!), we took the *Udfart* slip-road off the coastal motorway and headed into another of my old haunts, Varberg, where there's a statue in the main square commemorating what I can only surmise to be the ancient Swedish custom of nudist mixed basketball, and the art deco *Stadshotellet* awaits. Another hotel with good memories attached – the first place I ever stayed on a business trip, when I was sent on a site visit during the commissioning of the nearby 'Ringhals Three' nuclear power station. We got freshened up after our long day and went down to John's Place, a beach restaurant out on the southern edge of town at

Apelviken, a famous windsurfing beach. By the way, *vik* in Danish and Swedish (and probably Norwegian, but I can't find my dictionary so I'm not a zillion per cent sure) means 'bay', as in Whitley Bay. So Sandvik, for example, means 'sandy bay' and Apelviken has to mean 'apple bay', I suppose – sae there ye gan! This was the first place I ever had a business dinner paid for by the company (wish I'd had seconds!). Back then, you drove your car down onto the beach and parked outside the log cabin. It's grown since, but I was so pleased to see it was still there after more than twenty years, and the dishes - especially the lamb and the steaks with baked potatoes - were as good as ever. The beer in Sweden seems to be not quite so extortionately priced as it used to be, either, so it was a great evening – good food and a beautiful Swedish west-coast sunset. Beats California.

One other thing you might notice as you travel around Sweden is how many towns are named after Ikea sofas, tables, bedspreads, and kitchen cabinets. I wonder why? Though they don't make a Bastad shelf unit, as far as I know. A Sandvik kiddies' sandpit kit might be a good idea.

We still had a couple of days' holiday before match day, so we headed up north of Gothenburg to the pink granite rocky archipelago region of western Sweden. Magical. Especially in the warm, bright spring sunshine when it's still a haven of peace before the summertime tourist crowds invade for a few short weeks in July and August. It was so quiet when we were there in mid-May, despite the beautiful weather. Each town only seemed to have one hotel and one restaurant open. It was as if they'd agreed amongst themselves that they should take turns to cater for the few travellers passing through, and let the others have the low season completely off. Luckily, we found one hotel open in Hunnebostrand, the 'Kaprifol', which is some kind of Swedish flower, as far as I could make out. Luckily, because the lady who runs it is a fantastic hostess – nothing was too much trouble, advising us on where to go, what to do. She made it a great stay, and even offered to lay on an evening meal for us (although she doesn't do meals except for the huge breakfasts), because the one restaurant that was open in the village was taken over that evening for a local company's private party - shades of *los estudiantes* in Mallorca. It turned out that she had lived in Brussels twenty years ago, not far from where we live, and she liked to practise a bit of her mostly forgotten French on us. She's Swedish, as you might have guessed, and married to a Norwegian who went to Newcastle University in the late sixties. Small world, though maybe you know that loads of Norwegians used to study there, certainly in my time; maybe they still do, despite Mrs Thatcher having a good go at putting off all foreign students from coming to the UK by steeply ramping up their fees in another example of short-termist thinking (may she spend the afterlife somewhere with a warm climate, bless her).

Apparently one of the reasons why these Swedish coastal villages feel so empty is that oil-rich Norwegians come down and buy up places to use as summer-houses, a bit like you used to hear happened with Welsh Humphries' cottages. Being Swedish, they don't burn down the Norwegians' acquisitions, though they do bristle at the Norwegian flags displayed on the statutory flagpoles in their gardens. Scandinavians love their flags – just about everyone has a flagpole - and they're very proud to display them. There's nothing of the negatives attached like in England, where an English flag displayed in anyone's garden would be more or less an admission of abominably fascist tendencies. It is striking, and refreshing, how few English flags you see in the North-East. Give me the Northumbrian one any day!

If you ever get the chance, you need to spend a bit of your time in Marstrand, Mollösund, Smögen, and Hunnebostrand, with the old fishermen's russet-brown wooden houses clinging to the sides of the granite cliffs and perching on stilts in the water. I bet you didn't know that one of the Feyenoord players in their '68 Fairs Cup team was from Smögen? I read it in the Chronicle's souvenir supplement. Smögen's also the place to go to eat fresh prawns. They come straight off the boats, into the fish auction and onto your picnic plate for your culinary delight as you dangle your legs over the harbour wall. You peel them yourselves, dip them into the herb mayonnaise (maybe on the end of a Swedish baguette) and wash them down with some Ramlösa or Falcon beer. It's so good that Abba have a seafood factory there. They do, honestly!

There was a stiff breeze the day we were there, and Brian's hat got blown off into the middle of the harbour. This is an amazing coincidence, as Pete lost a Panama hat in exactly the same way while on holiday in Sweden a couple of years earlier. What is it about the Swedes and tourists' hats? We half-heartedly attempted a rescue and had given up on it until we saw the harbourmaster's boat coming along. He was already heading over to investigate what mysterious black creature could be floating around in his territorial waters (could it be yet another Russian sub?) when we waved and pointed at Brian, making the gesture of pulling a hat down over his head. The harbourmaster kindly obliged and fished the hat out and brought it back to dry land. Catch of the day.

If you're somewhere you're not likely to go back to soon, and an idea pops into your head of something you wouldn't mind seeing, doing, or going to while you're there, but which might be a little bit difficult or time-consuming or strenuous or inconvenient, but at the same time rather attractive, what do you do? For a start, you should shorten your sentences! Because when you get back you will think to yourself, 'Maybe I should have ... while I had the chance.' I used to think, 'Oh, I'll do it another time.' But now I just do it; time's maybe running out! (Same goes for writing a book.) So, with it being a sunny and warm though windy day, and with the crystal-clear waters of the Ramsvik (ram's, or maybe lovers') bay inlet in front of me, no matter that they were pretty glacial, Long Sands style, I jumped in for a swim, persuading Emilie, Sarah and Brian in ascending order of reluctance to follow suit. Now when I think back, I say 'I did it', and I'd do it again next time too. And when I say glacial and Long Sands style, I mean: that small!

On match day, we made our way back down the coast to Gothenburg with a detour to Torslanda for a trip around the Volvo (that's Latin for 'I roll') factory. Swedes certainly are patriotic - what with their flags everywhere and seemingly half of them driving either a Volvo or a Saab (that's a Latin acronym meaning something very rude). I know they've been swallowed up by Ford and GM, but if we'd done the same, maybe there would still be such things as a Riley or a Wolseley. On second thoughts, maybe we did the right thing. It was all very professionally done with excellent speakers, and a tour on one of those little tourist trains around the ultra-clean and organised factory. More than a quarter of the workers are girls, and very nice they are too. Makes you think of those Cuban cigar factories where they're supposed to roll the best leaves on their thighs. What bit of a Volvo could you roll across your thighs? Maybe the gear knob? It almost makes you want to buy one. Maybe I should have done while I had the chance? So I did.

The Gothenburg *Fiesta* (no, not a Ford) was well under way when we arrived in mid-afternoon. We had a short bout of verbal wrestling with a Swedish traffic warden who had managed to find time to spot our car and call a truck to tow it away while we took our bags into the centrally located but difficult-to-park-outside City Hotel. He bowed to reason in the end and used his mobile phone to call off the dogs of the tow-away racket. Though I am still wondering whether we are going to end up with a parking fine via the hire car company some months into the future.

It wouldn't have been the first time I'd had our car towed away on a football mission. We went to Selhurst Park to watch us play Wimbledon the week before the Man Utd Cup final – I think it was the year before they went down (the Wombles, that is, unfortunately not Man U.). The match itself was the one thing that nearly went right – we drew and the atmosphere was manic with a 'Ruud Gullit's Black and White

Army' chant that developed into a kind of religious frenzy and lasted the entire second half of the match, just like against Spurs in the semi-final. Plus, the pre- and post-match gatherings in the Green Tree just opposite Norwood Junction station were also a bit special, as always. It was so black and white, with a home-from-home atmosphere, that you almost expected to step outside into the Bigg Market.

On the Friday night we'd parked our car in a meter zone on the south bank outside the old GLC buildings. I knew I had to put some cash in before breakfast the next morning and when I went out a few minutes after the start of the metered time at half past eight, the car was already gone. I eventually got it back from some hell-hole of a car dump in what I suppose must have been Lambeth, because I ended up sending in my complaint to a council of that name, if my memory serves me right. I'd wasted the whole morning and also it had cost about a couple of hundred pounds for the fine and the towing charge.

The crux of the matter is that you're allowed fifteen minutes to collect some change to put in the meter before they can even start to think about giving you a ticket, and the time on the ticket was within those fifteen minutes. The tow-truck had obviously been lined up with all its pals ready to do the dirty deed, because when I arrived on the scene before the fifteen minutes were up, not only had our car been taken, but so had all the others in the same row. Someone told me that they scout around in the early hours and set up the streets they're going to scavenge from well before the meters start ticking. Which is not at all in the spirit of the law. Anyway I won and got all my money back and a nice apology. But watch out, there's a thief about. Especially in the smoke.

What a weekend that was. Just about everything that could go wrong did exactly that. It was a series of disasters. It started with Nathalie, Brian and me sitting opposite the railway station in a bar in the corner of the Place du Luxembourg, which confusingly is a square in Brussels. We ordered drinks, only to have them presented in stinking dirty glasses. The place has since closed down. We were waiting for Pete, but his train to Brussels was delayed due to engineering work near Namur, so we set off late for the Channel Tunnel and missed the train we were booked on, and so got into London late for our meet-up with Chris, Sarah, Neale, Eric and Big Brian at Porter's in Covent Garden. Then there was the car getting towed away.

Plus, we'd left three tickets at the reception of the hotel for our friends to pick up, as we were going off into London and had arranged to meet them inside the ground instead. Unbelievably, the reception staff had seen the envelope with our friend's name on, had checked the register and found someone staying in the hotel with the same name, Kelly, and posted the tickets under their door. So when our friends got there, the tickets were nowhere in sight. Luckily they got into the ground anyway, but what a disaster!

Then the best bit of all: leaving England through the Eurotunnel, I somehow couldn't find my passport while we were waiting in the queue for the UK customs control. We pulled over to the side and emptied the car out but couldn't find it anywhere. But we had to get back, so we rejoined the queue and explained our predicament to the English passport inspector, who had spotted that we'd been looking everywhere and clearly understood it was an honest error. He gave us a piece of advice: 'I'll let you through and when you have to stop at the French checkpoint (which was just a hundred yards farther on), just show them your wad of passports, and they probably won't even notice that one is missing. They're French after all!' I don't know how we managed to get across those hundred yards without turning into quivering wrecks, but with the encouragement of British officialdom backing us up, we gave it a go. And it worked! God bless British *sang-froid* and French shoulder-shrugging *bof*.

Having escaped the clutches of the Swedish tow gang, we parked up in a giant car park on the way to the Ullevi and made our way back the short distance to the city centre. We bumped into someone selling more of those souvenir split scarves, this time half Marseille, half Valencia. It turned out that he wasn't Spanish or French, he was English and that it was his brother-in-law who runs the whole of this souvenir scarf business for European and International matches as a sideline from his insurance job. Back in the days of gangsters and prohibition, he could have gone by the name of 'scarf-face'. He'd been over in Japan for the World Cup and had sold out three thousand pounds' worth of scarves in half an hour. I checked the Marseille end of the split scarf and showed him that it still had the same spelling mistake in the logo 'Droit au Butt', as on our semi-final souvenir, and he quite liked the idea that it meant 'right up the arse.' Anyway, their sideline's done pretty good business out of us this year; six or seven scarves, I make it.

Walking to the ground, Sarah was impressed with the blue and yellow 'UEFA Cup Final Gothenburg 2004' flags hanging on every lamp-post and flagpole, and got it into her head that she had to have one. As I walked along I checked, and only the ones directly outside the stadium were on proper flag lines that you could take down; all the rest had deliberately been put up using ladders, well out of reach of any souvenir hunters' clutches.

There were lots of despondent-looking ticket touts with wads of tickets, not cash, in their paws. The going rate was anything between 'half face value' and down. This made a welcome change from the likes of *Tigrou*, and as we got closer to the ground and closer to kick-off time, there were more touts and also lots of normal fans forlornly trying to off-load their spare tickets, and the price was going down. The last we heard before we went through the turnstiles, tickets were going for ten euros. For a Cup Final! These two teams didn't deserve to be in it. Imagine what it would have been like if it had been us against Celtic. Don't these teams have more than a few thousand true fans? Talk about 'Sell all your tickets, you couldn't sell all your tickets,' it makes you sick!! Note for your file: if you fancy going to a major European Cup Final, as long as it's between a couple of teams who can't raise more than a few thousand true fans from the ungrateful, uninvolved, and unenthusiastic masses, so in other words with no English or Scottish teams involved, just turn up on the night and you'll get in for next to nothing.

The Ullevi is a nice modern stadium, except it's not! It's actually nearly fifty years old, but typically for Scandinavian design, it must have been way ahead of its time when it was built for the 1958 World Cup, with its tasteful lines and flowing curves, modelled after the bodies of Greta Garbo and Ursula Andress, someone said. Unfortunately the pitch is remote from the crowd because it also has a running track, so you feel a long way from the action. One clever idea is that the stands curve up to the highest point at the halfway line, meaning that a good proportion of the spectators are concentrated on the sides in line with the centre circle. We were, so we had a great view. The stands behind the goals are very small in comparison, so the majority of the people in the ground have a very good sideways-on view. Surprisingly enough for a place which must be as wet and cold as England and Scotland, and probably more so, there is no roof to speak of.

According to the programme, the biggest crowd ever at the Ullevi was not for a World Cup match or some big athletics championship, but instead had been for a couple of concerts given by Bruce Springsteen, on the same tour when he also pitched up at St. James's. If anyone ever asks you what was the finest line-up you've ever seen at our home ground and you're weighing up whether to say the '95-'96 or the '96-'97 teams, or even the '68-'69 team or the Supermac, John Tudor, Terry Hibbit, Tony Green, Jinky Jim teams of the early 70s, could it be that the real answer is The Boss along with the E Street Band? Maybe you went like me to the London double-header of the Man Utd Cup Final followed by Bruce Springsteen at Earls Court. Brother Ian couldn't make it to the concert at the last moment and I ended up having to sell off his ticket outside, just like at a match!

I'd been half-expecting astronomical catering prices in the Ullevi, with it being a big event, and with three children expecting to be plied with regular re-fills of fizzy pop, hot dogs and crisps, I'd stocked up on cash. We were pleasantly surprised to find that prices were lower inside the stadium than out on the street, so like the Milky Bar Kid nearly used to say, the hot dogs were on me.

The baldy Italian Collina was the referee, so it was to him that fell the great pleasure of sending off the equally baldy Barthez. You can't have too many baldy gits on the pitch at the same time! It's just a pity that Barthez couldn't have done something equally dumb against us in the semi-final – instead of making a jammy save from Shola with his trailing shin after ten minutes of the first leg, why couldn't he have gone out and grabbed him by the ankles like he did to the Valencia centre forward? Up till then, it had been fairly even, with Valencia looking slightly more the likely lads, but after the penalty it seemed all too easy for them as Marseille took off their best player on the night, Meriem, whose first name is Camel. Drogba was shackled Woodgate-style by Ayala, though Woodgate had used his brains whereas Ayala now used only his brawn.

By the way, the UEFA Programme was pretty biased in our favour, getting very close to saying that we would have been in the final if it hadn't been for all the injuries. We all had a soft spot for Valencia already, from having seen them in their Mestalla home ground demolishing Lokomotiv Moscow in the Champions League a few years before, when we'd been down there on holiday and found by coincidence (honest) that they were playing. The terracing in the upper reaches of the Mestalla is as Eddie-the-Eagle-steep as it was in the temporary stands at Charleroi, and for the same reason; it's hemmed in by narrow streets in a residential part of the town (sound familiar?).

Before the match, we were treated to an Abba tribute group called Waterloo, who rolled (volvo'd) back the years, and at half-time we first got an eyeful of the Carlsberg Cheerleaders from Copenhagen (probably the best cheerleaders in the world) before our eyes were assaulted by the sight of a big hairy arse climbing over the barrier just a few rows down from us as he set off to streak across the pitch. Pity the cheerleaders had by then left the scene, otherwise it could have been an interesting encounter. Over on the far side of the ground I saw a big blue and white banner announcing that the 'Fanatics' were there supporting Marseille. They were the supporters club whose tickets we'd bought off *Tigrou* for the semi-final. I don't know if *Tigrou* was there, but I rather doubt it judging by his eagerness to off-load his semi-final tickets to us at ten times the proper price, and all the empty seats around the ground. In front of us there were three empty seats, and there were another four just behind and to our right. It was the same everywhere.

When it was all over and Valencia had deservedly won, the teams got their medals on a podium hastily erected down on the pitch, with Collina getting the biggest response of all (boos from one side and cheers from the other) aside from the actual lifting of the trophy. I didn't know until Sarah and Emilie started jumping up and down and shouting 'There's a mouse' that Valencia have a man in a Bat get-up as their mascot. I wonder why?

On the way back, Sarah was determined to have her flag but all the reachable ones were in direct view of officials, so we didn't manage it, even though we went back to the hotel and then went back out again for another hunt around after midnight. The next morning though, I got up early when the streets were deserted because it was a national holiday (*Kristi Himmelfart*, remember?) except for workers dismantling things from the day before, and I managed to get a gigantic 'UEFA Cup Final Gothenburg 2004' banner that was being taken down. It looks great in the garage. Still, it wasn't a flag, so to please Sarah we went back round by the Ullevi on our way out of town, and Nathalie spotted some people busy at the VIP and Officials entrance. With the kids in tow, she went in and asked if there were any souvenirs. The people were generosity personified, and the kids ended up with a programme and an official UEFA coat each - a bit big, but they'll grow into them!

We crossed back from Sweden into Denmark using the Helsingborg to Helsingør ferry, from which you can enjoy a great view of Hamlet's castle which guards the straits of the Öresund, and rounded the trip off by spending a couple of days with our friends Eric and Nina and going on a tour of the places where I used to live and work. I lived not too far away from (supra-Carlsbergly speaking) definitely the best art museum in the world, Louisiana, perched on the cliffs overlooking the Öresund straits to Sweden at Humlebaek. You can't beat sitting in the sculpture garden on a warm sunny day like we had, watching the boats sailing by behind the mobiles (the dangling variety, not the ones you talk into) swaying in the breeze. It also has the single most perfect room in the world – in the shape of a cube with one whole side a window looking out onto a still pond in the woods, the other walls all white, and populated only by two emaciated bronze figures. You have to go when the place is deserted and just be there by yourself and take it slowly in.

We bought our breakfast of Danish *wienerbrød* in the bakery at Tisvildeleje along with two weeks' further supply of Danish pastries to take back with us. It's funny how the Danes call them *wienerbrød*, which means Viennese bread, while everyone else in the world calls them Danish pastries. Some irony there. Though it's no more ironic than Newcastle Brown Ale not being a brown ale at all, but a Viennese Copper. So maybe in Vienna they call a Danish pastry a Newcastle pasty, who knows? At any rate, I love the pastries they call the 'baker's bad eye', because the big dollop of raspberry jam in the middle of the white icing sugar reminds them of a bloodshot eye. The sesame seed ones, the chocolate ones, and the almond ones are pretty good too. They're sweet, sticky, and bad for you, but you cannot whack them. We couldn't resist eating a few in the car, but we kept some for a relaxed breakfast in the executive lounge at Kastrup airport, washed down with the complimentary orange juice and coffee, before catching the plane back. This is the aesthetic (and certainly not ascetic) side of the pilgrim talking to you here.

Well, we're back home now, and it's all over for another year. It had been a long season, just not quite as long as we would have liked, though. Out in the harbour beyond the *Vieux Port* of Marseille lies the Count of Monte Cristo's *Château d'If*. We'd foundered on its rocky 'if's'. 'If' we had got through the semi-final; 'if' we hadn't had all those injuries; 'if' baldy Barthez hadn't made his jammy save from Shola; 'if' everyone had recovered by the time of the final, would we have won? I don't know. I do know, however, that Valencia looked like a very good team. I also know that a lot of people, not just us, would have liked to see us in the Final. Maybe they will next year. We can but hope! Pigs might fly. Get prepared to follow the pilgrim street to the Syrian or Siberian borders and put this date down in your diary: Wednesday, May 18th, 2005 - the Final in Lisbon. So the theme of next year's pilgrimage is 'Fatima' (i.e. it would be a miracle!!) - join us along the way.